After Dawn

After Dawn

Hope after State Capture

Mcebisi Jonas

Foreword by President Cyril Ramaphosa

PICADOR AFRICA

First published in 2019 by Picador Africa
an imprint of Pan Macmillan South Africa
Private Bag X19, Northlands
Johannesburg, 2116

www.panmacmillan.co.za

ISBN 978-1-77010-675-8
e-ISBN 978-1-77010-677-2

Editing by Sally Hines
Proofreading by Russell Martin
Indexing by Christopher Merrett
Design and typesetting by Triple M Design
Cover design by publicide
Author photograph courtesy of Government
Communication and Information System (GCIS)

Contents

Foreword

Reading Mcebisi Jonas's manuscript, *After Dawn*, I was again struck by the historic moment that we are facing in South Africa – a moment that is in many ways not too dissimilar to the bitter-sweetness of the early 1990s when we were negotiating the country's future through multi-party constitutional negotiations.

Coincidentally, the national election of May 2019 fell almost exactly on the 25th anniversary of the first parliamentary sitting of the Government of National Unity when we adopted the Interim Constitution on 9 May 1994. It was an exhilaratingly historic day, and I think we have forgotten just how momentous it was. At the time, we knew that we had work to do but we had no idea of the mountainous task that lay ahead – building consensus on the blueprint for the country, our final Constitution, which was promulgated two years later on 8 May 1996.

The constitutional negotiations that we embarked upon to draft the Interim Constitution, as well as the Constitutional Assembly negotiations to draft our final Constitution, were difficult, fraught with ideological and political battles and threatened by forces that did not want to see change and wanted to use violence to impose their will. Making the Constitution was no less complex – our ideological differences prevailed as each party carefully considered how to protect their own interests. Dissension was rife over things such as whether South Africa should be declared a Christian country, as it was during apartheid; the role of traditional leaders; the division of power between central government and the provinces; the shape and powers of the judiciary; the location of parliament; our electoral system; which of the many languages spoken in South Africa should be considered as being official languages; education; capital punishment; labour rights; and ownership of property and land.

As all negotiations are often fraught with differences and disputes, we adopted two mantras – 'sufficient consensus' and 'there is no problem without a solution' – to shepherd the constitutional talks, and, miraculously, by the middle of 1996 we had what I described then as 'the birth certificate of the nation': our final Constitution.

The outcome of the negotiations restored political rights, democracy and dignity for all, as well as the founding of democratic institutions to secure and advance democracy and human rights into our future. But, it is equally true that the settlement did little to rearrange economic power. It was, for example, silent on the need for ownership changes in major corporations. It also said little about the need to reverse injustice in land and asset ownership.

The brittleness of our country 25 years ago, and the adversarial nature of the negotiations, meant that the compromises we made then were necessary to avoid full-scale political implosion.

I am invoking the memories of the negotiations process because I think we are at another defining moment in our country's history. Mcebisi Jonas's book comes at this critical juncture: he puts a pivotal stake in the ground to remind us that, despite the miracle of the rainbow nation, our 1994 consensus risks unravelling precisely because we have failed to utilise the settlement for what it was – a vehicle of transition for far-reaching changes, not an end point in itself.

After Dawn explains to us why and how this has happened. On the one hand, the book leaves us with answers to the deep sense of disorientation and fatigue that we have experienced as a nation over the past decade or so. On the other hand, and more importantly, it makes a vital contribution to our future trajectory by proposing practical and implementable solutions. Mcebisi is blunt about our failures but offers us hope in return: *After Dawn* goes beyond rhetoric to set out where we went wrong (and in many cases what we did right), cutting across political and ideological divides to propose how to restore effective and accountable governance, and how to build a faster growing and more inclusive economy.

Since the State of the Nation Address in February 2017, South Africans from all walks of life have heeded the call of Thuma Mina. Most of us recognise that our country stands at a crossroads, in which we have the opportunity to set our economy and society on the path to prosperity. Indeed, part of the Thuma Mina call is for citizens to engage in a project of reimagining and rebuilding an inclusive and fast-growing economy, and a more just and equal society.

We have a long history as South Africans of making tough choices in precarious moments. Time and time again, we have pulled ourselves back from the brink of despair and inspired hope, renewal and progress. Today, we are faced with such a moment. And it is our profound responsibility to live up to it.

May we take this important book as a guide to dialogue and engage with each other as we make the difficult trade-offs required to reach our dream of a non-racial, non-sexist and prosperous South Africa. There will likely be differing views on some of the issues raised in the book, but it provides a solid basis for a wider conversation and for consensus-building.

President Cyril Ramaphosa
May 2019

Preface

Why This Book Now?

We learn from history that we do not learn from history. — Georg Hegel

In October 2015, the Gupta brothers offered me the position of minister of finance in exchange for R600 million.

I had already become aware of a festering nexus between certain business people and politicians. I knew that the ruling African National Congress (ANC), like most transitional political parties, was facing internal challenges and I knew patronage and access to state resources were used by political brokers to rally support behind leaders and factions.

I had put these issues down to the cut and thrust of an emerging democracy. I have been active in the struggle for democracy since I was 14 and I did not question the resilience of the ruling party to shepherd the country through these challenges.

But the afternoon I was offered the bribe crushed this belief. I felt a deep sense of loss and disorientation as it dawned on me that the rumours of a parallel state were not only true but had assumed a scale so audacious that South Africa's state-building project had fallen headlong into the hands of business interests whose value system seemed directly opposed to that of the ANC that I knew. I thought of the years we had spent fighting for democracy; we lost our youth and we suffered at the hands of the apartheid state. Now we were faced with this – a mafia state that threatened to usurp everything we had fought for. In many ways, unlike apartheid, this felt like an invisible coup. I felt deeply disempowered. I felt like a puppet in a much bigger game that I could not comprehend.

I turned down the bribe and navigated the months that followed in a state of incomprehension about the future of our country. My sense of mission did not wane during this time. But it was an intensely lonely period. I could trust only a handful of people. Everything that I had held as sacrosanct for 45 years was suddenly disintegrating. I began to examine my basic assumptions about what democracy meant in South Africa. Who were we as a nation? How did we reach this point? I read widely, I studied other countries that had faced similar crises and I sought the international experience of the likes of Dr Daniel Kaufmann and Dr Joel Hellman, experts on state capture. Conceptually this helped, but it also confirmed to me that there was no clear precedent to help us chart the way.

The election of President Cyril Ramaphosa in December 2017 was a victory, and progressive South Africans breathed a well-deserved collective sigh of relief. But Ramaphosa was almost immediately burdened with the insurmountable expectations attached to 'Ramaphoria'. When, after 100 days in office, he had not delivered the impossible, newspaper headlines screamed 'From Dawn to Dust – The Implosion of Ramaphoria' and 'Ramaphoria to Ramaphobia', and so on.

This was a far-reaching mistake we made as a nation. Such was our enthusiasm for everything to be all right, and such was our relief that state capture had not pushed us over the precipice, that we failed to acknowledge the complexities that had driven us to the point of near collapse.

This was not something that one man, however well-positioned, could fix. Indeed, the current propensity to over-personalise our politics – whether it is a focus on Jacob Zuma who 'created the problems', or Ramaphosa who 'can fix the problems' – means that we risk overlooking the much more dangerous structural and systemic nature of our crisis.

This crisis sits at the heart of our current system, which places politicians at the centre of our economy and in so doing also puts politics in the middle of economic policy-making and implementation. As a result, the short-term management of constituencies and the retention of political power and control – determined by our electoral cycles – have come to define our political and economic trajectory. A long-term inclusive growth agenda has become incidental. We have failed to maintain the independence of key institutions, in part because meritocracy has not prevailed, and in part because political deployment has trounced administrative independence in state institutions and the public service.

During the first 15 years of our democracy, our economy was large enough to support excessive politics and interference. Up until the 2008 global financial crash, our economic surplus, driven mainly by the commodities super-cycle and policy stability, kept the imbalances in our society in an uneasy equilibrium. From about 2009, this began to unravel because the surplus required to balance the interests of the various competing constituencies that make South Africa was no longer present. This system now threatens implosion.

This is a book about the political economy. It is a book that determines how politics has shaped our economic choices and our fortunes, which now lie at the heart of our growth challenge. There have been many studies of our economy in isolation from our politics; this book acknowledges that the two cannot be delinked. But in acknowledging this, I would argue that we need to create a system that is able to move the country from dependence on a political elite to one that promotes innovation and administrative independence. We must move from a system where we once celebrated old monopolies to a system driven by technology, competition and global links.

The essence of my argument in this book is that the 1994 consensus – the social contract that enabled us to peacefully transition to democracy and which bound us together in the first two decades of freedom – is unravelling.

I argue that this consensus was built on four pillars.

1) The historic elite or what we could call established wealth. This group was accommodated through macro-policy stabilisation and the political management of expropriation risk through, among other mechanisms, specific constitutional provisions.

2) The aspirant black elite. This group was accommodated through a thin albeit powerful layer of boardroom Black Economic Empowerment (BEE), through public sector jobs and access to state-business patronage networks.

3) Organised labour. This group was accommodated through supportive

labour legislation, collective bargaining and public sector unions, which have become increasingly larger and more powerful within the labour federations. They were incorporated through above-inflation wage increases with little emphasis on productivity.

4) The poor and unemployed. This group was accommodated through fiscal redistribution as a result of a rapidly expanded welfare net. This ensured that the poor and unemployed remained more or less supportive of the transition, accommodative of the market-led policy choices and less susceptible to national or ethnic populism.

This system is now unravelling (or rather has unravelled) and we could be on a path towards major disruption.

The historic elite have grown frustrated with mixed policy signalling, corruption and the rising costs of business. They are withholding investment and investing elsewhere, or investing in liquid rather than fixed capital markets where jobs can be created.

The new black elite have grown increasingly frustrated at the limited opportunities for inclusion in the concentrated and stagnant real economy, and, more recently, some sections of this group have become frustrated at the closing spaces in the patronage economy resulting from reduced fiscal resources, improved governance in state-owned companies and growing anti-corruption sentiments in society.

Lack of growth and consequent fiscal constraints have limited the available resources for buying acquiescence from public sector unions. Continued above-inflation increases for public servants seem highly unlikely in the short to medium term.

And the lack of jobs, coupled with the fact that levels of fiscal redistribution cannot keep pace with cost of living increases, has created heightened levels of grassroots discontent, which is illustrated in growing service delivery protests and populism.

In simple terms, this unravelling is being driven by three things: firstly, the model itself has been anchored on growth, which we have failed to achieve since 2008/9. Secondly, it was based on assumptions about the effectiveness and efficiency of the state, which have proven misplaced as we have slipped backwards in this respect. Thirdly, the constituent elements of the 1994 agreement – business, labour, government, society and political parties – have become increasingly self-serving and concurrently dislocated from their base. In essence, we have a leadership crisis, combined with an existential crisis as a nation. We have no clear identity and no clear vision for where we are going.

This means that the scene is set for disruption. But what remains unclear is the form that this will take, what the likely outcomes are and the strategies we need to adopt to ensure a path to a constructive future.

This book makes a modest contribution to better understanding the nature of the systemic challenges we face and what we need to do to transition to a new kind of politics and economy.

Seven sets of actions must bring together the programme for constructive disruption:

Firstly, constraints to competitiveness and investment must be quickly removed so that the economy can grow and our fiscal crisis can be resolved. Here we need bold measures and new institutions to enhance productivity and the competitiveness of firms. We must also strengthen our historical competitive advantages – manufacturing, agriculture, mining and tourism. This will quickly result in heightened confidence in the economy, especially among those with established wealth.

Secondly, we need to put jobs at the centre of economic policy while we restructure towards higher productivity competitiveness. This will require new policy measures and transitional packages, including subsidies and incentives to encourage labour-intensive production. A number of suggestions on how this can be done have been made in the book.

Thirdly, we must rapidly expand new technological capacities and knowledge to quickly transition to a twenty-first-century economy. Key to this will be to develop instruments that incentivise investment in research and development and innovation, as well as initiatives with the banking sector to expand access to financial instruments. This is vital to create a black innovative and productive class.

Fourthly, and linked to our transition towards a higher productivity economy, we need to expand human capabilities at scale, both through addressing our skills and education failures, as well as importing critical skills to provide us with the necessary technical and entrepreneurial capabilities in the immediate term.

Fifthly, we need new sets of trade-offs and measures to accelerate economic inclusion. This must be done with the established private and banking sectors. As I argue, this must be done in a manner that does not compromise investment, output and employment growth.

Sixthly, we must develop a corruption-free, high-performance state built on meritocracy and innovation. This will require a new compact with public sector unions. In the short term, we need to strengthen the independence of existing institutions and, where needed, create new institutions as centres of excellence – possibly semi-autonomous and cushioned from political interference – to drive economic restructuring.

Seventh, the nature of politics must change. This includes ANC reform, as well as a realisation across political structures of the existential crisis we are facing as a country and as constituent parts. Dynamics within the governing party will be a major deal-breaker. The ANC remains highly fractured around competing interests and ideological persuasions. But as a country, we cannot be held hostage to the possibility that the ANC may reform and modernise itself.

The agenda suggested in this book must be embedded across various social formations such that the governing party becomes led by society as much as it leads society.

Come with me as I take you on two journeys. The first will take you through the badlands of political and economic failure as I attempt to diagnose the problems besetting the country. The second will take you through a series of solutions – some complex, some easier to achieve – that I believe are necessary if we are to power South Africa up so that it becomes the vibrant, dynamic and job-creating country from which all citizens benefit.

Abbreviations

ACSA	Airports Company South Africa
AfDB	African Development Bank
ANC	African National Congress
ASEAN	Association of Southeast Asian Nations
BBBEE	Broad-Based Black Economic Empowerment
BEE	Black Economic Empowerment
BEX	Business Expansion Structured Products
BLF	Black First Land First
CNR	China North Rail
COSATU	Congress of South African Trade Unions
CST	Colonialism of a Special Type
DA	Democratic Alliance
EFF	Economic Freedom Fighters
FDI	foreign direct investment
4IR	Fourth Industrial Revolution
FF+	Freedom Front Plus
GDP	gross domestic product
GEAR	Growth, Employment and Redistribution
GLC	government-linked company
ICT	information and communications technology
IDZ	Industrial Development Zone
IP	Internet Protocol
IPAP	Industrial Policy Action Plan

IPP	independent power producer
IT	information and technology
JSE	Johannesburg Stock Exchange
MEC	Member of the Provincial Executive Council
NECC	National Education Crisis Committee
NEET	Not in Education, Employment or Training
NERSA	National Energy Regulator of South Africa
NGO	non-governmental organisation
NGP	New Growth Path
NPA	National Prosecuting Authority
OBE	Outcomes-Based Education
OECD	Organisation for Economic Co-operation and Development
PRASA	Passenger Rail Agency of South Africa
RDP	Reconstruction and Development Programme
SAA	South African Airways
SABC	South African Broadcasting Corporation
SADC	Southern African Development Community
SADTU	South African Democratic Teachers' Union
SARB	South African Reserve Bank
SARS	South African Revenue Service
SEZ	Special Economic Zone
SME	small and medium-sized enterprise
SMME	small, medium and micro-sized enterprise
SOE	state-owned enterprise
TIMSS	Trends in International Mathematics and Science Study
TLGFA	Traditional Leadership and Governance Framework Act
UK	United Kingdom
US	United States

Introduction

Can We Prosper?

Nostalgia for the economic past is not just about money, though; it is also about diminishing hope. — Yascha Mounk

I am sometimes asked: can South Africa survive? The answer is easy. We will, of course, survive. A much better and forward-looking question is: can South Africans prosper? Will we be able to create a system of government and economy that will realise the hopes and aspirations of South Africa's citizens? Or are we doomed to struggle forever through apartheid's terrible legacies of exclusion, division and inequality?

I believe the answer is: we can. But to realise a more positive future, we have to face a number of hard truths and act on them.

The first, and perhaps most important of these, is that the political and economic consensus that brought about the tremendous political changes of the early 1990s and the subsequent period of stability is no longer fit for South Africa's prosperity purpose.

This bargain safeguarded the interests of the existing (largely white) economic elite essentially by ensuring South Africa did not nationalise; it placated the black elite primarily through state employment and rents in the form of preferential ownerships and procurement schemes; and it brought labour on board by securing the rights of organised labour and putting in place a regime of protective labour laws. Those who were outside this bargain looking in were placated with the rolling out of a comprehensive welfare system for the poorest South Africans. This political-economy deal is represented in Table 1.

There is no doubt that the 1994 consensus – especially the welfare-spending

1

Established Wealth	The New Elite
Accommodated through macro-economic policy stabilisation, and the political management of expropriation/ nationalisation risk	Accommodated through boardroom BEE, public sector jobs, and access to state-business patronage networks
Organised Labour	**The Poor and Unemployed**
Accommodated through supportive labour legislation and collective bargaining	Accommodated through fiscal redistribution through a rapidly expanded welfare net

Table 1: The political-economy deal of the early 1990s

component – brought significant social returns in reducing extreme poverty and vulnerability, and extending access to basic services. And there is also no question that our robust system of accountability and the democratic institutions we have established provided critical checks and balances to those entrusted with the means of state administration and coercion.

But we must accept that the 1994 consensus has become unviable and is unravelling. Sustained low rates of economic growth, especially since 2008, have limited the volume of income for redistribution. Graduation of millions from this scheme also remains very difficult for a number of reasons. Inequality has not reduced, ownership of the economy remains highly concentrated and higher economic returns continue to accrue to those already endowed with capital and skills. Our poor education and training outcomes have not helped. Education spending as a percentage of our GDP is higher than the United Kingdom, the United States and Germany – more than 6% of South Africa's GDP is spent on basic and higher education combined. The UK spends 5.7%, the US 5% and Germany 4.9%.[1]

In all of this, an ambitious project to create a developmental state to transform the apartheid economy has been hamstrung by the absence of the necessary coherence and capability, as well as the existence of patronage, corruption and state capture. As a consequence, short-termism and populism are on the rise, along with political fatigue, especially among younger South Africans – all of this fed by the growing restlessness of our people who are not blind to the obscene inequality that abounds and who are losing hope in the vision of a future of shared prosperity.

Our failure to grasp the importance of inclusive economic growth means we have been unable to create jobs, invest in infrastructure and skills, raise wages and productivity, and embark on ambitious social welfare projects at a pace fast enough to meet the needs of a growing population. If you are not growing, you are falling behind. This stark fact can be seen in terms of South Africa's declining per capita share of global income (see Figure 2).

The importance of growth

Economic growth is one of the most important indicators of a healthy economy. Positive growth drives long-term prosperity, which, in turn, has an upward impact on national income and employment. This increases the standard of living for the bulk of the population, giving people not only material security, but a sense of identity and connection with their country. It is the flywheel effect.

The opposite has happened in South Africa. Unless this changes, our country will fail to deliver on the needs and aspirations of its people. While catastrophic failure is unlikely, the alternative is just as damaging in the long term: a continuous erosion in a downward spiral of slow growth, uncompetitiveness, increasing exclusion from the formal economy, inequality, institutional decay and disinterest, and growing reversion to extra-parliamentary forms of protest, which could ultimately manifest in Venezuelan-style populism and democractic collapse. This is otherwise referred to as the 'frog in the pot' or the 'slow-puncture' effect, a gradual, insidious decline from which it is harder and harder to return given the corrosive effects and lost years. This happened during the years of the Jacob Zuma government. It is the task now of every vested South African to put the country into a different cycle defined by inclusive growth, productivity and competitiveness, investment in people and assets, and prosperity.

Confronting and transforming our social, political and economic realities, however mountainous, is necessary to avoid a reoccurrence of state capture. At the time of writing this book, our growth and inequality levels were akin to those in war-torn countries.[2] State capture undoubtedly exacerbated this, but the near-systemic failure of our state cannot be blamed on capture alone.

Nor can state capture be dismissed as an anomaly of our history – rather it is a consequence of our collective failure to define a common national agenda to meaningfully pursue growth and the transformation of South Africa. Here, there is a another tough truth: while the effects of state capture cannot be minimised, our economy was ripe for capture given the combination of weak institutions, divisive leadership, fragmented loyalties and, notably, low growth.

Our economy was ripe for state capture

Since 1994, our annual economic growth rate has averaged 2.76%, well below comparative developing nations and the global growth average of 3.1% over the same period. In the decade between 2008 and 2018, South African growth averaged 1.8% and global growth averaged 2.4%.[3]

The effects of this cannot be overstated. We are falling behind in a global context and in meeting the hopes, now, of two generations of South Africans.

We may be tempted to claim that this poor performance is down to our unique colonial history, which has, no doubt, played a part. But, compared to other diverse societies, such as Singapore and Malaysia, South Africa has

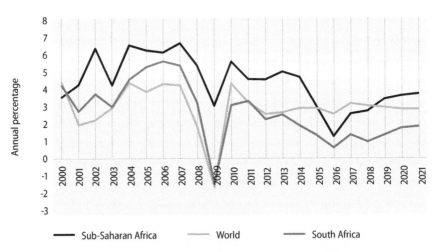

Figure 1: GDP growth in sub-Saharan Africa, the world and South Africa

(SOURCE: WORLD BANK WORLD DEVELOPMENT INDICATORS)

performed relatively poorly in terms of national income per capita as a share of global per capita income in the first quarter-century of its liberation.

While South Africa's per capita income has increased since 1994 by 37.5%, incomes in Singapore increased by 437% over the first 24 years following independence in 1965; in Malaysia by 188%; and in Vietnam by 241% between 1986 (when its Doi Moi[4] policy reforms were launched) and 2010.[5] While South Africa's apartheid legacy presents a significant challenge, there are few who have had to overcome Vietnam's challenges of four periods of colonial control over 1 000 years, 54 ethnic groups, a difficult neighbourhood and topography, three million dead and utter infrastructure devastation during the 21 years of the American phase of its liberation struggle. Our excuses pale by comparison.

Part of South Africa's failure to grow is the fact that we remain locked into a historical growth path, and we are overly dependent on commodity prices and demand and financial portfolio inflows. Yet, we have also made poor strategic policy choices driven by short-term supposition. For example, at the very moment the world entered a Chinese-led commodity super-cycle, our mining industry shrank because it was regarded by the government as

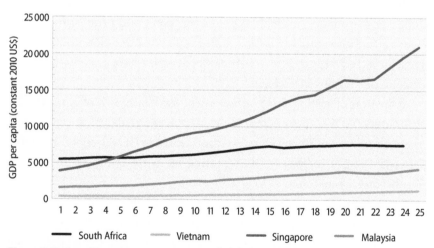

Figure 2: National income as a percentage of global per capita income: first 25 years of independence.

(Source: World Bank World Development Indicators; Author's calculations)

an apartheid relic, a 'sunset' industry in the terminology of the time, and little new investment was made. Long the foundation of our economy and employment, with a million jobs at its height, the industry has subsequently halved in size and, with it, many more jobs were lost in its associated industries and service sectors. Such is the cost of poor choices.

Some consequences are the inevitable product of our development stage. South Africa is in a typical middle-income trap where we cannot compete in the low-productivity, low-cost sectors, and we do not have the technology and human capabilities to compete in the high-productivity space. Where we do compete, such as financial services and the services sector, the benefits accrue to the highly educated. To compound this, our education system is not producing the skills we need to graduate as a country from our low-productivity, low-wage trap.

Again, however, just like others who emerge, growing, from this trap, we have to face up to the same realities that they have tackled. Growth requires investment, especially private investment, particularly when, as in our case, the opportunities for public sector investment (from revenue and debt) have narrowed considerably. Currently, levels of public sector fixed investment have dropped, and private sector fixed investment has not increased. Domestic corporates are withholding investment and/or are investing in liquid as opposed to fixed capital markets. Levels of foreign direct investment have reduced and other African economies have become preferred destinations for this investment.

At the time of writing, South Africa's debt was nearly 60% of gross domestic product (GDP). The measure of the ratio of external debt to exports had risen from 90% in 2009 (when external debt was US$80 billion) to 160% (around US$200 billion) in 2019, putting us in the company of Malawi, Zambia and Zimbabwe.

The reasons for our declining levels of fixed investment include rising costs of doing business, electricity supply constraints, our skills crisis, declining productivity and competitiveness, labour volatility, and policy and political uncertainty.

A case of the chicken and egg

Corruption and state capture played a significant role in our economic decline. Weak political and economic governance directly impacted on investment confidence. The growing tendency of national populism, as well as the narrative of radical economic transformation, increased expropriation risk and led to policy confusion.

Overarching plans, such as the National Development Plan, were not implemented or have been partially implemented at best. Under state capture, effective governance, especially of state-owned enterprises (SOEs), was sacrificed, a pliant and factional security cluster was established and state capacity was hollowed out as organs of state were repurposed to serve corrupt patronage interests.

In a vicious cycle, declining levels of capability and legitimacy undermined the capacity of the state to play a developmental role with respect to growing and transforming the economy. Corruption reduced fiscal resources for service delivery and infrastructure, and mismanaged SOEs brought serious contingent liability risk to the fiscus, potentially compromising national sovereignty. It is a startling fact that, at the time of the May 2019 national election, the electricity public utility Eskom was in debt to the tune of half a trillion rand. Once one of the world's most profitable and largest energy utilities,[6] Eskom's revenue is no longer sufficient to cover the cost of servicing this debt.

The incremental weakening of the security organs of state and the prosecuting authority also enabled widespread capture at provincial and local levels, often brokered by political barons. While some insights have come to light in the various commissions of inquiry, including the Zondo Commission, the Nugent Commission and the Mokgoro Commission, the shape, scope and scale of these networks cut across factions and the political spectrum. This intersects with and compounds the country's political, economic and social fragility.

It follows that addressing rampant and systemic corruption is a prerequisite to develop state capacity to drive growth.

But this is only a necessary first step. It is not enough if it is not complemented by a programme of careful state reforms, both to eliminate and

7

reduce the opportunities for state capture in the future and to improve the performance of government administrations across the state. Our system of government procurement and public service appointments are two obvious places to start, but there are others.

Politics fit for the task

The state capture project has unfortunately led to a binary polemic driven by the mainstream media, among analysts and within the urban echo chamber, resulting in the African National Congress (ANC) being torn between saints (reformers) and sinners (capturers). This is unhelpful.

Business-political patronage networks and rent-seeking is inevitable, especially in transitional societies where governance is weak and politicised. But herein lies the paradox. Dismantling business-political networks and shutting down wealth-creating opportunities of the patronage economy will trigger widespread resistance towards incumbent political leadership.

However, if we do not dismantle these networks, growth and state capacity will be undermined. This suggests that the needs of the aspirant elite must be accommodated in the productive economy to compensate for lost space in the patronage/clientele economy.

Policy since the end of apartheid has been confused. This is mainly because it has been iteratively designed to accommodate the varying and sometimes contradictory needs of diverse sectors of society, without the benefit of an overarching vision and mandate.

In 1994, the ANC had to confront a crisis-ridden and highly inefficient economy, the extent of which took it, and South Africa, by surprise. The country had been in economic stagnation since the mid-1970s; we were dislocated globally; poverty and joblessness were on the rise; we had worn capital stock, falling net investment, an uncompetitive industrial sector and massive skills deficiencies. The structure of the economy was highly unequal, and there was virtually no black wealth. At that point, the country was running, in an eerie portent of things to come, a budget deficit of 6.5%, and total government debt was estimated at 52.5% of GDP (including debt of the former homelands).[7] Then, as now, the deficit and debt had risen more rapidly than GDP.

In exile, the ANC had not prioritised economic policy, and by the early 1990s it did not have a well-worked-out post-apartheid economic policy. The 1992 'Ready to Govern' document was woefully short on detail, and the reality since 1994 is that there has never been an economic policy framework that has enjoyed the full support of all stakeholders.

Early tensions were evident in the Tripartite Alliance over the Reconstruction and Development Programme (RDP) and the Growth, Employment and Redistribution (GEAR) programme. The RDP presented a broad framework for the transformation of South African society and was designed primarily to address the basic needs of the poorest South Africans by focusing on poverty and socio-economic inequalities. In 1995, shortly after its formulation, the ANC's National Executive Committee announced that government's focus on delivering basic services, as outlined in the RDP, would not succeed without first concentrating on economic growth. The RDP office closed and some of the socio-economic components of the plan were incorporated into government's fiscal redistribution programme, with mixed success.

GEAR, in turn, was focused on macro-stabilisation, job creation through labour market reforms and inserting South Africa into the global economy. Though GEAR was criticised for enabling capital to leave the country, and for its fiscal prudence and tight inflation targeting, the programme achieved its stated objectives of eradicating apartheid debt and achieving price stability by keeping long-run inflation in check.

Under GEAR, economic growth was targeted at 6%. Growth reached a high of 5.3% in 2005. GEAR was followed by the Accelerated and Shared Growth Initiative for South Africa (2002), the Medium-Term Strategic Framework (2009), the New Growth Path (2010) and the National Development Plan (2012).[8]

Apart from GEAR, economic policy in South Africa has generally lacked the political will to make the difficult choices it demands. The Integrated Manufacturing Development Strategy (2001), the Micro-Economic Reform Strategy (2002), the National Industrial Policy Framework (2007) and various iterations of the Industrial Policy Action Plans (2014–18) have not gained any meaningful political traction to grow output and address structural weakness in the economy. More recently, under former President Zuma, the New Growth Path, the president's Nine-Point Plan, and the National Development Plan also failed to strengthen and unite the state, the private sector, society and organised labour around a coherent vision to grow investment, growth and jobs. There has been no coalescing 'Big Idea' around which the country can galvanise and which can explain the difficult choices and the short-term costs they invariably impose.

The ANC-led government has partly succeeded in creating a new black political elite through access to state employment and access to state-sector markets. This was enabled through, among other pieces of legislation, the Preferential Procurement Policy Framework Act (2000). However well-intentioned in terms of addressing South Africa's racial wealth profile, and however effective in terms of creating a new black elite, this class project, particularly post-2009, came at a price. As state resources dwindled, because of the global economic downturn, increasing policy uncertainty and political opportunism, so ANC factionalism escalated, state capacity diminished, resistance to the rule of law grew, and populism escalated.

The phenomenon of personality politics in South Africa also risks distracting us from finding sustainable solutions to our challenges. Over the past 15 years, our politics have been marked by an 'anti' sentiment upon which political party leaders have risen (and fallen) – Zuma was pitched as 'anti-Mbeki', Ramaphosa as 'anti-Zuma', etc. We are already witnessing the rise of new groupings in the form of what is broadly called the 'fight-back' campaign in the ANC, and which is, in essence, anti-Cyril' and his reform agenda.

South Africans must not allow the growth of the country to fall victim to the fickleness of political personalities, nor should political leaders solely be burdened with the success or failure of the country. Simultaneously, the importance of strong and uncompromising political leadership cannot be underplayed. Visionary leadership capable of mobilising support across interests and sectors and managing spoilers is required. But building a country is not the task of one person alone.

The established elite, the new bureaucratic class and labour need to accept that uncomfortable trade-offs will be necessary to mount a consolidation period as a first step to building a new consensus. An unwavering, cohesive civil society is central to this. Political parties and government should no longer fear an active citizenry. Instead, an active citizenry should be embraced, for this is where change will come from.

The future of the country is a matter that should concern every one of us and I strongly believe that it rests with every vested South African, regardless of where we come from, to collectively build, drive and safeguard an alternative future. We have no choice. It is to this challenge, and the suggested solutions, that this book now turns.

Part One

A Diagnosis of the Problem

1

Eight Economic Realities

Unhappy is the land that is in needs of heroes. — Galileo

Chapter summary

- South Africa has been falling behind. Compared to other countries in their first 25 years after political reform (Vietnam, China, Singapore and Malaysia, for example), South Africa's GDP per capita has declined in relation to world GDP per capita.

- The net rate at which people have entered the job market has exceeded the rate of job creation. Between 27% and 37% of South Africans are unemployed, depending on the definition.

- Technological change is not taking any hostages. We need to either adapt our economy and specialise effectively, or risk falling ever further behind.

- Government reform is a critical and undeniable part of this. Rather than serve corrupt interests, SOEs must be primarily focused on driving the economy through the competitive provision of reliable and cheap services.

We must constructively critique our first quarter-century of progress, but it would be a mistake to diminish the 1994 transition, particularly given the scale of our inherited challenge.

South Africa had considerable success in the first 15 years of democracy in reducing poverty and improving basic services. Three million homes were built; potable water and health clinics were provided to far-flung corners of the country; townships were electrified; local and national infrastructure was developed; free health care and schooling became a reality for millions of people; and we created a world-class taxation system.

The second decade of our democracy battered us, leaving us damaged, fatigued and disorientated. Our history demands of us now that we reshape, redefine and reimagine a different future.

On 26 June 1955, the Freedom Charter was adopted at the Congress of the People in Kliptown, near Johannesburg. The Charter committed the liberation movement to a non-racial South Africa in which all would enjoy equality and prosperity. It pledged to 'strive together, sparing neither strength nor courage' to achieve this vision.[1] It provided the cornerstone of the political emancipation we achieved in 1994.

The question that I ask myself is: to what extent have we given effect to the vision of the Freedom Charter? Is our National Democratic Revolution still on track? How do we regain lost ground and reset our national compass towards economic liberation?

The Italian theorist Antonio Gramsci argued for the need to overcome ideological rigidity to ensure greater relevance to new political demands.[2] In every political organisation, there is a danger that ideology, mythology and the need for solidarity serve to obscure objectivity and empiricism when assessing the record of delivery and future policy options.

I think one of our biggest weaknesses as the governing party is that we have become ideologically puritanical and blinkered to the many blind spots that contradict our efforts to build a faster-growing and more equitable economy. I was always intrigued as a politically deployed MEC of Economic Affairs in the Eastern Cape that industry players – the local captains of industry so to say – were so appreciative that I met and engaged with them. Seemingly, this had not been standard practice. I recall one particular session with the larger industry players in Nelson Mandela Bay where one CEO, of the second largest private sector employer in Port Elizabeth, lamented that he had spent the last six months trying to get a meeting with the executive mayor. How did we get our priorities so wrong? Or not necessarily our priorities, because jobs have always been our priority: rather the role we ascribe to private sector firms in addressing our priorities.

Granted, the established private sector might not be part of the ANC's core constituency and it would probably not get their vote. But it will get significantly more votes from the poor, working and middle classes if our economy is growing jobs, and if we are growing revenue to redistribute to the poor and indigent.

We have already fallen victim to this policy mythology and need to guard against further self-deception in order to pursue policies that will succeed in reducing unemployment, poverty and inequality.

It is in this spirit that I have written this chapter. Without an honest appraisal of our current realities, we will not achieve the inclusive growth and development path to which we aspire.

Reality one: We are locked in a jobs crisis

South Africa has the highest unemployment rate in the world among middle-income countries. This directly feeds our other two major crises: poverty and inequality.

For two decades, economists and policymakers have been trying to make sense of our unemployment conundrum. Why is our unemployment rate so high? What can be done about this? There are no simple answers to these questions, given the complexity of the problem. Our unemployment crisis mirrors South Africa's racialised history, but it is also reflective of the breakdown in trust since 1994 between the four broad class groups, which I described in the introduction to this book.

Since 1994, six million people have entered the job market, yet the economy has only created four million jobs.[3] Total employment in South Africa is about 16 million against a labour force of 22 million people. This means that the net rate at which people have entered the labour market has exceeded the rate of job creation. The post-apartheid era resulted in increased labour market participation, which is positive, but only insofar as the economy could absorb the numbers. The results are common cause – a narrow unemployment rate of about 27% (an increase from 16% in 1995), which in real terms means that more than one in four South Africans actively seeking work are unemployed. This rate of joblessness rises to nearly 37% if those who have stopped looking for work are included.[4]

Unemployment (%)	1995	2005	2017
South Africa	16.9	23.8	27.3
Brazil	9.9	11.4	13.3
Sub-Saharan Africa	7.6	8.0	7.3
Russian Federation	9.4	7.1	5.2
China	4.6	4.1	4.7
India	4.0	4.4	3.5
Middle Income Country Mean	5.9	6.2	5.4

Table 1.1: Unemployment rates, by comparator country
(Source: World Bank Indicators)

It is, of course, very difficult to transform any society without creating the conditions that generate jobs. If we do not drastically and sustainably reduce unemployment and increase the size of the working population, the stability of the country will be threatened.

Apartheid labour policy, which was premised on deliberately preventing black people from acquiring skills or getting professional, higher-paid jobs, benefited the owners of South Africa's key economic sectors at the time, agriculture and mining. However, as these two industries became more mechanised and capital-intensive, and less labour-intensive, and as our economy evolved from primarily agricultural or resource-based, millions of unskilled or under-skilled people fell out of the system, with no transitional policy and plan for them.

This history, however, only partly explains our unemployment problem. The other reasons relate to the sectoral transition of our economy, which anomalously all but bypassed the developmental stage of having a large manufacturing sector. Manufacturing, which should be the engine of job creation for a low- and medium-skilled country such as South Africa, has instead consistently contracted here. To my knowledge, no country has evolved from middle- to high-income status without the presence of a

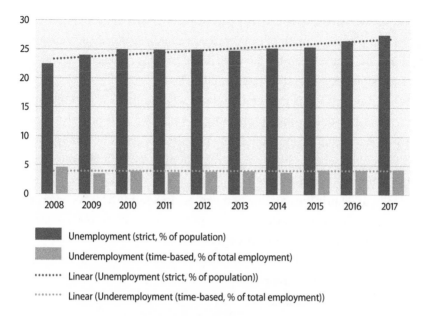

Figure 1.1: South African unemployment statistics
(Source: Stats SA; South African Quarterly Labour Force Survey; Author's calculations)

vibrant manufacturing sector.

In quantitative terms, since 2001, our primary sectors have shed 500 000 jobs. The secondary sector has stalled – only one million jobs have been created, of which just 99 000 have been in the manufacturing sector. Almost five million jobs (90% of net job creation) have emanated from the tertiary sector, with the biggest job generator being the public sector and financial and business services sectors.

The substantial growth of South Africa's finance and services sectors is not necessarily a bad thing, but it becomes self-defeating in an economy like ours where there is a mismatch between our skills distribution and the skills that our economy needs. The implications for our inequality crisis of a growing services sector alongside a shrinking manufacturing sector are self-evident because there is an ever-widening earnings distribution driven by high wage growth for people with tertiary qualifications. This obviously links directly to our education crisis.

The growth of the black middle class, which is often cited as a key success of the post-apartheid South African government, and which intuitively drives some of the growth of our services sector, is unsteady. Data from the National Income Dynamics Survey shows that just one quarter of South Africa's population is in the 'stable middle class'.

What concerns me is that among those who do make it into the middle class, there is a one in four probability of relapsing into poverty. In other words, a significant proportion of the population that is normally counted as middle class remains highly vulnerable to poverty, with obvious implications for unemployment levels.[5]

Finally, and fairly inexcusably in my mind, in South Africa we have one of the smallest shares of informal sector employment in a sample of comparator countries – 18% in South Africa versus a global average of 61%.

At the most basic level, our unemployment problem shows that the demand for labour is incompatible with our abundance of unskilled labour – that is, our dominant skills profile.

Labour market economists cite several reasons for this.

Firstly, South Africa's skewed economic concentration levels mean that only a few players dominate the key sectors of our economy. This results in a lack of competition, high barriers of entry for new, small firms and stifled innovation – the latter being a critical driver for economic growth in developing economies.

Secondly, we have a chronically low-trust society as a result of our history. According to Vimal Ranchhod, a professor of economics at the University of Cape Town's School of Economics, 'this manifests in excessive bureaucracy and labour disputes that are costly to both workers and management. The effect of this is that employers can become highly risk-averse when considering applicants with little work experience or lower levels of qualifications ... the net effect is to reduce employment below its potential.'[6] The ongoing debate over the National Minimum Wage is indicative of this.

Thirdly, investors have become increasingly skittish about policy and political risks to their return on investments. This includes threats to property rights, social instability and corruption. Without investment, we will not create jobs, however laudable our labour policies might be.

Fourthly, our industrial policy has become synonymous with excessive bureaucracy and inefficient targeting, instead of promoting investment and creating jobs. Our industrial policy should drive a dynamic and innovative economy where people are rewarded and supported for entrepreneurism and risk-taking. In South Africa, we have somehow instilled a culture that creates a fear of failure. In Silicon Valley, for example, the prevailing culture is one where start-ups are allowed to fail, and indeed are expected to fail, as a rite of passage.

Finally, and self-evidently, we need a high-quality educational sector that is accessible to everyone and which responds to the natural evolution of our economy.

Reality two: We are locked in an inequality crisis

The net effect of our employment crisis is that nearly half of all South Africans remain below the poverty line. For half of our population, in other words, the world has changed very little, despite the transition to democracy and seismic shifts in the global economy.[7] Many people have never secured a decent place to live. Some people do not own the land they work. Access to decent schooling and skills remains limited. Above all, in a system where our future depends on the accumulation of skills and capital, few people have the means to ascend the ladder of opportunity.

Since 1994, South Africa has implemented the largest welfare programme in Africa, with relatively higher rates of fiscal redistribution than countries such as Brazil, Chile, Colombia, Indonesia and Mexico.[8] South Africa has redistributed assets (primarily land), albeit at a limited pace, scale and success rate, and has adopted a range of regulatory measures aimed at addressing racial inequality (including affirmative action, preferential procurement and Broad-Based Black Economic Empowerment). Yet, the Gini coefficient, which measures the gap between rich and poor, has only reduced slightly since 1994. Inequality among black South Africans has increased over the same period.

The last quarter-century has seen significant change in the pattern of earnings, though less so in patterns of wealth. Over the past 20 years, the income earned by black people has gone from roughly one-third to just over

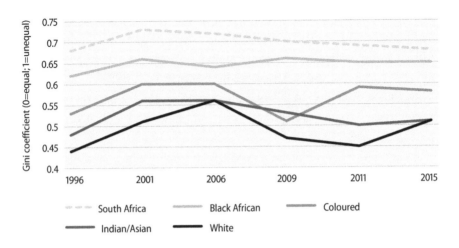

Figure 1.2: Inequality (income per capita) by racial group
(Sources: Stats SA; Supplementary data obtained from Southern Africa Labour and Development Research Unit)

half of national income. But while the black share of income has increased, the black share of wealth in the economy has not really increased. This suggests that access to assets and savings remains disproportionately skewed towards white South Africans – a legacy of historical wealth.

Inequality is also reflected and reproduced in the provision of social services. Our health and education systems are characterised by extreme dualisms in which citizens (and their children) from the elite classes receive private services of a globally high standard, while the townships and rural poor continue to receive sub-standard public services. Similarly, how safe we feel in our homes is directly related to the affordability of private security contractors.

Unfortunately, race remains the central determining factor in socio-economic status, which presents a significant challenge to our agenda of constructing a non-racial narrative of development and change.

In this respect, wealth inequality and inequalities of opportunity present a persistent threat both to the dignity of our citizens and to the strength and security of our society. This also provides fertile ground for divisive populist rhetoric.

Reality three: We are locked in a low-growth trap

Until 2012, South Africa's growth performance broadly tracked that of the global economy – when the global economy was growing at close to 5%, we were growing at slightly above 5%.

Since then, we have grown at a much slower rate than an already slowing global economy, and significantly slower than our benchmark peers.

Since 2012, global growth has averaged approximately 3%, while our growth has averaged just 1.5% and has at times been negative.

In 2016, the economy grew by just 0.57% and in 2017 by 1.3%, much lower than in comparable emerging economies, such as India at 7.1% and Ethiopia at 7.6%. This remains well below the 5% target, established by the National Development Plan, which is required to sustain rates of job creation that are commensurate with our current population growth.

South Africa's lacklustre economic growth over the last two decades reflects structural, spatial, skills and policy constraints. In response, and under pressure, the government has relied on creating jobs within its own ranks, using the public sector budget to consume rather than to invest. This has caused our debt-to-GDP ratio to climb inexorably from 27.8% in 2008 to 50.1% in 2018. Furthermore, this has led to another problem, identified by leading South African labour economist Professor Haroon Bhorat, which is a key new labour segmentation between the strength of unionised public and private sector workers in South Africa. According to Bhorat's research, the public sector's formal workforce membership has risen to 66% since 1997, while the private sector's share has declined to 18%. Unionised workers earn more on average than non-unionised private sector workers. Bhorat finds:

> In the South African labour market, public sector unionised workers earn the highest wages. In the middle of the distribution curve, the public sector wage premium is, relative to non-unionised private sector, the highest. Private sector workers in the middle of the distribution suffer the most from a lack of real earnings growth, given in part their small union wage premium.[9]

This has obvious implications for our low-growth trap. The public sector cannot sustainably be South Africa's largest employment creator. We need growth-producing, productivity-enhancing employment drivers spearheaded by an investment-hungry private sector and supported by the public sector.

Reality four: We have a crisis of falling investment

A crisis of falling investment is underpinning our dismal growth performance. South Africa's fixed capital investment as a percentage of GDP is only 19% and has been in a period of sustained contraction over the past two years. Fixed investment in China, by comparison, is 43% of GDP, and in South Korea, it is 30%.

Foreign direct investment (FDI) inflows into South Africa have remained well below their potential and have been insufficient to create momentum. According to the Reserve Bank, 'in 2017, South Africa fell from being the second largest recipient of FDI in Africa to the sixth largest, receiving only 3% of FDI into Africa that year. This was mainly a result of lack of confidence in the economy. In 2018, South Africa's FDI inflows rose to a five-year high off the back of confidence in President Ramaphosa. However, portfolio

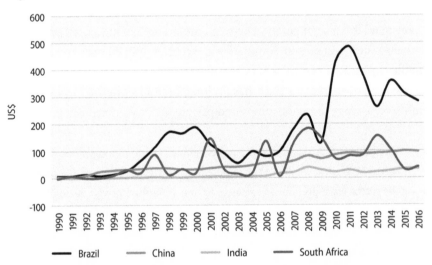

Figure 1.3: FDI inflows per capita across developing countries, 1990–2016

(Source: World Bank World Development Indicators)

investment inflows fell to R90 billion in 2018 from R278.8 billion the previous year, demonstrating our ongoing vulnerability to financialised markets,
as opposed to the stability of fixed capital investment.'[10]

Our crisis of investment is not a private sector problem alone. The South
African government owns 46% of the total fixed capital stock of the economy. Despite this, over the past two decades, it has accounted for only 20%
of net investment. There is a need to open this sector – including the ownership of our state-owned enterprises (SOEs) – to greater competition so that
our SOEs can become meaningful engines of economic growth and development. I provide more detail on the critical role of SOEs in this regard in
Chapter 12.

Reality five: We are not competitive enough

For all the global rhetoric about declining trade flows, we live in an age of
unprecedented interconnectedness between the economies and societies of
the world in a way that those present at the adoption of the Freedom Charter
in Kliptown could not have imagined. To succeed in today's world, competitiveness is key.

As a percentage of total global GDP, cross-border trade in goods and
services has nearly doubled since 1990 to 56%. Trade between China and
Africa, for instance, rose from less than US$1 billion in 1995 to over US$120
billion in 2016. The world is increasingly one large, integrated market, a fact
that no country can afford to ignore.

Local firms can now rapidly reach worldwide scale by tapping into international markets for goods and services and by integrating into global value
chains. Rapid and exponential growth for South Africa would be the net
result, but only if supported by the right domestic policies and institutions.

In addition, globalisation gives countries access to technologies and
financing (investment and loans), which promote development and industrialisation. Globalisation, when properly managed, can lead to generational
poverty reduction, as it has done in many Asian countries. In South Africa,
we subscribe to the Doha Declaration, which states: 'International trade
can play a major role in the promotion of economic development and the

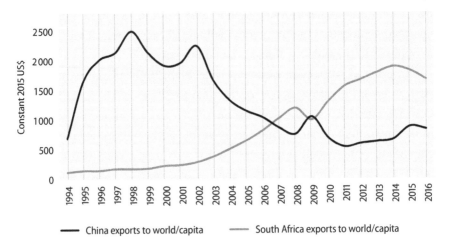

Figure 1.4: Outward trade per capita
(Source: World Bank World Development Indicators)

alleviation of poverty. We recognise the need for all our peoples to benefit from the increased opportunities and welfare gains that the multilateral trading system generates.'[11]

In this regard, it is also a universal truth that globalisation produces winners and losers. Winners are those who specialise early on, according to some comparative advantage, such as geography, demographics or resources. Losers are those who fail to specialise – often due to trade barriers such as tariffs and subsidies – and are left to manufacture locally at a higher cost to consumers.

Unfortunately, we have not done enough to reduce our binding constraints on investment and growth and on our opportunity costs for competing in the global trade game. South Africa ranks 82 out of 190 countries on the 2018 World Bank's Ease of Doing Business Index, but ranks 136 for starting a business, 112 for getting electricity, 107 for registering a property, 147 for trading across borders, and 115 for enforcing contracts. We were placed 61 out of 137 economies in the 2017/18 World Economic Forum's Global Competitiveness Index, slipping 14 places from the previous year.

We cannot hope to secure our place competitively if we keep scoring own goals in terms of becoming the best we can.

One of our greatest competitive advantages used to be the cost of our

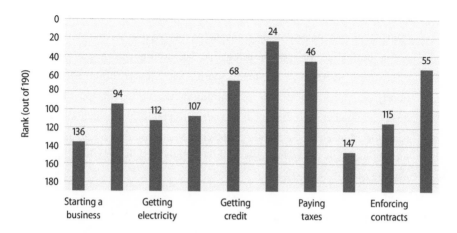

Figure 1.5: Rankings on doing business topics in South Africa
(Source: World Bank)

electricity. Electricity tariffs have increased by 356% in the decade since 2007, even though total inflation over the same period was only 74%. In 2018, electricity in South Africa was the least affordable of all the BRICS nations (Brazil, Russia, India, China, South Africa).

Existing power generation relies heavily on baseload coal, despite the fact that new power from solar and wind would be at least 40% cheaper overall.[12] Expensive electricity raises the operating costs of small and medium businesses and represents a serious obstacle to major investments in mining and industry.

We are also falling behind in the cost of our transport infrastructure, limiting access for businesses to the global economy. The average cost of transporting a shipping container in the Southern African Development Community (SADC) is US$2 148 for exports and US$2 745 for imports, compared to US$823 and US$800 respectively in China. Documentary and border compliance takes on average 168 hours, compared to almost zero in the Organisation for Economic Co-operation and Development countries.

An additional problem in this area is that road and rail infrastructure is designed to support the natural resource sector alone. The World Bank recently argued:

Rail continues to be designed for bulk transportation in South Africa (with tariff structures putting transporters of cargo at a disadvantage versus bulk transporters), meaning that non-mining businesses have to rely on road freight, while many South African ports continue to be poorly equipped to deal with non-mining merchandise, with port fees 88 percent higher than the global average. This results in a system where transportation costs contribute to pricing many South African non-mining products out of business in international product markets, and making imports expensive.[13]

Our inadequate infrastructure also exacerbates the difficulty of accessing regional and global markets. Regional integration remains low, with intraregional trade representing just 10% of total trade in southern Africa (compared to 60% in Europe, 40% in North America and 30% in the Association of Southeast Asian Nations). Exporting manufactured goods and services into the SADC region, where they are highly competitive, is crucial to achieving economies of scale, increasing levels of production and eventually penetrating global markets. In addition, ease of access to the region is an important factor in attracting FDI flows. However, barriers to trade – most notably, insufficient infrastructure and 'soft barriers' in moving goods across the border – prevent the growth of regional connections.

South Africa will need a larger network of logistics infrastructure, lower transport costs, and faster and less onerous customs procedures to facilitate the movement of goods. In turn, the country will need to position itself as a hub for international trade and as a competitive location for multinational corporations to produce goods for export.

No economy has historically been able to generate high levels of economic growth without the private sector as a partner. Small enterprises are the economic oxygen that we need to grow the middle class. We therefore need to utilise economic incentives (such as preferential procurement and lower interest rates) and create better or less regulation to grow the small and medium enterprises sector. The costs of doing business remain stubbornly high, especially for small and medium-sized enterprises.

A significant regulatory burden is placed on formal businesses, which

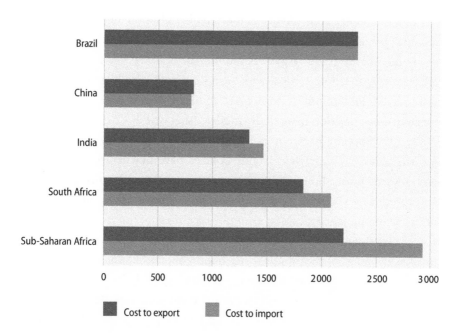

**Figure 1.6: Cost of moving containers across developing countries
(US$ per container, 2014)**

(Source: World Bank World Development Indicators)

must navigate complex company registration procedures, onerous regu-lations to access credit, long waiting periods for registering property or receiving electricity and water, and a plethora of requirements to comply with labour law, which are managed by different agencies.

While government has its role to play in setting the conditions for growth, rapid, inclusive and equitable economic growth is directly correlated to the number and size of local businesses in an economy, which, in turn, requires an environment that is conducive to entrepreneurship.

Historically, this has been the driver of sustainable growth in almost every successful economy around the world. Turkey's annual economic growth of over 11% has relied on tax breaks and billions in loans to small and medium businesses through the National Credit Guarantee Fund. These businesses can create higher-paying jobs and grow quickly, but they will not emerge if the barriers to creating them remain so high.

In the late 1990s, South Africa embraced liberalisation, removing many of the tariff protections for agriculture and textiles at a faster rate than expected by the World Trade Organization, but the country has not specialised effectively. Our failure to deal with structural problems by converting our resource-based economy into a more modern competitive economy has weakened our position in a rapidly modernising world.

Our flip-flopping over our policy regime has chronically damaged our growth trajectory. Our rigid labour policies have not helped, particularly with regards to our failure to create a meaningful manufacturing sector to absorb our low-skilled labour force. Our limp mining sector, once the cornerstone of our economy, is an example, regardless of the fact that it is seen as a 'sunset industry' – in other words, a dying sector. We have simply failed to take advantage of commodity price booms and attract the commensurate foreign investment needed to sustain economic growth. In 2005, during the previous mining boom, Australian mining companies reported a near doubling of pre-tax profits, compared to just 12% in South Africa. In the latest commodity price boom, South Africa again performed weakly, at just 4% growth in production compared to Australia's 26%.[14] Our failure to benefit from higher commodity prices is typically associated with the constantly changing Mining Charter and lower-than-needed investment in the sector due to regulatory uncertainty.

South Africa's inability to retain international investors or attract new ones is a failure of policy more than a failure of markets and returns. In fact, we boast some of the highest returns in the world, with the annualised real returns (percentage) on the Johannesburg Stock Exchange outperforming all the world's stock exchanges over the long term.[15] Yet, we have experienced unprecedented capital flight as investors lost confidence in the government's ability to ensure the political stability needed for economic growth. FDI picked up in 2018 in response to President Ramaphosa taking the reins and instituting a global investment drive, but that was before a new round of electricity load shedding dampened investor enthusiasm in early 2019. Political uncertainty and threatening populism have increased the cost of capital and the risk premium required by investors. It is particularly telling that investors would rather earn near-zero returns in European markets than invest in higher-yielding markets in South Africa.

Reality six: We have failed to prepare our youth adequately

We will never transition to high productivity competitiveness if we do not completely overhaul our education and training system.

Almost six million South Africans aged 15–34 are unemployed, of which 38% (more than one in every three young people) are aged 15–34.[16] This crisis has its roots in the performance of the education system. South Africa's education system is one of the weakest in the world, despite public spending of 6.4% of GDP, compared to the European average of 4.8%. Government delivery on education has been a chronic failure over the last three decades, which has resulted in a structural skills deficit in key sectors with high growth potential. Our youth have not been adequately equipped to start their own ventures, or to secure more skilled work in higher productivity sectors. I expand on this in Chapter 13.

Reality seven: We are being left behind in the Fourth Industrial Revolution

Technological change is shaping the nature of the global economy. Computing power available today is more than one trillion times greater than it was 50 years ago. Goods, services and information move faster and at a lower cost than ever before. Only those countries that adapt to these trends, and seize new opportunities, will thrive in this context.

Technological disruption is creating profound economic changes around the world. Automation and artificial intelligence are expected to replace human labour in many sectors, resulting in job losses and depressed wages. Even in the advanced economies of North America and Europe, there has been a public backlash at perceived threats to employment. In the decades to come, these trends will have a marked impact on the South African economy. In order to prepare for and endure these changes, we must adapt now and lay the foundations for a flexible, modern economy that is equipped for a technology-driven century. This is our long-term imperative and the policies that we implement now must be designed to anticipate such change.

Right now, we are falling critically short in this regard. We currently spend 0.76% of GDP on research and development and technology, compared to 4% in South Korea and 2% in China. Hi-tech goods make up just 4.5% of exported manufactured products in South Africa, compared to 43% in Malaysia and 26% in both China and South Korea. We have lost critical design and engineering capability through deindustrialisation and we risk being left further behind in the Fourth Industrial Revolution (4IR).

In the First Industrial Revolution, water and steam power were employed to mechanise production. Electricity drove the Second to create mass production. Automation was the outcome of the Third through electronics and information technology. The 4IR uses the fusion of digital and other technology to change not only the way we interact but the relationship between biological and physical realms. The extent of the changes created by the 4IR has the scope to transform entire systems of production, management and governance.

Countries that have already made this transition have shielded themselves against the tumultuous effects of the 4IR. India, for example, has positioned itself as a forerunner among developing countries in technology, with space exploration, pharmaceuticals, biotechnology and renewable energy taking preference in government-driven investment programmes. The nearly US$170 billion IT services industry in India is expected to grow by between 7% and 9% this year and add as many as 250 000 jobs to the economy.

These threats are real, but they are not insurmountable. There are a number of positives from the new 4IR world, some of which offer particular advantages to developing countries. According to McKinsey & Company, for instance, 4IR is expected to create up to US$3.7 trillion in value to global manufacturing.[17] If we are willing to embrace this opportunity through nimble and pragmatic policies and single-minded leadership, it could be a game changer for South Africa, which up to this point has failed to create a path-changing manufacturing sector.

Reality eight: We have failed to build a capable and corruption-free state

Over the past decade, the state has been compromised by capture by narrow political-business complexes, its lack of policy focus, and insufficient technical capacity. Our SOEs should be primarily focused on driving the economy (by providing cheap and secure electricity, efficient port handling and other services), but have instead been repurposed to serve corrupt interests. In countries such as Singapore, the state was *the* critical catalyst in economic reform, but the prerequisite for this was zero-tolerance for corruption and patronage.

Building a capable, professional and corruption-free state has to be our priority over the short to medium term. At the outset, this will require significant restructuring. Government itself is currently sprawling and inefficient, and places an unacceptably high burden on the national budget while simultaneously preventing rapid and well-coordinated policy implementation.

Ramaphosa has started this process by slimming down the size of his Cabinet, and has indicated that he intends to streamline the size of government even more. The new Cabinet is now made up of 28 ministers and 34 deputy ministers and a number of ministries were merged. Before this restructuring, South Africa's Cabinet comprised 72 people – an outlier among countries of the same size and economy. The size of South Africa's Cabinet has ballooned over the years, from 50 members under Thabo Mbeki to 72 members under Jacob Zuma.[18]

The expansion of government has led to increasing bureaucratic complexity, many redundant levels of administration and overlapping institutional mandates. Crucially, job creation that is propelled only by public sector expansion is not fiscally sustainable and does not represent meaningful growth in the economy. We need to build a streamlined and capable state, which can create an environment for social mobility and economic productivity rather than providing jobs for and of itself. This view is supported by a growing consensus in the international literature that economic growth and development needs capable government administrations to work. We need not overcomplicate this fact with ideology and competing political ideals.

Conclusion: Not all doom and gloom

There is a temptation, when confronted with the range of problems outlined in this chapter, to believe that there is little hope of turning the South African political-economy around. It sometimes feels as if the challenges are overwhelming, particularly with so many moving parts under the control of so many different players with conflicting agendas.

The truth is, I really believe our strengths and opportunities outweigh our weaknesses. I would not be engaging in a debate about the future of South Africa if I believed otherwise. We have a highly developed infrastructure, a sophisticated and capable business and banking sector, and deep markets. We are incredibly well placed to leverage off Africa's future trade and development opportunities.

The unleashing of our potential will, however, only happen when the state, institutions, markets and citizens cohere more deliberately around a common purpose and set of interests. Not the interests of big corporate capital. Not the interests of a political elite. And not the interests of the people, at least as defined by the growing number of populist pretenders who claim to speak – loudly I might add – on behalf of the downtrodden. Defining these common interests, and distilling the necessary trade-offs, must be the outcome of intense dialogue and consultation, underpinned by evidence and shared analysis. New institutional mechanisms need to be forged to develop and sustain this new economic ecosystem. This, in turn, will require leadership and resolve among core stakeholders that we have hitherto lacked.

In Part Two of this book suggestions to make this possible are elaborated on.

2

The Developmental State Remains Elusive

Conceptually we have a problem – because most of our thinking processes have not gone beyond the 1980s, yet our society has been transformed quite fundamentally. — Tito Mboweni

Chapter summary

- We need to situate South Africa's experience of government since 1994 in the context of two historical processes: state-building and economic transformation.

- In the first phase, which began properly with the establishment of the National Treasury and SARS, the state is there to enable economic growth and transformation.

- In the second phase, which coincided roughly with the Zuma period, the state itself is regarded as an economy, especially an economy ripe for radical transformation.

- State capture arose when the imperative for economic transformation, especially in the state-owned enterprises and through the system of public procurement, trumped the imperative to build effective public institutions.

Corruption and state capture in South Africa, beyond what they tell us about the values and morality of the political elite in the country, are symptoms of deep character flaws in the organisation of government. We are in danger of overlooking these structural elements if we continue to treat corruption and capture as the work primarily of bad apples or of criminals. Certainly, there has been shocking and massive criminality in government and among politicians, especially from the ANC. These individuals need to be exposed and dealt with, with the full force of the law. But it does not end there.

The Zondo Commission of Inquiry into State Capture will only have limited success if it stops short at exposing guilty parties. The commission's terms of reference invite it to make findings and report on the nature and extent of corruption, especially as it relates to the awarding of contracts and tenders. The commission has a historical opportunity, in other words, to help develop an agenda for change in the wake of state capture.

What is needed is a more complex understanding of what has happened in government and among the political elite since 1994. We need to situate recent events in the context of two major historical processes. The first is state-building. The second is economic transformation.

After 1994, state-building and economic transformation were understood as related but, nonetheless, distinct historical projects.

The first concerned overcoming the legacy of apartheid that had, at the level of the state, fragmented the country into literally dozens of parallel and separate administrations and governments. 'Whites', 'Coloureds' and 'Indians' were governed via distinct administrations with regard to education, social welfare, housing, local government, arts, culture and recreation, which were formalised after the 1983 Constitution in the Tricameral Parliament. Through the 1950s and 1960s, Africans fell under the remit of the notorious Department of Native Affairs and then, through the 1970s and 1980s, increasingly through either 'self-governing' homelands (KwaZulu, for example) or through the nominally 'independent' states of the Transkei, Bophuthatswana, Venda and Ciskei. Each had its own departments and administrations for education, health, housing, and so on. Many of these governments and departments were hopelessly inefficient and there was gross and widespread corruption.

In order to improve the effectiveness and responsiveness of the state, two broad initiatives unfolded after 1994. One was the move to public management, with a view to give greater autonomy and discretion to senior government officials to make decisions in their respective areas. Another was the deliberate politicisation of the administration by making, for example, recruitment into the public service a responsibility of the political executive, often without proper regard to experience and to qualifications. This combination of managerial discretion and politicisation is precisely what has ultimately compromised the effectiveness of government administrations and made them vulnerable to state capture.

The second historical project undertaken by the ANC was one of economic transformation. Since at least the 1950s, the centrepiece of thinking in the ANC and the Tripartite Alliance was that the winning of political power by the black majority was the 'first stage', with a 'second stage' – a thorough-going transformation of economic relations in South Africa – to follow. The Colonialism of a Special Type (CST) thesis opened up vigorous and extremely productive political and scholarly debates about the relationship between race and class right through the 1970s and 1980s.[1] In the 1990s, feminist interventions expanded these debates to include the relationship between race domination, class exploitation and patriarchy.

Given the way that race domination was embedded in the workings of the capitalist economy, black majority rule was always understood to have major consequences for (and was inextricably linked to) the structure of the economy and capitalist social relations in particular. What such a 'post-apartheid' economy would consist of has been one of the central areas of tension and disagreement within the ANC itself and between its Alliance partners. On the one hand, the 'left' of the ANC interpreted CST and the theory of National Democratic Revolution to support a move towards socialism, or, at least, to imply a substantial role for public ownership in a 'transformed' economy. It is not difficult to see how elements of this thinking have been taken up in the Economic Freedom Fighters' call for the nationalisation of the commanding industries in South Africa and for state ownership of all land.

Under Thabo Mbeki, in particular, CST was interpreted differently. Economic transformation took the form not of nationalisation but of Black Economic Empowerment within the framework of a market economy. Sometimes this was referred to as a South African model of the developmental state. What is easily missed in the heated contestation over the Growth, Employment and Redistribution (GEAR) programme, introduced in 1996, and widely regarded on the left as a concession to neoliberalism and a betrayal of the ANC's traditional values and politics, is that 'left' and 'right' conceptions of the post-apartheid economy saw a major role for the state. Indeed, they agreed, even if implicitly, that state-building was an essential ingredient of economic transformation.

Contemporary governance in South Africa has to be seen in the context of these challenges of state-building and economic transformation. From this perspective, we can identify two distinct periods.

In the first phase, which began properly with the establishment of the National Treasury and the South African Revenue Service (SARS), the state was there to enable economic growth and transformation. In the second phase, which overlapped with this first period in many parts of the government but was given formal political expression after 2007, the state itself was regarded as an economy, especially an economy most ripe for radical transformation.

State and economy

When the ANC came to power in 1994, it was alarmed to find that the country's finances were in a terrible condition. In the 1994/5 fiscal year, public debt had risen to nearly 50% of GDP, up from 30% ten years before. The global economic recession had taken its toll as had international sanctions. In the main, however, it reflected the crippling costs of the war in Angola and Namibia, as well as the price of internal repression. What is more, financial management systems had broken down, especially in the former homelands.

These were not circumstances propitious for the financing of the Reconstruction and Development Programme (RDP) – an ambitious project of state-funded investment in infrastructure and in basic service delivery. The establishment of the National Treasury was a response to the dire financial situation but also to the colonial legacy of apartheid. Economic growth and development depended on a process of state-building.

The 1993 Interim Constitution made fiscal consolidation a priority, and Department of Finance officials were given the work of producing a single revenue and expenditure framework by combining the budgets of all of

South Africa's various administrations. This was no simple accounting task. It required nothing less than stitching homeland administrations back into the fabric of a united South Africa and bringing them under the sovereignty of a democratic, national government.

The right to raise taxes was withdrawn from homelands and former provincial administrations as they were slowly phased out. New provincial governments were established with limited financial and fiscal powers. The Constitution placed the National Treasury at the centre of a new, intergovernmental system, responsible for coordinating and developing financial management and budgeting processes. The difficulty with the Treasury's mandate, however, is that it could not be realised through legislative or regulatory fiat. Provinces and local governments are protected in the Constitution as autonomous spheres of government. In this context, fiscal consolidation had to take place in a situation of widespread institutional decentralisation or what came to be known in South Africa as a framework of 'cooperative governance'. Failure adequately to adapt to this institutional environment had severely undermined the RDP Office. Officials from other departments and spheres of government frequently failed or refused to submit their expenditure plans, undermining the Office's role as some kind of 'super-ministry'. Fiscal consolidation and decentralisation went hand-in-hand with moves to outsource more and more of government's work to the private sector.

The new Treasury was formally established in 2000 after the passage of the Public Finance Management Act, which merged the departments of finance and state expenditure. It had core responsibility for budget management, intergovernmental relations, macroeconomic policy and asset and liability management.

The constitutional constraints on the National Treasury's powers were largely overcome through institutional and political arrangements. In the first place, the National Treasury quickly developed a reputation for technical competence in its field, employing and retaining highly qualified staff who were usually able to persuade politicians and other officials by the force of their arguments and/or the sophistication of their tools.

Whereas other departments in government experienced very high staff turnover rates, especially at senior levels, the National Treasury was remarkably stable during this period. This helped create a robust intellectual culture within a collegial environment, generating the conditions for what became known as 'Team Finance'. Secondly, the close relationship between the finance minister, Trevor Manuel, and President Mbeki complemented the department's status. This was further supported by the fact that Mbeki saw the Treasury as a key driver of state-building in South Africa and in a privileged position to steer the implementation of the GEAR strategy. Thirdly, without the legal authority simply to give binding instructions to provincial officials, the National Treasury developed a complex intergovern-mental system that relied as much on formal power as on social capital to achieve its aims. The flagship process in this regard was the Medium-Term Expenditure Framework, which devolved management authority to state institutions subject to the Public Finance Management Act.

The Medium-Term Expenditure Framework sought to create a collabo-rative system of decision-making by bringing officials from the National Treasury together with their counterparts from provincial departments. Ministers, Members of the Provincial Executive Councils and the Budget Forum, comprising the minister and deputy minister of finance, MECs of finance and senior officials, aimed to coordinate the plans across the vari-ous spheres of government. The principle that informed the model was that departments had discretion to determine their own spending priorities, though within a framework of spending limits determined by the National Treasury.

This model of financial and fiscal governance was successful in bringing coordination and discipline to public accounts across the state (with the exception, perhaps, of local government) – earning the department high plaudits internationally. From 2000, government spending rose dramati-cally, sustained by impressive growth in government revenue (especially from 2003).

At stake was a model of a South African developmental state. State-building involved efforts to establish powerful government administrations, especially on the economic front, which were able to regulate and incentivise appropriate developmental behaviour in the market and in other parts of society. Beyond the National Treasury and SARS, the government's record was extremely uneven, and in many sectors, including education, health and in local government, it was largely disastrous. Some of this was related to the new spirit of 'managerialism' that infected public administration scholars in the 1990s and 2000s, which drove organisational changes in many government departments. Emphasis was placed on developing a leadership core that was strategic and innovative, rather than one that was stable, appropriately trained and well insulated from political interference.

Improved financial and regulatory powers in the state, however, were not having the desired developmental effects, especially in the economy. So even though economic growth was relatively strong up until the financial crisis of 2008, wealth remained concentrated in white hands and unemployment remained high. In general, growth reproduced apartheid-era patterns of racialised inequality and economic exclusion.

From the early 2000s, the National Treasury started attracting criticism for overly controlling the budgetary process and, effectively, setting government priorities. In particular, the Congress of South African Trade Unions (COSATU) baulked at the fact that money bills were not submitted to parliament for review and amendment. Treasury officials had justified this state of affairs in the name of fiscal discipline. The People's Budget Process, a partnership between COSATU, the South African Council of Churches and the South African NGO Coalition, was established to try to redress this situation. From the provinces, there were complaints arising that even if the Treasury did not have *de jure* authority over the provinces, it exercised *de facto* control of provincial spending priorities. Several scholars worried that 'provincial governments have been turned into provincial administrations'.[2]

This relationship between the centre and the provinces was managed to the benefit of the National Treasury as long as the minister of finance enjoyed strong support from the president. This was the case during Mbeki's Presidency. Furthermore, Mbeki increasingly concentrated political power into the expanded office of the Presidency, reducing the influence of provincial politicians and others outside of an inner circle, including senior office holders in the ANC. This situation changed dramatically after the election of Jacob Zuma as president in 2009.

Coalescing around provincial politicians were a variety of powerful regional forces that felt stymied by the centralised fiscal system. Among them were senior officials in the ANC. The growing influence of provincial power bases versus national leaders was later expressed through the so-called 'Premier League'. The momentum and force of these provincial and regional players (together with support from the South African Communist Party and COSATU) is what brought Zuma to power. Today, three of the 'Top 6' officials of the ANC are provincial politicians.

Concern about the role of the National Treasury in setting government's priorities was coming from the Cabinet too. Early into his presidency, and prior to the establishment of the National Planning Commission, Zuma had gone far to put in place what was called at the time an 'outcomes-based' system of government. It involved defining priority areas for government and then pressing departments to plan accordingly. Key performance indicators were defined in relation to desired outputs and these were then used to draw up performance agreements between ministers and the president. Ultimately, however, the move to outcomes-based government was an attempt to reduce the power of the National Treasury in defining government's priorities.

State as economy

The pre-Polokwane model of development was largely rejected after the ANC's Conference in 2007, if not in words, then certainly in practice. Opposition to Mbeki had been growing through the 2000s because of a host of reasons, including perceptions that he was putting the state above the ANC due to his supposed neoliberal policies. In particular, it was argued that the South African economy worked to exclude black people and Africans, in particular. Black Economic Empowerment was described by proponents of this narrative as having been co-opted by the new bogeyman of 'White Monopoly Capital' so as to reproduce the existing patterns of capital ownership and control. Gwede Mantashe, then secretary general of the ANC, referred to a 'cappuccino' economy, white on top and black all the way below. Black businesses found the rules of market competition extremely prejudicial, especially as existing white firms could rely on high economic concentration, access to capital, recognisable brands and established supply chains to make the costs of entry prohibitively high. Black employees and women employees faced discrimination in the workplace and the heavy weight of the not-so-glass ceiling. The rules of the economic game were rigged against black workers, but also against black entrepreneurs and black capitalists.

What we saw in the phenomenon of state capture, whether it occurred in state-owned companies, in metros and provincial governments or in local municipalities, was the preparedness of some business people, politicians and officials to tear up the rule book altogether.

In the search for a more radical route to change, we have seen the return of two unexpected pasts. The first is of 1950s' socialism, premised on large-scale nationalisation and state ownership. The second is of 1950s' Afrikaner nationalism and the way that parastatals were used as instruments of Afrikaner economic empowerment – both to create an Afrikaner bourg-eoisie and also to eliminate white poverty. During the Zuma Presidency, this model of economic transformation was especially prominent.

From this perspective, the role of the state was positioned not so much to enable capital formation through the market and then to direct it towards particular sectors or actors, or even more ambitiously, to incentivise eco-nomic activity in sectors deemed important by the political class. Rather, the state was itself thought of as a major economy in its own right, specifically to enable new black firms to shoulder their way into established markets.

As the authors of *Shadow State* argue, the trouble with this develop-ment trajectory was that it set radical economic transformation up against the Constitution.[3] As politicians, business people and government officials were increasingly prepared to break the rules, so they needed also to cap-ture and weaken key state institutions, including the police and the National Prosecuting Authority. The National Treasury was always the big prize in this regard. In this way, the project of economic transformation came into contradiction with the project of state-building.

The consequences have been serious. There has been a steady decline in the effectiveness of government administrations. We will consider the state-owned enterprises more closely in Chapters 4 and 12 as well as the state of education in South Africa in Chapters 5 and 13. There is very little aggregate data on the performance of government in South Africa and the Department of Planning, Monitoring and Evaluation offers no such general view. Reporting on the results of the 2017 review of municipal audit outcomes, however, the auditor-general, Kimi Makwetu, observed: 'When we released the [...] municipal audit outcomes in August 2013, we highlighted, amongst others, a lack of decisive leadership to address the lack of accountability by ensuring consequences against those who flouted basic processes that hampered effective municipal governance.' Five years later, he lamented, 'we are still faced with the same accountability and governance challenges we had flagged throughout these years. There has been no significant positive change towards credible results; instead we are witnessing a *reversal* in audit outcomes' (emphasis added).[4]

Irregular expenditure had grown from R16.2 billion in the 2015/16 financial year to R28.4 billion in 2017 – an increase of almost 60%. More than R2 billion of this amount included prohibited contracts to other state officials. As a whole, the auditor-general found that in the vast majority of municipalities (nearly 70%) tendering practices were unfair and uncompetitive. It is impossible to reduce this phenomenon to poor financial administration or to corruption.

The Mo Ibrahim Foundation, which publishes a comprehensive evaluation of overall governance on the African continent, found that government performance had generally declined between 2008 and 2017. It had no finding, however, for the effectiveness of the public service. The World Bank's Worldwide Governance Indicators recorded a general decline in 'government effectiveness' between 1996 (when it started) and 2017. The index scores countries between -2.5 (weak) and 2.5 (strong). In 1996, South Africa was scored at 1.02. In 2017, the World Bank rated government performance in South Africa at 0.28.

Conclusion

State-building, as we know from historians and sociologists, is a project of the longue durée. It is also a difficult and brutal undertaking. The tendency to reduce it to a question of technical fixes is to overlook the legacy of colonialism, apartheid and capitalist development on the structure, person-nel and cultures of government. In the age of globalisation and environmental crisis, we also have to be realistic about what can be achieved at the national level. There are several important reforms that are urgently needed and that are within our capacity to make.

The first relates to the need to decide which levels of the public service are appropriately staffed by political appointments and which are staffed by professional appointments. We need to draw a clear line between them.

Secondly, the recruitment of professional public servants and of munici-pal officials must be taken out of the hands of politicians and be subjected to meritocratic assessments, which might include a universal entrance exam for, at least, senior managers and promotions based on grade assessments. This was the historical role of the Public Service Commission. Maybe it should get this function back.

The third relates to the fact that public servants and officials need instru-ments and tools to protect themselves from undue political interference. Public service unions need to be more active in this regard.

Fourthly, public procurement is in urgent need of reform. This work has already started in the form of the Office of the Chief Procurement Officer. We need to rethink the current decentralised model of supply-chain man-agement and procurement officials need better training, status and oversight wherever they are.

Lastly, we need a proper debate about rents and rent-seeking. I have dis-cussed at length the apartheid legacy and its effect on the economy and especially on the ability of black enterprises to compete in the market as it is currently structured. State procurement is an excellent way to subsidise new black companies as they develop their institutional capacities. This requires that we acknowledge that certain kinds of rents are legitimate, for example, when they stem from competitiveness. However fraught with dangers such a development would be, it is time to debate the question openly.

3

Successes and Failures of Policy

The crisis consists precisely in the fact that the old is dying and the new cannot be born; in this interregnum a great variety of morbid symptoms appear. — Antonio Gramsci

Chapter summary

- Democratic constitutionalism has held firm, but is under threat as constitutional provisions, a free media and an independent judiciary are seen as obstacles to transformation.

- Social policy has significantly improved living conditions for South Africans since 1994. This said, huge dualisms exist in the quality of services offered, and policy continuation is threatened by fiscal constraints.

- Macroeconomic management has been largely effective. There is, however, major scope for improvement in credit extension (to support inclusive growth), and current fiscal risks need to be carefully managed to protect national sovereignty.

- The biggest single policy failure has been around inclusive growth. Policies to grow, restructure and deracialise the economy have all had very little impact.

The South African economy is in limbo. The old economic order is dying, but the new is yet to be born. South Africa's failure to make the structural changes needed to place the economy on a new growth-intensive and inequality-reducing footing has been the subject of much agonising, and much policy-making, over the last three decades.

It is important to understand that policy choices are the outcome of class and political contestation. The state rules and enforces collectively binding decisions in the 'common interest', but how this common interest is defined depends on the capacity of competing social forces to exercise influence and control over the state. There are winners and losers in policy decisions – insiders and outsiders who benefit or do not.

Policy is used for political gain. Because the ruling Alliance – between the ANC, the South African Communist Party and the Congress of South African Trade Unions (COSATU) – is everything to everybody, it has become easy to define and redefine the common interest around the needs of political leaders and their jockeying within the Alliance.

Shaping policy less by the cult of personalities, and more by a new common and embedded interest, is really what inspired me to write this book. My time in politics and the state bore witness to the fact that many of the key decisions we take as leaders have less to do with the evidence-based correctness of a particular choice, and more to do with narrow and short-term political expediency. I think this has worsened over the past decade as the intellectual and strategic capacity in both the ANC and the state has withered. In fact, many of the skirmishes between the National Treasury and various organs of state have been very much about this.

Policy is shaped by history. There is no escaping that the core policy issues we seek to address are shaped by our colonial and apartheid past. The common interest during the colonial period was very much defined around the interests of the imperial powers (the Dutch and the English). This legacy is ever-present – our logistics system is still primarily mine-to-port, and we are not geared to trade and do business with our neighbours on the continent.

The brutal politics of segregation and subjugation were honed under apartheid, a system where the common interest sustained the needs of historic English capital, while generating enormous wealth accumulation for newly formed Afrikaner capital and a new Afrikaner middle class.

This policy history bequeathed to us in 1994 a racially polarised society and highly inefficient and unequal economy and spatial form that required fundamental transformation. And because of the closeness of the state and capital under the apartheid regime, our history also bequeathed to us a mindset in the new ruling Alliance that capital, and by implication markets, were our adversary. This really limited the extent to which we were able to draw capital into a project to industrialise and restructure the economy to serve the new national interest.

Policy post-1994 closely resembled the Convention for a Democratic South Africa deal, which was designed to achieve a new national consensus built around the following core pillars:

- Democratic constitutionalism (built around the Constitution);
- Social policy (RDP and fiscal redistribution programmes of the state);
- Macro-stability and globalisation (GEAR);
- Labour rights (labour legislation); and
- Black class formation and racial transformation (employment equity, state employment and BBBEE).

It is time, having passed the 25th anniversary of democracy, to examine the achievements, constraints, contradictions and impacts of our policy to ensure we keep the right mix of continuity and change going forward. As the old adage goes, we mustn't fix that which ain't broke, but we must be bold enough to tackle those policy holy cows that hold us back in our quest for shared prosperity.

Democratic constitutionalism and the threat of populism

There is no doubt that the Constitution, with its mechanisms for accountability and built-in checks and balances, has provided a solid basis for a 'fair and good society'. The Constitution should be defended at all costs, although constitutional amendments are perfectly acceptable, provided they are well considered and in keeping with the overall spirit and intent.

The last few years have seen democratic constitutionalism under threat. Youth unemployment and increased social discontent have fed the growth of populism both within and outside the ANC. The situation has been further compounded by weak and confused leadership in the governing party and the state, which has not been able to manage the twin outcomes of redistribution and growth.

A narrative has developed over the past decade or so that constitutional provisions, such as a free media and an independent judiciary, have become constraints to transformation. This narrative was fuelled by the forces of corruption and their spin doctors (the public relations firm Bell Pottinger, among others). Fortunately, our institutions of democratic accountability proved resilient, supported by a core network both within the Alliance and civil society. But high levels of social discontent remain, as do the other objective conditions fuelling growing populist sentiments.

An Afrobarometer survey conducted in 2018 shows that 63% of South Africans say they would be willing to forgo elections if a non-elected government or leader were able to impose law and order and provide housing and jobs.[1] This is startling.

As trust, both within the ruling party and among economic stakeholders, has declined, so economic populism has increasingly taken root in our country. Like the global resurgence of populism, this should be of concern to us, with its disdain for democratic accountability and its dismissal of well-considered policy choices. Populism works best in low-trust societies and encompasses a range of ideologies, left and right wing.

The essence of populism is to define friends and enemies, and it demands that the state takes sides and behaves in a partisan manner even if it breaks its own rules and bypasses the institutions established to uphold law. We saw hints of this in 2018 in the varied reactions to the land debate. By its nature, populism denies complexity, denies constraint and denies risk. It distracts attention from the real issues that must be addressed, and, as has been evident over our recent past, closes down space for democratic dialogue and conversation. It offers, and I quote Alex Harrowell from his article 'The Populist Papers: 29 Years of Populism', 'absolute creative freedom to the bullshitter to come up with whatever the audience would enjoy hearing'.[2] Hence, its appeal to desperate politicians and the massive traction it enjoys among electorates. We need the wisdom and the courage to resist this trend, especially when it divides us as South Africans and is an attack on our democratic constitutionalism.

Social policy

Socio-economic rights took centre stage during the Reconstruction and Development Programme (RDP), which sought to direct state resources to make up for apartheid-era backlogs in housing, schooling and health, among other issues.

Ministers and departments were expected to account to an RDP Ministry under the leadership of Jay Naidoo about how they were redirecting spending towards addressing apartheid's infrastructure backlogs. The Ministry was based in President Nelson Mandela's office, signalling that it was not to be trifled with.

Just 15 months after its inception, Mandela announced that economic growth, rather than an expanded budget focused on social redistribution, would become government's main priority. This shift in priority was premised on concerns about how the RDP, and the fiscal risks associated with the apartheid debt, would be financed. The Growth, Employment and Redistribution (GEAR) strategy followed, which resulted in key economic programmes envisaged in the RDP Base Document being shelved, such as the establishment of a people's bank and subordinating monetary policy to income redistribution.

As detailed in Chapter 2, the National Treasury replaced the RDP Office as the apex of policy formulation, and was tasked with managing the complex interplay between the macroeconomy and social redistribution.

Many of the RDP social programmes were incorporated into the fiscal redistribution programmes of government – a fact largely ignored by the left elements in the Alliance who labelled the policy shift as a sell-out and labelled it as the so-called '1996 class project'.

The safety net package of social grants, access to basic education and health care, subsidised housing and free basic services for the poor and indigent has had a significant impact on South Africa's levels of poverty and deprivation in the country. According to Stats SA, the proportion of black Africans living below the lower-bound poverty line in 2006 was 60%, dropping to 47.1% in 2015.[3]

Improvements to housing, electricity and water access are shown in Table 3.1.

Indicator	1996	2016	Change (number)	Change (proportion)	Average daily change
Total number of dwellings/ households	**9 059 606**	**16 921 183**	**7 861 577**	**86.8%**	**1 077**
Formal	5 794 399	13 404 199	7 609 800	131.3%	1 042
Informal	1 453 018	2 193 968	740 950	51.0%	102
Access to piped water	7 234 023	15 218 753	7 984 730	110.4%	1 094
Access to flush or chemical lavatories	4 552 854	11 436 619	6 883 765	151.2%	943
Use of electricity for lighting	5 220 826	15 262 235	10 041 409	192.3%	1 376
Use of electricity for cooking	4 265 305	14 012 036	9 746 731	228.5%	1 335
Use of electricity for heating	4 030 850	6 370 000	2 339 150	58.0%	320

Table 3.1: Living conditions, 1996 and 2016
(Sources: Stats SA; Census 2001; SAIRR)

These safety net measures have been vital in mitigating the impacts of poverty and vulnerability, and have also resulted in significant resource transfers to less developed parts of the country. This has stimulated aggregate demand in these regions, albeit with impacts limited mainly to the trade and financial sectors.

Even in the current tight fiscal framework, social wage allocations have been protected. But quantum leaps in efficiencies are now required. Health and education systems are still characterised by extreme dualisms in which citizens (and their children) from the elite classes receive global-standard private services, while the township and rural poor continue to receive substandard services.

These dualisms – coupled with extreme levels of joblessness – are the daily experience of the poor and provide fertile ground for the rise of populist social movements. The past ten years have seen a marked rise in social protests.

Data collected by Municipal IQ's Hotspots Monitor shows that 2018 was a record year for service delivery protests with some 237 recorded.[4]

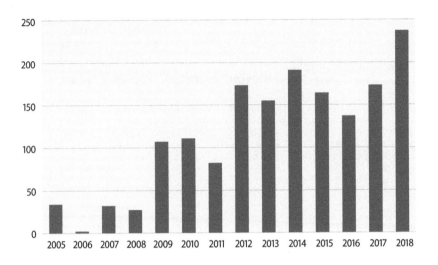

Figure 3.1: Major service delivery protests, by year
(Source: Municipal IQ Hotspots Monitor)

According to Municipal IQ: '2018 had already eclipsed previous annual records for service delivery by the end of September. [Figure 3.1] shows the unequivocal peak, with 2018 tallying 24% more protests than the previous 2014 record-holder.'[5] The protests were spread around the country.

These protests have, in the past, been caricatured as being orchestrated political campaigns masquerading as genuine protests. While this might be true in some cases, it seems that a better explanation is that they are the cry of marginalised and disillusioned people expressing their anger outside of the formal political system.

The link between service delivery protests and the country's economic malaise is plain to see. Karen Heese, an economist at Municipal IQ, says:

> The dual economic pressures of a recessionary environment and rising unemployment seem to be feeding into service delivery protests. Over the course of 2018, a growing number of protest grievances included the demand for municipalities to create employment opportunities, or unhappiness with how these were allocated. It can be concluded that it is crucially important for reinvigorated and equitable economic growth

to mitigate the social and financial pressures manifested in many service delivery protests.[6]

Macroeconomic performance

South Africa's macroeconomic performance since 1994 must be considered in terms of monetary and fiscal policy.

On the monetary policy side, the past 25 years have been a resounding success in terms of protecting the value of the rand, which is defined by the Constitution as the primary objective of the South African Reserve Bank (SARB). Historically, South Africa has avoided hyperinflationary episodes, in contrast to most Latin American countries and others elsewhere, which highlights the dangers of economic populism and ill-conceived policy decisions. We must protect this discipline because hyperinflation will surely further impoverish the majority of our people.

South Africa has a highly efficient national payments system managed by the SARB together with the banks. This electronic system (which was still paper-based 25 years ago) is crucial for the functioning of any monetised market economy such as ours, and must be protected.

South Africa is also globally praised for the strength of its banking system and the quality of its oversight and supervision. We avoided a significant financial sector crisis in 2008, one of the few countries in the world to do so. Our banks have a capital adequacy ratio (own capital in relation to credit advanced) of about 17%, compared to ratios as low as 1% of some global banks prior to the 2008 crisis. The Basel III ratio is 6.4%. Our macroprudential management must not be tampered with.[7] We are the financial centre of Africa and need to think how we can better leverage this.

Other successes in monetary policy speak to our foreign exchange regulations regarding pension funds and other institutional investors, which stipulate that 75% of their assets must be invested in the domestic markets. This is useful to increase the supply of funds in the domestic capital market. And we tripled the country's foreign exchange reserves over the last few years to over R700 billion. These assets must be protected.

Where monetary policy has had less impact is in the area of credit extension. I believe much more should be done to direct credit to the emerging black entrepreneurial stratum.

To prevent rand depreciation and consequent price inflation, we have deliberately kept interest rates high to induce portfolio capital inflows. Total credit extension in South Africa is about R4 trillion,[8] of which about 50% is to the household sector (mainly for mortgage loans) and 50% is corporate and investment banking.[9] A very small proportion of credit extension goes to small business and new start-ups. Our private equity and venture capital sector is very small, making up just 5% of total bank credit extensions. High-earning households and corporates remain the main recipients of bank credit, with obvious consequences for those individuals, homes and businesses that fall outside of the 'credit-worthy' net.

The other component of macroeconomic policy is fiscal policy, which must be considered from both a tax revenue and fiscal management perspective.

To date, our progressive tax system has worked well, although it has faltered of late with the mismanagement of the South African Revenue Service. Taxes of about 30% of GDP are collected, with two-thirds of these monies being directed towards social spending. I think more could be done to use our tax system to promote inclusive growth; for example, incentivising labour-intensive sectors, incentivising employee stock ownership plans, or incentivising local content in various value chains, as we have done with the auto industry. The recent tax breaks for Special Economic Zones are a step in the right direction, although they have taken years to come into effect.

The National Treasury's professional control of fiscal spending over the past 25 years is to be commended. South Africa is a global leader in budget transparency, according to the Open Budget Index, and the Treasury has to date avoided a gross misallocation of state resources (for example on nuclear energy) in spite of political pressure to do so.

We have been less successful managing debt.

Since the 2009 global recession, we have engaged in counter-cyclical fiscal policy. That is, we purposely ran a fiscal deficit to inject more demand into our economy in order to compensate for the lower demand caused by the global economic downturn. Our massive infrastructure programme lay at the centre of this approach. We avoided recession, but the low-growth

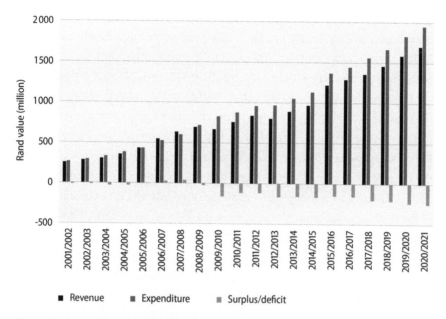

Figure 3.2: South Africa's fiscal policy over time
(Source: National Treasury Annual Budget Reports, 2000–2019)

scenario lasted much longer than anticipated. We now find ourselves with higher government debt, higher debt-service costs, higher dependency on foreigners for fiscal borrowing and, therefore, we are more beholden to the ratings agencies than we were previously. Gross debt has not yet stabilised and is only expected to do so by 2023/24 at 59.6% of GDP. The mismanagement and pillaging of our state-owned enterprises (SOEs) have not helped. Coupled with existing debt, the contingent liability risk of SOEs, such as Eskom, presents a significant threat to national sovereignty.

Even a modest acceleration in the inflation rate will be alarming for fiscal sustainability, given that close to 35% of government debt is either inflation-linked or denominated in foreign currencies. Currently, the space for looser monetary policy or expanded fiscal policy simply does not exist. Unfortunately, I am not sure the gravity of this situation is appreciated by and shared among key role-players in leadership.

I am on record with my views that the current drive to nationalise the SARB is, at best, a red herring; and barely contributes to the debate on how to grow the economy. The image presented of an institution controlled by outside forces that do not behave in the national interest is wrong. In fact, SARB shareholders have no real power. The only thing they do is vote for seven board members with knowledge of labour, agriculture, mining, industry, commerce and finance. The other eight board members are appointed by the president (including the governor and three deputy governors).

The governor meets periodically with members of the Parliamentary Portfolio and Select Committee on Finance. The SARB is accountable through the minister of finance to parliament, and thus to the people of South Africa. The SARB has an immutable constitutional mandate and is governed in terms of the 1989 Reserve Bank Act (as amended and in terms of regulations flowing from the Act), as well as other pieces of legislation, such as the 1990 Banks Act. And while it is to be expected in a constitutional democracy that the institution's policies and practices are subjected to contestation and 'democratic public reasoning', it is imperative that the SARB is politically protected and empowered so that it is able to achieve its constitutional mandate. This includes any pressure for 'debt monetisation' whereby the SARB is directed to create money to purchase government debt – a well-trodden route to hyperinflation, as practised by Germany's Weimar Republic, Zimbabwe and Venezuela.

Labour market interventions

South Africa is only partially industrialised and has exceptionally high unemployment rates and low labour market participation rates by international standards.

Labour market policy over the past 25 years has had a mixed impact. Key pieces of labour legislation, such as the Labour Relations Act, the Basic Conditions of Employment Act and Employment Equity Act, have been more about correcting apartheid wrongs and extending worker protection than about preventing job loss or increasing employment and labour market participation rates. This trend has continued with the latest significant policy – the National Minimum Wage. While the Commission for Conciliation, Mediation and Arbitration functions efficiently, the Labour Courts remain highly inefficient and take years to finalise cases. The case management

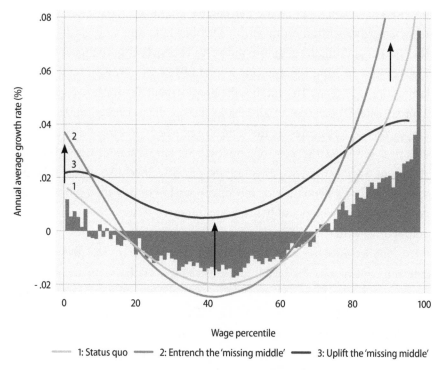

Figure 3.3: Real wage growth in South Africa, by percentile, 1997–2015
(Source: Development Policy Research Unit)

system in the Labour Courts remains non-digitised.

Research by the head of the University of Cape Town's Development Policy Research Unit, Professor Haroon Bhorat, shows interesting trends with regards to real wage growth in South Africa over the past 20 years.[10] Real wage growth has been experienced by bottom-end workers, primarily as a result of sectoral minimum wage legislation for vulnerable workers in domestic work, farm work, trade, security, contract cleaning, etc. High-income earners have also experienced real income growth, benefiting from the skills-based economy. But, workers in the middle have experienced a decline in the growth of real earnings.

The only policy that has incentivised demand-side employment has been the Employment Tax Incentive, which is aimed at offsetting the costs of hiring young, inexperienced workers. The Employment Tax Incentive provides an income tax rebate per eligible employee aged 18–29 years for those employees hired on or after 1 October 2013 and who earn less than R6 500 per month. To date, the incentive supports 686 402 jobs, up from 134 923 jobs in 2014, representing a total of 15% of jobs held by the youth cohort of 18–29 years. This implies the Employment Tax Incentive supported approximately 5 per cent of all jobs in the tax dataset based on individual employee tax certificates in the 2014/15 tax year.[11] The incentive has been effective, reducing the cost of employment and simultaneously building skills and work experience of young people. This incentive needs to be put to scale, and new demand-side incentives need to be designed to reduce the costs of employment, possibly in labour-intensive sectors where we could be competitive with the right policy support.

As detailed in Chapter 1, the changing labour market has also had significant implications for trade union dynamics. Public sector trade union membership rose from 35% in 1997 to 69% in 2013, while the private sector's share declined from 55% to 24%.[12] This has been driven primarily by deindustrialisation and a massive employment decline in mining and manufacturing, together with the growing size of the public service. This has important political and strategic implications, including for policy prioritisation, within the governing ANC and broader Alliance, and will require bold leadership to navigate.

Inclusive growth

South Africa has had some success with macroeconomic management and social policy, as well as with the worker protection side of labour market policy, but the same cannot be said for driving inclusive growth. The economy, despite numerous policy attempts over many years (GEAR, the Accelerated and Shared Growth Initiative for South Africa, the New Growth Path, the Industrial Policy Action Plan and the National Development Plan), has failed both to grow *and* become more inclusive.

South Africa's inequality is staggering. If our GDP were to be equally distributed among all households, then each household would receive about R260 000 per year or R22 000 per month. But, about two-thirds of all households earn less than a quarter of this. Only 9% of black African households have monthly expenditure of more than R10 000, while 65% of white households do.[13] No wonder our politics continue to be so racialised. Also, the wealthiest 10% of the population own 95% of all wealth.[14]

More than 25 years into democracy, serious questions need to be asked as to why we seem unable to grow the economy above 1% or 2%, and why we have been unable to deracialise ownership of wealth and assets.

Several core reasons account for this. We have accumulated insufficient capital to employ all our people. Present rates of private investment are not much larger than depreciation. This again points to the need to increase rates of real investment in our country, both public and private. Our high costs of doing business, policy uncertainty and lack of skills, among other reasons, are why we are not able to attract and retain fixed investment. Over the past ten years, this has worsened, indicative of the fact that we have fallen on a number of global competitiveness rankings.

We are uncompetitive, and are becoming less competitive, in the low-productivity, labour-intensive tradable sectors. Our competitiveness is developing in the high-productivity, skills-based sectors, which only benefits a narrow labour market segment of those endowed with skills. Over the past 20 years, the economy has experienced the decline of mining, manufacturing and agriculture – all sectors that traditionally generated low- and semi-skilled jobs. The economy is now dominated by the services sector, which accounts for well over two-thirds of GDP. In particular, over the past 20 years, the finance, insurance, real estate and business services sectors have seen rapid growth. We need to ensure that this sector becomes more responsive and relevant to increasing fixed investment in infrastructure, small and medium-sized enterprises (SMEs), new start-ups and new entrants. The Industrial Policy Action Plan does not have a sufficient focus on jobs.

Our education and training system, as well as active labour market interventions, has not enabled sufficient labour market participation, nor reduced costs of employment.

The economy is dominated by large-scale capital and capital-intensive industries. By international standards we have an unusually low contribution by SMEs to economic activity, and low new business start-up rates and

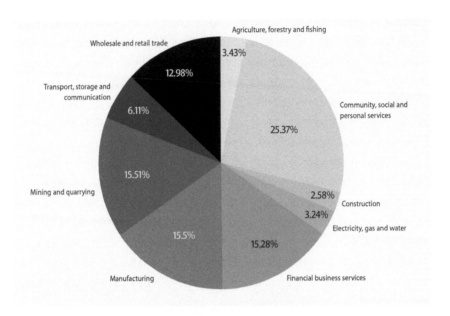

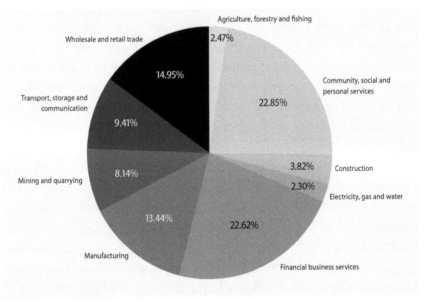

Figure 3.4: Sectoral composition of GDP, 1994 and 2018
(Sources: SARB; Development Policy Research Unit)

entrepreneurship rates. Our informal sector is also very small by comparative standards.

Efforts to enhance black participation in the economy – employment equity, preferential procurement, land reform, etc. – have not seen the emergence of a 'class' of black innovative and entrepreneurial business people. This new class formation process requires the development of a rich and networked ecology, which has yet to evolve. Existing private sector players, including financial corporations, non-financial corporations, development finance institutions, universities and science councils, regional innovation systems, incubators, among others, need to drive the coalescing of this networked ecology.

The role of big business in this process cannot be over-emphasised and must form a crucial component of creating the space for the consolidation of this class of black innovative and entrepreneurial business people. Up to this point, this space has remained largely closed, resulting in the public sector becoming the only meaningful employment alternative – an unsustainable situation given the fiscal and productivity consequences. One of our major policy failings post-1994 has been our reluctance to accept that we need big capital, and require its mobilisation in support of industrial diversification to unlock the competitiveness of new industries where we have comparative advantage. The creation of this new wealth is critical to the successful deracialisation of the economy. Leveraging private capital behind inclusive growth is even more important, given the fiscal constraints we face. Unfortunately, leadership in both the state and private sector remains moribund, and we need a reality check in how business and the state can work together in the interests of national development.

Finally, the state itself is uncoordinated and disjointed with regard to microeconomic and industrial policy implementation. The 1990s was characterised by trade liberalisation outside of any significant state support for manufacturing restructuring and strengthening firm-level competitiveness (outside of the auto sector). The Industrial Development Zones (IDZs) were established outside of any coherent industrial or export strategy.

I have vivid memories of fights we had with national government in the late 1990s and early 2000s when we were setting up the IDZs in the Eastern

Cape. Government could not make up its mind about whether IDZs were a good or a bad thing for the economy. Some officials and politicians wanted fully fledged Special Economic Zones with relaxation of labour legislation, specifically around the rights to hire and fire. Given our history, this was never going to fly, and COSATU quickly blocked this. Others were opposed to IDZs getting any kind of incentives, I suppose on the basis of some kind of free market logic that only the competitive should survive (never mind that we already had an automotive incentive in place).

Regional politics also came into play, with some seeing the Ngqura deep-water harbour and back-of-port Coega IDZ as competition for Durban. As the Eastern Cape government, we took a bold decision to fund the IDZs ourselves, and were successful in advocating for the deepwater port. National government came on board in funding the IDZ infrastructure, but the incentives package that would have made them globally competitive was never implemented. It is only now, with the new Special Economic Zones Act, that this is set to change.

The nineties and 2000s were characterised by a host of microeconomic planning frameworks, all subject to a high degree of political jostling and consequent inertia. These included the Integrated Manufacturing Development Strategy, the Micro-Economic Reform Strategy, the Accelerated and Shared Growth Initiative for South Africa, the New Growth Plan and the Industrial Policy Action Plan, all of which were unable to coordinate the supply-side support measures of government (infrastructure, skills, research and development, development finance, etc.), let alone with private industry and other role-players.

Having experienced at the coalface the impact of policy confusion and inertia, we argued in the build-up to the Polokwane Conference for the development of a national plan. After all, at provincial level we were required to have Provincial Growth and Development Strategies, and municipalities were required to have binding institution-wide Integrated Development Plans: why did the same not apply to the national sphere? A key instrument of successful developmental states is a national plan that functions as the overarching coordinating node of government and other key stakeholders like the private sector. The 2012 National Development Plan was meant to be exactly this, but it was hamstrung from the start by the lack of political championship. The declining technical capacity in the Presidency also contributed to its ineffectiveness as evidence-based planning increasingly took a back seat to political expediency in the previous term of government.

Conclusion

Progress has been made over the past 25 years, particularly around social policy, although serious concerns with the quality of social spending continue. The macroeconomic management and worker protection side (as opposed to worker participation side) of labour market policy have been largely successful.

But the single biggest policy failing since 1994 has been around economic growth and inclusivity. South Africa has declined in competitiveness, and has not been able to attract levels of investment required to fully industrialise and create jobs. Fixing this will require major interventions to address the binding constraints on economic growth: a low skills base, costly and unstable power, inadequate infrastructure to facilitate trade, high costs of doing business, and an expensive and inefficient public service, in addition to pervasive policy uncertainty. Previous policy proposals and programmes have failed to decisively remove these constraints and unshackle the economy. Instead, they have been characterised by timid adjustments at the margins.

This is indicated in the array of well-intentioned policy plans developed by successive governments to boost the economy, but which have, in fact, resulted in very little real change to our deeply unequal economic structure. The result is that the country has been unable to shift onto a permanent high-growth, low-inequality trajectory.

I think it is now generally recognised that low growth and high inequality are mutually reinforcing, and unless we deal with them in conjunction with each other, we will deny future generations their place in this country.

4

State-Owned Enterprises and the Growing Burden of Debt

Debt is such a powerful tool, it is such a useful tool, it's much better than colonialism ever was because you can keep control without having an army, without having a whole administration. — Susan George

Chapter summary

- SOEs can only be effective vehicles for development if they are well managed and economically productive, and if they do not have a monopolising or stifling effect on the private sector.

- South Africa's SOEs are actively subverting our development agenda by requiring repeated bailouts and guarantees, running at a consistent loss, siphoning public funds to corrupt criminal networks and providing poor-quality services to the public.

- At the root of corruption in SOEs lies the appointment of corrupt and politically aligned figures to management and board positions.

- Restoring SOEs requires rooting out corruption and appointing capable and honest managers.

At the end of November 2015, we held the National Treasury's Annual Strategic Management Planning Workshop in Centurion. This workshop was attended by about 25 ministry and Treasury officials.

When we convened that day, we were, in my experience, in the midst of one of the most intense periods in South Africa's democratic history and we in the National Treasury were trying to hold the line, without presidential or Cabinet support, against an economy teetering on the edge of recession, while various crises unfolded at some of the state-owned enterprises (SOEs).

The month before, I had received the bribe offer from the Guptas, and so I was, by the time of the planning workshop, acutely aware of what we were up against. But such was the culture of fear and uncertainty that we were facing that I had not yet told anyone about it, apart from Minister Nhlanhla Nene and Minister Pravin Gordhan. I, however, felt very strongly that I needed to convey to the Treasury officials at the workshop that day, who were among the most experienced and dedicated civil servants I have worked with, the extent of the threat the country was facing. The ministry, and the nation at that point, had not yet fully understood the gravity of state capture. As part of the planning workshop, we placed on the programme a session to identify possible events or changes to both the economic and political environment, which, in the event of them materialising, would warrant certain leadership interventions from the National Treasury. The plan was to deliberate these as a team. As the discussion progressed, while robust, I realised that we were failing to see the elephant in the room. In the course of writing this book, a former Treasury colleague shared the notes he took that day, which recorded what I said and which are a jarring reminder of how close we were to the edge of collapse, the repercussions of which we are dealing with today. When my turn came to address the workshop, I decided to speak to the issues directly:

> Unfortunately, there are things we are not debating and discussing, the elephant in the room as it were, and how this is impacting on our work. Firstly, the issue is that we have a captured state: the levels of corruption are far higher than we've been able to articulate and this is holding back a whole range of things. The vested interests that have captured the state view Treasury as a block and are therefore intent on delegitimising the institution. The nuclear story is real and what you hear about the SOEs – these are the big issues that are going to sink us. If we can't deal with SOEs in a decisive manner we are heading for a reversal. We'll slide backwards, and this even goes for those SOEs that are said to be performing well. We are moving backwards, the capacity of the state is regressing. To be more

direct, we are in an environment where politics of recession is reigning supreme and we have not interrogated and analysed how this is playing out and what the impact will be. One of my overriding concerns is the weakness of the centre, which is veering towards populism, and with this, good governance, control and thinking are being delegitimised.

We must ask the question: what are the implications for Treasury? The biggest threat is that we lose the capacity, the coherence and the confidence that we have here today. Our danger is that we lose all of that. That would kill us.

The rest, as they say, is history. Less than two weeks after the workshop, Minister Nene was fired and replaced momentarily with Des van Rooyen and then Minister Gordhan. A year later, he and I were fired. The story of the SOEs really sits at the heart of what we were up against during this time, the consequences of which today remain the biggest threat to our stability.

The role of state-owned enterprises in South Africa

Historically, SOEs have been central to the development trajectory of South Africa because of their direct economic and social impact and their indirect effect through procurement from the private sector. Their official responsibilities are broad and include investing in economic infrastructure, promoting industrial policy, increasing the competitiveness of South Africa's economy and assisting to 'stimulate inclusive growth'.[1] Importantly, SOEs have been a powerful vehicle to drive economic transformation in post-apartheid South Africa. In 2017, SOEs had a joint aggregate turnover equivalent to 12% of South Africa's GDP. This makes them systemically important and central to the economy. Unfortunately, they became an economy in their own right.

Today, the South African government controls 715 SOEs (including subsidiaries), although public attention usually focuses on the largest ones. The most important and prominent SOEs are those listed in Schedule 2 of the Public Finance Management Act of 1999, which includes Eskom, Transnet, SAA, Telkom, Airports Company South Africa (ACSA), the Central Energy

Fund, Denel and Armscor. A few other major public entities are listed in Schedule 3(b), which includes PRASA and many of the water boards.

Using the 2016/17 financial statements for the 11 largest SOEs in South Africa, the Development Policy Research Unit[2] at the University of Cape Town estimated that SOE capital expenditure (capex) alone in 2017 stood at R116 billion.[3] This is equivalent to 7.5% of total annual government expenditure. The majority of this investment spending is by Eskom, which had a total capital expenditure of R66.5 billion in 2017 – accounting for over half of total capital expenditure by the SOEs.

SOE	SOE capex	% Total SOE capex	% Total Gvt. Expenditure	SOE Revenue	% Total SOE Revenue	% Total Gvt. Revenue
ACSA	893	0.77	0.06	8 583	2.25	0.63
City Power	1 800	1.55	0.12	15 727	4.13	1.16
CSIR	144	0.12	0.01	2 712	0.71	0.20
Denel	66	0.06	0.00	8 057	2.12	0.60
Eskom	66 578	55.51	4.31	177 136	46.51	13.09
PetroSA	779	0.67	0.05	10 357	2.72	0.77
SAA*	14 863	12.84	0.96	30 385	7.98	2.24
SAPO	54	0.05	0.00	4 539	1.19	0.34
SITA	497	0.43	0.03	5 681	1.49	0.42
Telkom	8 654	7.48	0.56	40 970	10.76	3.03
Transnet	21 438	18.52	1.39	65 478	17.19	4.84
TOTAL	115 766	100.00	7.50	380 822	100.00	27.31
Total Gvt. expenditure	1 543 800					
Total Gvt. revenue	1 353 500					

Table 4.1: Capital expenditure and revenue, selected SOEs: rand millions, 2016/17
(Source: Development Policy Research Unit)
* SAA capex data only available for 2015/16 financial years. Rand values are presented in nominal terms.

To understand the current state of SOEs – and, of course, to determine what must be done to rescue them now – it is necessary to trace their history in the apartheid economy and how they reached this point.

Present-day SOEs have their origins in the early efforts of the colonial and apartheid state to facilitate industrialisation and to reduce dependence on foreign mining companies. In the 1920s, the Union government (under Jan Smuts and later J.B.M. Hertzog) established two major state corporations: the Electricity Supply Commission (Escom, later to become Eskom) and the Iron and Steel Corporation (Iscor). Escom and Iscor were intended to build a stable energy supply to support nascent industry and to invest in new steel and manufacturing capabilities. They continued to grow in size and importance after the National Party assumed power. Historian Nancy Clark explains: '[Nationalist leaders] sought to broaden the base of the South African economy so as to meet the revenue needs of the state and provide more jobs for white workers ... a key development of this interventionist approach was the direct participation of the state in production.'[4]

The original SOEs operated under the tight control of the apartheid regime, and their secondary function was to provide sheltered employment for white workers in order to secure political support for the National Party. Of course, the irony is inescapable of far-reaching state intervention in an economy that was viewed by Western powers as a bulwark against communism during the Cold War. Clark goes on to point out 'the paradox of dominant state enterprise within a country that claimed to be the last bastion of capitalism in Africa'.[5]

As international pressure on South Africa grew and the anti-apartheid movement gained momentum, SOEs played a crucial role in sustaining an economy under siege. Sasol, then the state oil company, ensured a stable oil supply after Iranian imports were stopped in 1979, though there were still massive sanctions-busting efforts to secure oil on the black markets. Armscor provided locally manufactured weapons for riot control and border wars. Through heavily supported state corporations, the apartheid regime tried to maintain a self-sufficient economy and prevent job losses.

This historical context is important, because it demonstrates the forces that shaped SOEs and the circumstances under which they were inherited by the first democratic government after the 1994 elections. Some SOEs, such as Sasol, which invented a technique for turning coal into liquid fuel, were innovative. But most were inefficient monopolies, often relying on outdated technology and employing large workforces. In the 1980s, for example, it became evident that Eskom had made huge mistakes in predicting electricity demand. The company had invested heavily in new generation plants on the assumption that the economy would grow steadily and that electricity demand would rise too. Yet, they had, somehow, not anticipated international sanctions. The resultant 'white elephant' plants dented the company's reputation and the De Villiers Commission of 1983 completed the humiliation. It recommended that Eskom be corporatised and that its wide planning and financial discretion be curtailed.

It was for this reason, together with high levels of inherited debt and international pressure to carry out dramatic economic reforms as South Africa opened itself to global markets, that the first ANC government began to pursue a significant privatisation agenda. Several SOEs were successfully privatised and entire sectors liberalised. Most notably, Telkom was partially privatised in 1997 in an equity deal valued at US$1.26 billion. Telkom is the standout success of liberalisation in the 1990s and early 2000s, with the state relinquishing a further 25% of its stake through an initial public offering in 2003 and establishing an effective competitor in 2007 in the form of Broadband Infraco. The 1998 White Paper on Energy Policy envisaged the creation of an energy market, with multiple players involved in generation. Independent power producers would be among them. Eskom would be broken up into separate generation and transmission companies.

In 2004, however, the government changed direction because the official strategy became to use SOEs to drive transformation as a central feature of national economic policy. Instead of pursuing aggressive liberalisation through equity partnerships and the sale of subsidiaries, SOEs were placed back at the centre of the developmental state. The Department of Public Enterprises was given a new mission: 'to drive investment, efficiencies and transformation in its portfolio of State-owned Companies, their customers and their suppliers to unlock growth, drive industrialisation, create jobs and develop skills'.[6] New capital investment programmes began, and the state tried instead to leverage SOEs for capacity-building in domestic supply chains and drive growth in small and medium-sized enterprises. This shift in approach is evident in the language used by government officials to describe SOEs and the increasing reliance on them for national development objectives.

This trend continued and was reinforced during the Jacob Zuma administration. In explaining the ANC's 2014 election manifesto with regard to changes in the procurement procedures at SOEs, Zuma announced that the state must buy at least 75% of its goods and services from South African producers. The state's buying power would support small enterprises, cooperatives and Broad-Based Black Economic Empowerment. Similar statements were made at the time by officials at the Department of Trade and Industry, as well as by the minister of public enterprises at the time, Malusi Gigaba, who said that in relation to SOE procurement spending the government was 'committed to the creation of a new generation of black industrialists'.[7]

Today, every relevant government planning document places SOEs at the centre of our economic policy regime. The National Development Plan emphasises the 'development potential of state-owned enterprises', and maintains that 'SOEs are central to advancing national objectives through providing economic and social infrastructure';[8] the most recent Industrial Policy Action Plan leans heavily on SOEs for the localisation of production and building capacity in domestic supply chains;[9] the New Growth Path calls on government to use SOEs 'to address backlogs in regional logistics, water and electricity infrastructure';[10] and the Medium-Term Strategic Framework highlights major investments by PRASA and Transnet to create jobs and expand our export infrastructure.[11]

There is no doubt that effective SOEs can pursue important policy goals, act in the public interest, advance development and generate revenue for the state. In a recent report, the World Bank argues for their strategic potential:

> Since 1994 SOEs have been a significant vehicle for achieving economic growth and poverty reduction. They are especially important vehicles for addressing market failure and for delivering key infrastructure services such as energy, transport, and water that allow the economy to grow

while ensuring equity through access and quality of social services to all citizens.[12]

There is truth in this vision for strategic state-owned firms operating in the economy to pursue public-minded objectives. But they can only be effective vehicles for development if they are profitable, well managed and economically productive, and if they do not have a monopolising or stifling effect on the private sector. If they instead require repeated bailouts and guarantees, if they run at a consistent loss, if they siphon public funds to corrupt criminal networks, if they provide poor-quality services to the public, and if they crowd out private competition, then they are actively subverting our development agenda.

Unfortunately, many of our SOEs fit this latter description perfectly. Indeed, failing SOEs and their growing levels of debt represent perhaps the greatest systemic threat to the South African economy today. The next section explains why they have collapsed, and what can be done to restore them to profitability and reduce their burden on the state.

Decline, dysfunction and debt

Corruption in our SOEs reached tragicomic proportions during the past decade, and now permeates several corporations from top to bottom. State capture manifested in the hijacking of the developmental functions of SOEs in order to enrich a politically connected elite.[13] The mandate of SOEs, as well as their very large capital budgets, rightly places them as drivers of economic growth in the country and a clear avenue through which the state can begin to redistribute economic opportunity away from a small group of established firms. But at the same time, as a country in transition, the SOEs are vulnerable to corruption because of their centrality to the economy, combined with their large procurement budgets, regulatory changes and the discretionary power of public officials who govern them. We are all aware now of how powerful bureaucrats, led by former President Zuma, took advantage of this situation and, together with a corrupt network, gained access to the large rents available at SOEs.[14]

The result is that over the last ten years institutionalised corruption has overwhelmed our key state institutions in South Africa, the full costs of which are impossible to quantify.

Examples abound, and range from small, almost laughable incidents to sophisticated fraud on a massive scale. Take, for instance, the widely reported theft of diamonds at Alexkor, the state-owned mining company. A 1999 article in *The Atlantic* detailed the daily smuggling of diamonds from Alexkor's operations near the town of Port Nolloth in the Northern Cape:

> Infamous in the [diamond] trade is the steady flow of stolen diamonds from Namaqualand, a sandy slab of South Africa along the Atlantic coast. Namaqualand's pan-hot desert and scraped little hills start north of Cape Town and run up to the Orange River, which forms the Namibian border. The ocean breaks on a forbidding shore. Not much happens in Namaqualand – except for the stealing of diamonds. In Namaqualand, stealing diamonds is the proper work of man.[15]

The American journalist investigating diamond theft found that the method of choice for employees of Alexkor was homing pigeons, which would be loaded with illicit diamonds and thrown into the air to be collected by collaborators in the town. At the time, Alexkor sources suggested that 30% of diamonds recovered from its 120-kilometre Namaqualand concession were stolen. Almost two decades later, a recent article in *The Economist* reports that 'as many as half of the diamonds it mines there fail to make their way onto Alexkor's income statement'.[16] Still today, pigeons are used to facilitate the theft, along with increasingly elaborate technical means and a deep-rooted system of bribery and corruption. No wonder Alexkor registered a loss of R82 million in 2015, R36 million the following year and a cumulative R78.7 million in 2017 – while its revenue for the year dropped by an astonishing 46% in 2018.

Alexkor serves as a useful representative example of the breadth and depth of corruption in SOEs. Small-scale theft of diamonds occurs throughout its operations and is allegedly perpetrated by criminals at every level of the company. At the same time, mismanagement and corruption at higher levels – perpetrated by its executive leadership – have virtually destroyed oversight procedures and led to massive losses every year. This is a formula that has been repeated in many SOEs. In 2017, then minister of public enterprises, Lynne Brown, appointed Lemogang Pitsoe as CEO. Prior to his appointment, while serving as general manager of Hernic Ferrochrome, Pitsoe had overseen the decline of the company into business rescue. At the same time, Hantsi Matseke was appointed as the company's chairperson. Matseke had until then been in charge of the Free State Development Corporation, where she was publicly linked to several corruption scandals involving the Estina dairy farm project and a failed property deal.[17]

Most concerning is the award of a sole-marketing contract to a shelf company called Scarlet Sky, which before receiving this tender had no evident track record in diamond sales. Diamond mines like Alexkor often use marketers to sell their output on to buyers. In the past, several known marketing companies – including the De Beers subsidiary Diamdel – had been responsible for Alexkor's sales. In 2015, however, a new contract was awarded to Scarlet Sky with no apparent justification.

According to an investigation by amaBhungane and Scorpio resulting from the #GuptaLeaks emails, Scarlet Sky is intimately linked to Salim Essa and the Gupta family. One of its directors is Daniel Nathan whose father, Selwyn, was linked to a corruption scandal at Transnet. At the time of submitting its tender, Scarlet Sky indicated that 'all communication should flow through their corporate advisers, addressed to one Marc Chipkin of Integrated Capital Management' – the same Marc Chipkin and ICM that have since been implicated in collusion with Essa to defraud Transnet.[18] The cost of subpar diamond marketing has been severe for Alexkor, whose stones have received on average US$450 less than the global market price for the past eight years. This has produced a combined estimated loss of at least R1.5 billion.[19] As the Alexkor example demonstrates, mismanagement and dysfunction – combined with corruption on both a petty and grand scale – have crippled many of the SOEs that should be creating jobs and contributing to national revenues. Almost every SOE, from the largest and most well known to the smallest and least prominent, shows signs of dysfunction.

Most dire of all, of course – and most prominent in public discourse – is the situation at Eskom. By April 2019, Eskom's debt burden had ballooned to

R475 billion because of massive annual losses. The resulting bailout by the National Treasury of R23 billion per year will contribute to pushing South Africa's debt-to-GDP ratio to above 60% in the next four years. As it stands, the country is borrowing R1.2 billion per day to keep up interest payments on national debt, a vicious cycle that is clearly unsustainable. The Public Investment Corporation alone holds R80 billion in Eskom debt, which threatens the government employees' pension scheme.[20]

Eskom's debt presents a systemic risk to the country's finances, but it is not the only crisis facing the power utility. Annual losses driven by high operating expenses, combined with old and faltering infrastructure in dire need of maintenance and upgrading, have placed a heavy strain on consumers paying higher and higher tariffs for electricity. In early 2019, Eskom requested a 15% hike in tariffs from the National Energy Regulator of South Africa (NERSA),[21] even though tariffs have increased by a cumulative 356% since 2008 (compared to inflation over the same period of 74%). These price increases hurt the poor and the vulnerable middle class most of all, but also potentially cripple heavy industries that rely on a stable and affordable power supply. In response to Eskom's application to NERSA, the Minerals Council of South Africa argued that a 15% tariff increase would reduce gold output alone by more than 120 tonnes and would result in the loss of 150 000 jobs in the mining sector.[22] The proportion of gold mines making a marginal profit or loss would increase from 71%, already too high, to approximately 96%.

These tariff increases are unacceptable and will strike a death blow to the economy. Citizens and firms are especially averse to paying them because of the well-documented theft and corruption at Eskom. The Special Investigating Unit is investigating the theft of R170 billion by contractors since 2005, although reports suggest that the actual figure could be as high as R500 billion.[23] This leaves Eskom in a crisis, with no apparent way out. On the one hand, it needs to spend additional resources on maintaining and improving its infrastructure and completing its new power plants to prevent ongoing blackouts and load shedding. Its debt burden is already stratospheric, and neither the state – already overstretched by its existing commitments – nor the taxpaying public can afford to cover its costs and improve its balance sheet.

Kusile and Medupi, the third and fourth largest coal power plants in the world, were supposed to come on line in 2014 and 2012 respectively. Together they would have supplied South Africa with an extra 9 600 megawatts of power. In 2019, both were still under construction. When their construction was announced by Eskom in 2007, the cost of Medupi was just under R70 billion and Kusile R80 billion. At the start of 2019, the cost estimates were R208 billion for Medupi and R239 billion for Kusile.[24]

Load shedding is an immediate result of this rampant mismanagement and corruption, but the long-term, anti-developmental repercussions cannot be overstated.

The collapse of Eskom is also a human story.

A manufacturer in Johannesburg's south, which employs 120 workers, described his realities. 'It creates chaos and all manner of untoward effects. Staff anger at the management wanting to go short-time is probably the most dangerous. You also can't talk load shedding to customers. If you don't have a generator you must be small fry, right? And if the generator fails, you cannot get anyone to repair it given the demand right now.'[25]

He adds that 'the biggest problem is manufacturing according to a just-in-time system. We don't have the luxury of production ahead of time, since we don't possess the storage space for our furniture, and yet we face penalties if we don't deliver the goods on time. We have become a third-world manufacturer operating according to first-world demands. But the worst aspect is that I have to look the staff in the face on a Friday and give them 20% less because of the short-time. He or she will have to then go and borrow money from a loan shark to make ends meet. They are sitting in town rubbing their hands. What happens when my staff cannot pay this money back, or cannot as a result get their ID books back?' he asks.

For our crop farmers, a critical resource for our economy, the Eskom crisis has been devastating, besieging commercial farmers and destroying small-scale farmers. A KwaZulu-Natal farmer described how his electricity costs increased by 296% between May 2008 and April 2018, but the price of yellow maize only increased 51%, wheat by 36% and soya beans by 33.5%. The cost of electricity, which was not even a line item in his financials ten years ago, is now his third biggest cost and has reduced what was once a thriving commercial farm to below break-even point.[26]

Industry leaders back up the concerns of these businesses.

Roger Baxter is the chief executive of the Minerals Council, formerly the Chamber of Mines, which represents the combined interests of 300 mining companies and their 460 000 workers in South Africa, totalling R400 billion in annual mineral sales. 'Electricity is such an important component of the mining sector, particularly deep level mining. It has to be plentiful and cost effective. The fact that South African electricity is more expensive than the US and Malaysia, among others now, means for one that smelters are migrating offshore. But the industry has never recovered from the 2008/9 electricity shortages, where supply was reduced by 10%, and which had a profound impact on all production, especially marginal mines. As much as 15% of production was shut down then and not recovered. The prognosis on Eskom remains bleak, so the mining situation remains bleak too,' he says.[27]

In 2018, mining contributed 8% to national GDP, down from 8.5% in 2014, and 46% of the country's exports.[28]

But Eskom is not alone.

At South African Airways (SAA), a R5-billion bailout from government in October 2018, together with R3.5 billion in commercial loans, prevented the imminent collapse of the state-owned airline. But, at the same time, SAA claimed that it would need an additional capital injection of R21.7 billion by 2021 to finance its turnaround strategy and has forecast operational losses until then (having made losses as high as R5.5 billion each year for the past decade). In short, the company is on the verge of bankruptcy.[29]

And there are perhaps even more egregious examples of the weight of corruption, state capture and incompetence.

The modus operandi is roughly similar in each case: a contract is awarded to a foreign company (with traceable links to some local entrepreneur or entity) by an SOE for an initial amount. Next, some disruption is introduced to the initial deal – perhaps a last-minute change of location or a new partner brought into the arrangement – under questionable circumstances. Due to the abrupt nature of the change, there would be little time and space for proper oversight. This disruption would lead to severe delays and incur costs of an order of magnitude well above the initial amount quoted.

The case of Transnet and China North Rail (CNR) serves as example. On 25 April 2015, CNR, a large state-owned firm headquartered in Shenzhen, signed a contract with Business Expansion Structured Products (BEX), a front company linked to Gupta family associate Salim Essa.[30] One year earlier, CNR had been awarded a major contract to supply 232 diesel locomotives to Transnet, one of South Africa's most important SOEs, at a cost of R9.9 billion.

The initial agreement between Transnet and CNR was that part of the manufacturing process would take place at Transnet's Koedoespoort facility in Pretoria. After the deal was signed, however, Transnet decided to shift production to its Durban facility instead. CNR's own internal projection for the cost of relocation was a mere R9 million.[31] Inexplicably, however, the deal that CNR finally concluded was that BEX would receive whatever Transnet paid for the shift in production over and above R580 million. The final figure was R719 million, a staggering 80 times higher than CNR's internal estimate. Ultimately, Transnet agreed to pay R647 million for the relocation, without performing any additional verification or requesting any changes.

How was all of this possible? At the root of corruption in SOEs lies the appointment of corrupt and politically aligned figures to management and board positions, where they have wielded their influence to facilitate grand larceny rather than the strategic objectives of the company. This has been made possible, in addition, by corporate structures that have allowed the undue influence of politicians in senior appointments and in operational matters. This is how Essa was able to earn over R3.8 billion in commission for securing another lucrative supply contract for China South Rail – representing R10 million of the R50 million that taxpayers paid for each new Transnet locomotive in the rail network.

Altogether, the corruption and looting at Transnet alone is estimated to have cost the public an astonishing R16 billion, of which at least R5.3 billion went directly to Gupta-linked shelf companies, both onshore and offshore, in the form of commissions and kickbacks. The total cost of irregular expenditure by the largest SOEs is estimated by the auditor-general at over R30 billion in 2017 alone.[32]

The South African Broadcasting Corporation (SABC) posted a loss of

R977 million in 2017 and R622 million in 2018, with devastating implications for local producers and artists whom the broadcaster is unable to pay.[33] The auditor-general last year issued a disclaimer on the SABC's financial statements, the most dire audit opinion available, and cited concerns about the failure of the organisation to hold anyone accountable for more than R5 billion in irregular expenditure (while giving bonus payments of as much as R10 million to former executives such as Hlaudi Motsoeneng).[34] At the time of writing, the SABC had requested a bailout of R3 billion from the National Treasury in order to pay the salaries of its core staff.

A report by Ernst and Young into SAA blamed corruption and mismanagement for its decline, with 60% of its largest contracts 'improperly negotiated, poorly contracted, or weakly managed'.[35] A combination of short-sighted decisions, poor fleet management, investment in unprofitable routes (often due to political interference) and massive corruption has completely crippled a once-profitable airline.

Denel, the state-owned arms manufacturer, was among one of the first SOEs to be implicated in state capture as a result of its failed joint venture with VR Laser Asia, a firm owned by Salim Essa. Last year the company posted a R1.7-billion loss, with over R2 billion in debt held by the Public Investment Corporation.[36] It required a R3.43-billion Treasury guarantee to stay afloat, without which it would have been unable to honour maturing bonds. The defence industry in South Africa sustains over 15 000 high-quality jobs in design, engineering and manufacturing, and many smaller defence companies have already folded as a result of Denel's non-payment and underperformance.[37] A panel of forensic investigators has been appointed by the new board to investigate major irregularities in procurement and appointments.

This is why President Cyril Ramaphosa has rightly called the SOEs 'sewers of corruption', and has made fixing them the priority of his administration.[38]

At the root of all of these pathologies lies one thing: political interference in the appointment of boards and management. Politically connected but otherwise unqualified and incompetent officials used their positions of influence to manipulate government tender processes and extract profits from the supply chains under their control, typically with policies like 'supplier development' and 'local content' as cover. At the same time, the departure of experienced and qualified managers hollowed out many SOEs and left them unable to effectively manage their finances or operations.

Over more than a decade, SOEs became a mechanism for dispensing political patronage – a symbiotic relationship emerged between a constitutional state with clear rules and laws, and a shadow state comprising well-organised patronage networks that facilitated corruption and enriched a small power elite. The latter fed off the former in ways that sapped the vitality from the formal institutions and left them empty shells incapable of executing their responsibilities.

They were ultimately no longer independent entities managed for profit and serving a strategic economic purpose, but rather a vast money laundering machine.

No single cause

Corruption has no single cause – it is a syndrome of many concurrent ailments. It is associated, on the one hand, with an individual psychology of self-promotion and enrichment. It is made completely routine and normalised: if everyone else is doing it, why not do it yourself? In the scramble for wealth and power, people take the short cuts that they are offered. In post-apartheid South Africa, in particular, many public officials imagine that they deserve financial reward, that it is their time to eat. As corruption and tender manipulation become more widespread as a means of securing power and privilege, many perceive that they have to participate in the racket in order to get ahead. In this way, corruption has a certain gravitational force – it is self-perpetuating.

On the other hand, corruption is structural in nature and is made possible by the institutions that structure our politics and our economy. Since 2009, SOEs were given a central role in driving economic development and job creation. The approach of political leaders changed from a focus on revenue and output, like energy or transport infrastructure, to a focus on leveraging the resources of SOEs to grow businesses in their supply chains and boost local economies. These 'developmental goals' were admirable in themselves but created an environment in which the officials in charge of managing

SOEs could use their power to suck those companies dry while enriching others and themselves. 'SOEs were not like private firms,' the argument went; 'they don't need to make significant profits, or to pursue ordinary corporate objectives. They need instead to spend money, to create jobs and to feed black-owned businesses in their supply chains.' In the right hands, this policy could have achieved legitimate economic goals. In the wrong hands, however, it led to the complete destruction of many of our most important corporations.

Lack of capacity and competitiveness

But corruption and mismanagement alone are not enough to explain the decline in the performance of SOEs in past decades, Eskom included. To appreciate how this crisis arose, we must dig deeper. After the election in 1994, the ANC government pursued an aggressive agenda of privatising SOEs and liberalising markets. The Department of Public Enterprises had a mandate to sell its portfolio of companies. As a result, anticipating major restructuring and a reduced role for the state in the economy, 'infrastructure SOEs were prohibited from investing in fixed assets and were induced to close down their capital procurement capabilities. In addition, major maintenance projects were put on hold.'[39] SOEs were, for the most part, prevented from growing or investing.

The story of Eskom is a good example of this approach. In 1998, the White Paper on Energy aimed to reduce Eskom's share of generating capacity to below 70%, allowing private sector firms to participate in generation. To facilitate this 'managed liberalisation', Eskom was 'prohibited from investing in new generation capacity in the domestic market and from building a new Capital Projects Capability'.[40] In the same year, 1998, Eskom approached the Department of Energy to insist on the necessity of starting a new build programme to avert power shortages by 2008, given projected growth in demand. In addition, Eskom asked that the tariff model should allow the utility to charge based on the actual cost of producing, to avoid sudden and inconsistent tariff increases in future years. The Department of Energy refused all these requests: its emphasis, together with the Department of

Public Enterprises, remained solely on phasing out the dominance of SOEs and bringing private firms into the energy sector.

In 2004, however, as mentioned earlier in this chapter, a major policy shift occurred, which placed a renewed emphasis on the importance of SOEs in general and Eskom in particular. As a result, the Cabinet decided that Eskom should be allowed to commence with new capital investments, and that none of its existing facilities would be privatised. The utility began construction of two large new coal power stations as a result, seven years too late.

This abrupt change in policy reflected, in some ways, the worst of all worlds. Ten years of underinvestment in construction or maintenance, and the erosion of Eskom's capital projects expertise, effectively incapacitated the company. When it was finally allowed to reinvest, it had already lost much of its former capabilities to the private sector and other countries, and the build project was too late to keep up with rising demand, as frequent shortages and load shedding quickly proved. Rather than consistently building and maintaining Eskom's infrastructure, or following through with the proposed privatisation of the company in whole or part, the government prevaricated and did neither. Eskom was caught in the middle, unable to properly carry out its core functions and without any private actors in the sector to relieve its load. Inconsistent and unclear policy has led to the company's current distress, in combination with gross mismanagement and corruption.

A similar story repeats across many SOEs, including Transnet. Our SOEs have for the most part lost their internal project management and governance capacity, leading them frequently to rely on consultants and outside contractors to carry out their work. This has two dangers: first, it leads to inevitable cost inflation and high contractor fees, and, second, it opens the door to large-scale corruption as more and more large projects are contracted out to external parties.

Examples of this abound and are again most egregious in Eskom's case. Eskom was told in 2015 that it needed to invest R27 billion to recapitalise coal mines close to its major power stations to secure its supply of cheap coal through long-term 'cost-plus' agreements. Instead of making this necessary investment, Eskom waited until these coal mines could no longer maintain a regular supply and was then forced to procure coal from further away at less preferential rates – from suppliers like the Gupta-owned Tegeta. Spending R27 billion five years ago would have saved the utility R90 billion in additional costs today.[41] Instead of carrying out routine maintenance and managing its assets carefully, corrupt executives at Eskom seem to have purposely run down its capacity to create a manufactured crisis that would benefit politically linked suppliers. This is an act of institutional sabotage, which would never have been possible if Eskom was filled with capable, independent and conscientious managers. Similarly, in one of the most startling stories of the state capture scandal, Eskom paid management consultants McKinsey & Company over R1.6 billion for only eight months of work towards an organisational restructuring, which seems to have produced no discernible results whatsoever. At least 35% of this fee went to the Gupta-linked firm, Trillian, which had arranged the contract and fronted as McKinsey's empowerment partner.

Restoring SOEs will certainly require rooting out corruption and appointing capable and honest managers – corruption and mismanagement have pushed out many of the remaining capable engineers, accountants and managers upon whom Eskom and other organisations relied for their survival and success. But it will also require long-term policy stability. Either an SOE must be adequately invested in and actively managed, or it must be privatised. To date, South Africa has neither properly sustained and invested in, nor relinquished, SOEs like Eskom.

The result, as anyone might have expected, is under-capitalised and incompetent organisations, ageing and insufficient infrastructure, and no one else to shoulder the burden of service provision.

Conclusion: Systemic effects and solutions

Fixing our SOEs is the single most important task that confronts South Africa today. Their combined debt is a threat to the national fiscus and to our credit rating. If Eskom defaulted on its loans, it would trigger a default on some government bonds, which could have serious fiscal repercussions, including triggering World Bank and International Monetary Fund intervention.

Beyond the mountainous burden of debt, which continues to grow as companies report annual losses year after year, SOEs have systemic effects on our economy. An unstable and insufficient power supply puts a definite brake on growth and prevents key sectors of the economy from being truly competitive. Similarly, Transnet's failure to provide efficient and modern port and rail infrastructure has held back our export industries, including mining and agriculture. Indeed, we largely missed out on the pre-2008 commodity boom because Transnet was unable to provide adequate infrastructure to sustain higher volumes of coal and other products. Simply put, these systemically important SOEs have to work if the economy is to grow and create jobs.

Ultimately, the failure of SOEs reflects a failure of politics, of policy imagination, of the relationship between the public and private sectors, of governance and the courage to make hard choices about the future. Fixing our SOEs remains the most pressing task facing South Africa.

In making these hard choices, we need to move beyond narrow ideological straitjackets. Wholesale privatisation is not the answer: with what is coming out of the Zondo Commission, imagine what trouble we would be in had we fully privatised some of our SOEs in the recent past. We must also shift quickly away from stubborn views that the state must own and control the whole value chain in core utilities. In any event, this has never been the case, with large components of outsourcing characterising all the SOEs. To date, the private sector has shared the profit but not the risk.

The private sector has the capital, expertise and capabilities that we need. We require a far more nuanced and pragmatic approach – horses for courses, so to say – in which space, where strategically appropriate, is opened up for co-investment and risk sharing. Negotiating these transactions to fix our broken enterprises will be a complex business requiring not only courageous political decisions and unwavering commitment to clean governance, but also exponential capacity development in the state to manage these processes in line with policy objectives and the national interest.

5

Schools but No Learning

Education is our most important economic and social strategy. From the early days the paradox was that we depoliticised the substance of education, yet we took a great political interest in creating an ethos of performance and autonomy in so doing. — Tharman Shanmugaratnam

Chapter summary

- By all objective measures, South African schools are performing extremely poorly. This is despite relatively high spending on education as a percentage of GDP, compared to other middle-income countries.

- We suffer from a serious lack of skills, both in teachers and at the managerial level in principals and school governing bodies.

- Schooling quality and labour market outcomes are inherently linked. Extreme skills scarcity perpetuates inequality through high earning differentials.

- Corruption in national and provincial education departments, along with the over-extension of the power of teachers' unions and school governing bodies, has played no small part in the collapse of our schooling system.

- Politicking at the expense of the education system must cease if we are to do what is right by the youth of South Africa.

If there is one area that is a microcosm of our vigorous battles – and our failures to overcome these – it is our education system.

While few people would disagree with this, I still find it confounding because education, more than any other area, really sat at the heart of our anti-apartheid struggle. Such was the focus on its centrality to achieving democracy that it was a rite of passage for all of us to work within the educational structures of the anti-apartheid networks, which fell under the National Education Crisis Committee (NECC). We viewed the struggle for education as inextricably tied to the struggle for a free, democratic and prosperous South Africa. The NECC taught us that 'people's education' and 'people's power' were intimately linked and, under their leadership, such powerful organs as Parent-Teacher-Student Associations and Student Representative Councils were formed as manifestations of the imperative of education for a successful mass democratic movement.

Following the unbanning of anti-apartheid political formations in 1990, the National Education Conference was convened in March 1992 just outside Pretoria by the ANC's Education Delegation. This delegation had been formed by Nelson Mandela in 1991 to participate in negotiations with the National Party to address the crisis and challenges in black education.[1] The conference called for 'people's power' based on the principles of 'people's education', and this spirit was carried through the negotiations:

> Education ... policy and practice shall be governed by the principle of democracy, ensuring the active participation of various interest groups, in particular teachers, parents, workers and students; and education shall be based upon the principles of co-operation, critical thinking and civic responsibility, and shall equip individuals for participation in all aspects of society.[2]

Twenty-five years later, our reality is that the education system has failed the most vulnerable in our society. It has failed to deliver equity, access and quality, and is failing to inculcate the basic capabilities needed to transform and build society – numeracy, literacy, analytical capabilities, critical capabilities and communication competencies. This is a fundamental indictment of all of us.

Our failure to educate

The crisis of education is a crisis of accountability (or the lack thereof). The children of today and tomorrow are being failed by political leadership, by bureaucrats, by teachers, by trade unions representing teachers and officials, and by their communities. Our collective failure to fix the education system condemns millions of working-class and poor children to a life of poverty and unemployment.

This will impact directly on our ability to grow and transform the economy, and will have serious consequences for political and social stability going forward. In this sense, education is a deal-breaker for the broader transformation project. Our continued failure to transform education means that the apartheid class structure will remain intact.

South Africa's extreme inequality is mirrored in its educational system – the top 3% of South African high schools create more distinctions in mathematics and physical science than the remaining 97% combined.[3]

It is an uncontested fact that our education system has not been sufficiently re-engineered since 1994 to support the upward mobility of poor children into labour markets. Our education system continues to support the reproduction of high levels of economic inequality, largely still along racial lines.

Although we have seen massive resource shifts to black schools and substantial reductions in differentials in years of schooling, qualitative differentials remain large (and may have increased). Most township and former homeland schools have continuing low matric pass rates and high drop-out rates. Good educational outcomes are restricted to private schools, former Model C schools and about 10% of historically black schools.

When we examine our basic education system, we can identify some general characteristics, including poor outcomes (as measured by international comparisons), high drop-out rates, relatively high fiscal allocations to basic education (in comparison to other middle-income countries and global averages) and a high component of 'cost of employees' within total education budgets.

According to educationalist Nic Spaull, only four out of every 100 students who start school complete a degree within six years of matriculating. In

Spaull's view, the problem begins with poor foundation skills in early child-hood development and primary school education.

The recent Progress in International Reading Literacy study showed that 78% of South African Grade 4 children could not read for meaning in any language – that is, they could not 'locate and retrieve an explicitly stated detail'. Comparable figures in other countries are 64% (Morocco), 35% (Iran), 13% (Chile) and 3% (United Kingdom).[4]

The teaching of mathematics is also very weak. According to the Trends in International Mathematics and Science Study (TIMSS), 61% of South African Grade 5 learners could not do basic mathematics; that is, they could not add and subtract whole numbers, have no understanding of multiplication by one-digit numbers and cannot solve simple word problems.[5]

Spending on education has been consistently high relative to other countries. Yet, compared to other countries of similar size, South African schools remain poorly provisioned and many do not have libraries or qualified teachers.

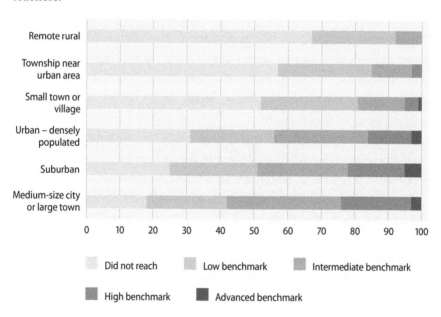

Figure 5.1: South African Grade 5 learner achievement of international benchmarks, by location

(Source: Progress in International Reading Literacy Study)

87

South Africa's regular curriculum changes (three iterations in the past 20 years) have resulted in 'curriculum change fatigue', which has negatively impacted teacher morale.[6] A full 49% of South African pupils cannot reach the lowest benchmark used in the literacy test.

A similar picture is painted by the TIMSS study, which measures the performance of Grade 9 learners in mathematics and science. South Africa ranked globally second from last in mathematics and last in science education.

Above-average spending per student does not translate into above-average outcomes (in contrast to, for example, Botswana and Mauritius). The problem begins with the way in which this spending is allocated. An astounding 93% of current expenditure of provincial Departments of Education goes to paying employees, leaving insufficient resources for scholar transport, nutrition and learning materials. As a result, South Africa's education system still reproduces poverty and inequality a quarter of a century after it was meant to start serving all the country's people.

To overhaul the education system is not easy. It is, however, possible. The solution to the crisis lies in a massive programme of political and social mobilisation, in new approaches to teacher development and support, standardised curricula and performance assessments, and in ensuring mother-tongue instruction at primary levels.

None of these solutions are new. We identified these elements of education transformation as far back as the late 1980s. Yet, we have failed to turn these ideas into reality. Bringing them to fruition is now more critical than ever before, given the intersection of multiple crises we face.

On the one hand, it is necessary to empower schools and communities to lead the transformation of education; they must be able to hold those tasked with education delivery to account. On the other hand, those responsible for education delivery must do so in a single-minded, goal-directed fashion; the diversionary self-interest that has bedevilled delivery to date must be allowed no space. I expand on possible solutions in Chapter 13.

Causes of our education crisis

The causes of the education crisis are historical and deeply rooted in the socio-economic and institutional disparities of apartheid. But 25 years after democracy, many of these structural features of apartheid have still not been sufficiently transformed and continue to reproduce social relations of underdevelopment and inequality.

Beyond the historical structural factors that bedevil our education system, the crisis can be broadly attributed to three interrelated sets of causal factors: the failure of policy post-1994; weaknesses in leadership and accountability; and the over-extension of vested interests.

The failure of policy

Since 1994, the overarching policy goals for the new education system in South Africa have been to increase access and quality, deepen democracy in structures and processes, redress inequalities of the past and improve efficiency within the educational system.

Education policy since 1994 has been through a number of stages. The first, during 1994–2001 or so, focused more on framing issues. The 1996 Constitution of South Africa guaranteed access to basic education for all as a fundamental right. The 1996 National Education Policy Act formalised relations between national and provincial education authorities; while the 1996 South African Schools Act provided for compulsory schooling and introduced a new school funding model to address issues of access, equity and quality.

The second phase, during 2001–4, focused more on implementing Outcomes-Based Education (OBE). During 2005–9, the focus was more on technical monitoring and evaluation and teacher appraisal (which indicated how badly schools were performing), while the current phase since 2010, framed in terms of the Curriculum and Assessment Policy Statement, has focused more on restoring basic functionality in schools in terms of the three Ts – Teachers on Time with Textbooks.

The current policy thrust also places more emphasis on separating basic education and post-schooling, with the new focus of post-schooling being on applied skills for growth and development. At the rhetorical level, no one can fault our policy intent. So where did things go wrong?

Five key factors account for our inability to realise our policy goals. Firstly, policy overload has seriously undermined strategic coherence and our ability to consistently focus on priorities. Since 1994, there have been some 161 education policy statements promulgated and introduced. These policies have been experienced as 'policy overload' by officials tasked with their implementation, especially when combined with the host of other policies regulating the public service (Public Finance Management Act, supply chain management, etc.) and the administrative burdens of teachers required to achieve the outcomes that the policies espoused. This has resulted in lack of focus and direction, and insufficient policy prioritisation with the 'everything at the same time' approach.

Secondly, policies were developed as a 'one size fits all', without any appreciation of the socio-economic and institutional disparities evident in the context within which the policies were applied. They further failed to ensure that the material conditions created by apartheid were coherently and synergistically addressed by all departments whose work impacts on education.

Thirdly, linked to the above, too little institutional support was provided to schools to ensure policies were implemented. For example, OBE assumed a particular level of educator capacity and orientation (mindset), which was sorely lacking in a large number of poorly resourced schools. Rather than providing hands-on capacity and support to schools and teachers, government has functioned as an unresponsive bureaucracy.

Fourthly, there was hopelessly inadequate monitoring and evaluation of implementation and of learner and teacher outcomes. Poor information systems and the absence of clear measurable indicators (with over-reliance on matric results as a measure of education performance) have weakened our ability to know where and why we are failing as well as failing to alert us to where we are showing success that can be built upon and put to scale.

Fifthly, these shortcomings have been exacerbated by inadequacies (of capacity, resources, commitment and will) among many of the civil servants charged with policy implementation. In a context rife with corruption and mismanagement, it is not difficult to appreciate that coherent policy implementation has been elusive.

Weaknesses in leadership and accountability

Despite high spending on education and on teachers, the quality of teachers remains astonishingly poor: 80% lack content knowledge and pedagogical skill to teach the subjects they are currently teaching. For example, 79% of Grade 6 mathematics teachers cannot get 60% on Grade 6/7-level maths tests.[7]

It can, in fact, be argued that one of the biggest failings in the education system to date has been in the area of teacher development. Collectively, we have completely failed to develop the kinds of teachers needed to revolutionise education in the country. Going forward, a clear teacher development and support plan is required to deal with the enormous capacity backlogs and the haphazard and uncoordinated approach to teacher development and teacher support. Tertiary institutions must be centrally involved in the development and execution of this plan, and must be held more accountable for the quality and orientation of teachers they produce.

The focus of teacher development initiatives must be better targeted. In the light of the last (controversial) Annual National Assessments and subsequent international benchmark tests, it is clear that subject-specific teacher education must be prioritised to improve teacher content knowledge.

Administration of the (national) Funza Lushaka Bursary programme, aimed at providing promising young people with access to teacher education, has been particularly poor in provinces where this is most needed, such as the Eastern Cape. Only a tiny fraction of the bursary holders that graduate each year are placed in schools in that province. This represents a significant waste of resources and opportunities.

A key source of support to teachers in understanding and implementing curricula and content changes in their classrooms should be the education district offices. Subject advisers and education development officers based in the district offices are expected to provide district-level connections between national and provincial education structures through to schools and classrooms. The extremely high vacancy rate in the education district offices renders this intended support link hypothetical. Recruitment and deployment of suitable support-providers is a critical component of transforming education.

This further implies a changed orientation from the adversarial relationship often cited by the South African Democratic Teachers' Union (SADTU) between education bureaucrats and teachers. Establishing teacher capabilities as an entry point to delivering support is fundamentally different from the perceived motive of undermining teachers. Again, the skill set required of this layer in the education system is not universally available, nor universally appreciated.

As much as South Africa suffers from a shortage of skills in teachers and education specialists, we also have a severe shortage of management skills in principals and school governing bodies, which must first and foremost be addressed.[8]

Over-extension of vested interests

The causes of South Africa's education and skills deficit partly lie in the poor quality of Bantu Education and the deliberate denial of black skills over generations, arguably the most pernicious legacy of apartheid. But the collapse of the public sector basic education system is also rooted in the 1994 political transition and the imperative to stabilise the country after the arduous struggle against apartheid.

Part of this stabilisation project involved incorporating vested interests:

- The protection of workers' rights and public sector workers in particular;
- Education being used for social control more than social mobility;[9]
- A realpolitik tendency to focus on short-term stability rather than longer-term growth and transformation; and
- Public education not being re-engineered to create quality education and genuinely redistributive outcomes (despite evidence of policy overload in this regard).

The current problem is that this stabilisation project is now well past its sell-by date, but it persists. The forces of long-term growth and transformation must replace short-term protection of vested interests. This is true of many parts of South African society, but is particularly crucial for the education sector.

The broad powers given to school governing bodies by the 1996 South African Schools Act has been a transformative step towards democratising state schools. Sadly, in many cases, it has also opened the door to mismanagement and even corruption, as politicised groups posing as concerned parents have effectively taken control of personnel appointments and school resources. In one example of this, the principal and school governing body of Glenvista High School in Johannesburg mismanaged millions of rands between 2012 and 2014, illegally using as many as eight bank accounts to channel school funds into individuals' air travel and holiday homes.[10]

It is no surprise that it is South Africa's broken politics that bedevil schooling.

Questions have also been raised about whether government has a free hand when it comes to the appointment of teachers and principals. The Ministerial Task Report found evidence of cadre deployment to ensure that high percentages of managers, decisionmakers and others with power and influence in education are placed in positions where they can prioritise certain sectional interests, for example of trade unions such as SADTU.[11] The matter is further compounded by the fact that key members of the education departments remain members of teachers' unions, causing serious conflicts of interests. As Spaull puts it:

> The interests of teachers and those of the government are often contradictory (for example managing a bloated budget on the one hand and wanting to increase teacher salaries on the other). If high level officials in the Department of Basic Education are paid-up teacher union members (as all the DDGs [deputy director-generals] in the DBE [Department of Basic Education] are) the union technically sits on both sides of the bargaining table. It is also not improbable to say that SADTU is using this managerial role to protect the short-term interests of its members rather than to support the longer-term interests of the country in growth and transformation through education re-engineering.[12]

Role-players will need to put their sectional interests aside and develop a broader vision for the sector. They must endeavour to see beyond their blind spots. Government must champion this plan, and demonstrate real success with respect to governance, leadership and community mobilisation.

For the plan to work, communities and schools must take centre stage: education transformation cannot be about securing jobs for bureaucrats and teachers. Education transformation must be about tangible changes in the conduct of teachers, the content of their teaching and the consistency with which resources are available. Such transformation demands that teachers put the needs of learners ahead of narrow personal and political concerns. Communities and schools are where these changes must be monitored, and where the success of such a plan will be evident.

Conclusion: Acknowledging youth and education

Good-quality basic education is both a development goal itself and a crucial ingredient of economic development. It is crucial to the supply of skills necessary to run a modern, complex, competitive and expanding industrial economy. Basic education (numeracy, literacy and other cognitive skills) is essential to vocational skilling.

There are several consequences of our collapsed public basic education system, including the growth of private schooling, a very low rate of post-school training qualifications,[13] an excess supply of unskilled workers coexisting with excess demand for skilled workers, and a huge pool of undereducated and unskilled youth. Of people unemployed (by the broad definition) it is estimated that more than a half are new labour market entrants (have never worked), are young (18 to 35 years) and lack basic numeracy and basic literacy.

Other consequences include a scarcity of critical skills, such as engineers, technicians and artisans, resulting in the need to import skilled workers. This translates into poor public sector management skills leading to poor service delivery. Skills scarcities also result in high returns to skills, which exacerbates income inequality, as inequality in South Africa is largely determined by labour market status and employment earnings differentials. High returns to skills, in turn, reduce competitiveness with countries that do not suffer from skills shortages.

It is clear that the challenges in our education system are deep-rooted and systemic. Visionary and decisive political leadership is required to address the crisis. Currently, the system is in a downward spiral, with various social forces pushing narrow sectional interests above those of the interests of the system as a whole.

South Africa's failure to properly educate its children is the result of allowing an important institution – the Department of Education – to fall under the spell of political compromise. By allowing trade unions a disproportionate say in teacher and school head appointments, politicians have mortgaged the future of generations of children in exchange for political pennies. This has got to stop if South Africa is to lift its youth out of poverty.

The education pipeline in South Africa needs to be fixed as a central component of the new consensus for inclusive growth. The system directly reproduces social inequality through streaming learners from poor rural and township schools towards unemployment, while streaming the children of elites towards highly paid professional and technical vocations.

Despite the relatively high fiscal allocations to the sector, our basic education system has very poor learner outcomes by international comparison (in literacy, numeracy, problem solving and especially maths and science). This requires a new national obsession with fixing our broken education and skills pipeline.

6

Youth Exclusion

Show me the heroes that the youth of your country look up to, and I will tell you the future of your country. — Idowu Koyenikan

Chapter summary

- The desolation of youth is the result of a collective failure of the education system and the job market. The dualistic education system translates directly into a dualistic job market.

- This has given rise to widespread disappointment, easily captured by populist and opportunist politicians.

- At the core of this populist movement is a hostility towards business, established wealth and 'foreign investment', favouring nationalisation and state control of resources.

- Meanwhile, there has been a decline in youth voters and a rise in political apathy.

If young people do not fulfil their potential, the nation will fail. Right now, South Africa's youth carry the intolerable burden of South Africa's unemployment crisis. The structure of our economy means that many young South Africans, especially if they are low-skilled, have almost no prospect of employment. The life chances of this generation will inevitably be greatly compromised by their failure to find a job and, accordingly, their families' dependence on social grants and informal sector subsistence. The National Development Plan notes the problem starkly: 'If youths fail to get a job by

24, they are unlikely ever to get formal employment. Unresolved, this trend poses the single greatest threat to social stability.[1]

The unemployment numbers for the final quarter of 2018 pegged unemployment at 27% and the 'expanded' rate, which includes job seekers who have given up hope, at 37%.[2] The pool of discouraged job seekers increased by almost 8% between 2018 and 2019.[3] The youth unemployment picture is far worse with in excess of 54% of those aged 15–24 out of work.[4]

Within our fragmented and unequal society, youth experience the highest levels of social dislocation and marginalisation in a socio-economic system that they perceive as unresponsive to their needs, identity and aspirations. In a very real sense, they are outsiders, not by choice, but by circumstance – in many instances, under-educated, excluded from the economy and living on the outskirts of urban centres with few services and opportunities to change their lives. These objective factors drive high-risk and anti-social behaviour (substance abuse, crime, unsafe sex, etc.), which, in a classic vicious cycle, further reinforces and exacerbates vulnerability and dislocation.

But the story of our youth is not just one about socio-economics. Youth are generally always at the forefront of social protest and change – think of the US hippie movement of the 1960s and the Vietnam solidarity struggles, the Soweto Uprising, the Arab Spring and Tiananmen Square. This is positive in that youth feel vested in the future of their country.

In South Africa, however, having such large numbers of youth in the country who have little or no vested interest in the socio-political and institutional status quo represents a significant risk to social cohesion (the so-called ticking time bomb), and provides fertile recruitment ground for populist political movements that could threaten our democratic gains.

The chief causes of youth unemployment are our poor education system, our highly inefficient labour market and the shift from labour-intensive to capital-intensive employment, without transition plans, as businesses seek to become globally competitive by introducing hi-tech efficiencies.

Our poor education system

Education is about more than preparation for the job market. Education

97

outcomes structure the possibilities (or otherwise) of creating new gener-ations of independent and critical thinkers as agents for social change in South Africa. Without quality education, young people will not fulfil their inherent human potential.

Education standards have a direct correlation to unemployment. The level of unemployment among South African graduates in the first quarter of 2019 was 31%, an increase of 11% from the first quarter of 2018.[5] While this rate is still unacceptably high, it is about 20% lower than the general youth unem-ployment figure. University enrolment has grown rapidly, from 495 356 in 1994, for example, to 938 201 in 2011 in public universities and universities of technology and more than one million in 2017.[6] While the chances of finding a job have historically been much greater even with a secondary matric qual-ification, the most recent data from Stats SA shows that this is declining with 55% of 15–24-year-olds with a matric out of work, and 32% of 25–34-year-olds with a matric out of work.[7]

One of the major reasons for our high youth unemployment rates is the lack of skills required for the job market. Only between 37% and 41% of students who begin Grade 2 eventually pass the Grade 12 school-leaving examination, according to the NGO Equal Education.[8] This is in stark con-trast to the Department of Basic Education's figure of a 70% throughput pass rate. In turn, of those 40% who pass Grade 12, 18% register at university, with about half dropping out of university before completing their studies.[9] This leaves a large majority of our youth who are not in education, with the obvious impact on the probability of them not obtaining employment or post-secondary training.

According to research by the Development Policy Research Unit at the University of Cape Town, South Africa's share of youth Not in Education, Employment or Training (NEET) is the biggest globally compared to coun-tries of a similar economic profile. 'Evidently, there is a large reservoir of untapped potential, who with the right opportunities and training, could make a significant contribution towards enhanced productivity and eco-nomic growth in the South African economy.'[10]

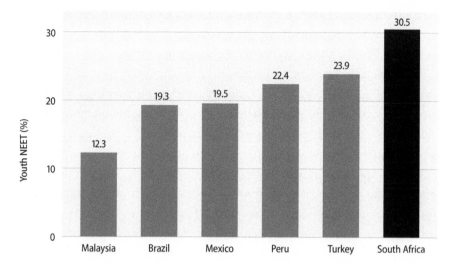

Figure 6.1: Share of youth Not in Education, Employment or Training (%)
(Source: ILO database; Development Policy Research Unit calculations)
Note: The share of youth NEETs was unavailable for China.

Youth in the labour market and economy

Youth dislocation in South Africa is directly linked to the structure of the labour market and the economy, and is the reason why we have been unable to absorb the growing numbers of unemployed youth as economically active citizens.

South Africa has a youthful population; those who are below the age of 35 years constitute about 66% of the total population. Nearly 18% (10.3 million people) are aged between 15 and 24 years, according to Stats SA.[11] About 29.5% of the population is younger than 15, according to the same study, which speaks for itself in terms of the shape of our future youth bulge.

Having a youthful population is often viewed as positive for unlocking growth and development potential – the so-called youth dividend. There is strong international evidence to suggest it is the youth who are the most innovative, the most risk-taking and entrepreneurial, and, as the new entrants into the economy, the most likely to stimulate both productivity and demand. But with growing structural unemployment and an economy stuck in a low-growth trap, the youth dividend can quickly turn into a youth burden.

Youth unemployment in South Africa among those aged 15–24 years is estimated at 55%. In simple terms, seven out of every ten unemployed people are young people. This is a crisis of epidemic proportions.

Paradoxically, the sectors where South Africa is currently most competitive – finance, knowledge services and advanced manufacturing – all require relatively high skills for entry. There is a structural disjuncture between our skills supply and skills demand profiles. Increased youth participation rates would require a drastic step-up in education and training outcomes.

One of the reasons why Germany has had relative success in youth employment is because of its training system, which prepares the youth for the labour market and entrepreneurial activities through experiential on-the-job training. Commitment to experiential learning is one reason why the Chinese have accelerated learning within their firms and ensured skills transfers (and technology transfer) from multinationals investing in China.

In the South African experience, skilling outcomes have been compromised by the poor performance of Sector Education Training Authorities, as well as the sub-optimal uptake of learnerships and apprenticeships by private sector firms. New incentives (for example, tax allowances) are needed to radically increase the uptake of learnerships and apprenticeships. Also critical are active employment services to improve efficiencies of job-searching and job-matching.

Youth also need to be streamlined towards entrepreneurship. Inclusive innovation and technology transfer, special support for start-ups through youth incubators, product development and market readiness support, and targeted financial support with customised instruments from development finance institutions and private banks should become non-negotiables. Overcoming regulatory constraints that limit small, medium and micro-sized enterprises, and which prohibit transitioning from informal to formal enterprises, must be prioritised.

Ultimately, however, our immediate challenge is to find employment opportunities for millions of unskilled and low-skilled youth who have been failed by our education and training system. This will require short- to medium-term rapid response transitional packages while we build a longer-term economy that is fit for our youth and therefore for the future. This could include a combination of upscaling direct public employment schemes, as well as opening up opportunities in low-skill, labour-intensive industrial segments. To achieve the latter would require some innovations in our labour market policies, possibly including wage subsidies and productivity-enhancing measures as an incentive for the private sector to increase employment. These innovations and their risks will require robust discussion among employers, government, labour unions and youth formations.

Youth mobilisation and leadership

Beyond the socio-economic implications of our youth crisis, I hold the view that we have failed to harness the energy (and militancy) of our youth to transform society. The youth are there to agitate and remind us that access to power is not the endgame. Instead, the exclusion of most youth from the labour market and tertiary education has led to growing social instability. As a result, the youth are vulnerable to populist politics.

In his seminal 1911 book, *Political Parties: A Sociological Study of the Oligarchical Tendencies of Modern Democracy*, sociologist Roberto Michels wrote about the 'iron law of oligarchy', referring to how leadership in various organisations in society and political parties hold on to their positions and ensure their continued occupation because of the resources and power that come with occupying these positions.[12] We are perhaps confronted by the iron law of oligarchy today where those who were the youth during the struggle and transition have moved into middle and old age and now hold on to positions of power and authority. If we do not find a way of enabling a youth transition in our society to accompany a fundamental economic transformation, we are likely to face worse social instability than we do today.

It is my view that youth social movements have not yet come into their own in terms of articulating and channelling their interests towards constructive arenas for engaging in meaningful social transformation. The uprisings of students first against symbols of colonialism (#RhodesMustFall) and then against the higher education system (#FeesMustFall) were unfortunately

101

unable to sustain momentum for driving a meaningful youth transformation agenda.

I would argue that this will only emerge if a new cadre of organic intellectuals emerges who can inspire youth mobilisation by linking the current youth experiences to an agenda of transformation welded to genuine foundations. This requires proper analytical work to prioritise issues and the appropriate strategic response. Reliance on instinctive idealism is unlikely to rescue the youth movement from the seductive populism currently doing the rounds and instead will drive it into its arms. When it emerged, the 1970s' student movement found a wide and deep range of analyses of the conjuncture – from historical materialist analyses of political economy, to strong statements of black consciousness, to archives of research on the South African labour movement and civil society. It also found a militant and active labour movement arising from the 1973 Durban strikes, with strong linkages to progressive university-based intellectuals, as well as community and cultural activists. This enabled the articulation of diverse struggles as one coordinated national liberation agenda, led by the ANC in exile.

In recent times, as our students arose in militancy, they were not supported by a critical mass of organic intellectuals who could help shape a real and sustained struggle. And they were not supported by a mobilised civil society that could both defend and advance their interests. Instead, the student protestors emerged as a rather fragmented mass, coordinated by social media tweets, but without an overarching agenda around which to build alliances with activists from other sectors of society.

Partly, this relates to one of the unintended consequences of our democratic transition. Key sites of accountability, including within civil society and youth structures, were inadvertently phased out with the emergence of a legitimate state. As a consequence, most donor funding was rechannelled away from the sites where organic intellectuals had been historically grown – organised labour, women and youth organisations, and community-based structures. NGOs and other civil society organisations adopted a survival strategy, and increasingly became agents of government service delivery.

In addition, organic intellectuals from communities were demobilised through movement into traditional intellectual positions within the state, and found themselves curtailed by regulations and bureaucratic hierarchy, far detached from the youth realities of today.

The challenge of restoring youth to their rightful position in society must begin by opening up the terrain where young organic intellectuals can thrive and grow, shaping the visions that will inspire other youth to follow and embrace the process of transformation and fundamental change. The basis of solving our youth crisis is a societal responsibility to encourage a socially legitimate, critical and inspirational youth leadership that consistently and deliberately influences our policy agenda and holds us to account.

Conclusion: Confronting the vicious cycle

South Africa is a country characterised by high levels of unemployment, economic exclusion and inequality. Within our fragmented and unequal society, the youth experience the highest levels of social dislocation and marginalisation in a socio-economic system that they perceive as unresponsive to their needs, identities and aspirations. In a very real sense, they are outsiders, not by choice, but by circumstance – in many instances, under-educated, excluded from the economy, and living on the outskirts of urban centres with few services and opportunities to change their lives.

The dualism of our education system is mirrored in a dualistic labour market, where graduates – the majority of whom come from former Model C or private schools – become high-earners while those who attended poor schools end up either jobless or in low-paying jobs, perpetuating a cycle of privilege and poverty. It is also mirrored in other elements of our dualistic society, such as our bifurcated health system, in which the poorest of the poor are denied proper health care, while those who can afford medical aid are served by a world-class private health care system. Only 10% of South Africans can afford private health care, while 15% suffer catastrophic health costs, where the cost of care is more than 30% of their income.

The challenge we need to urgently confront is how to deal with this dualism and disrupt what has become a vicious cycle.

South Africa has the luxury of a potential youth dividend, which ought to bring new vigour, innovation and drive to the economy. But, instead of finding ways to get the youth economically active, leaders have kept them on the margins, facing a bleak future with poor education and no jobs. Steps must be taken to turn the tide so that the youth can reach their full potential.

7

Politics

The More Things Change, the More They Stay the Same

The disengagement of people from the institutions of society is the defining feature of contemporary political life. — Frank Furedi

Chapter summary

- Political parties see the object of attaining and retaining power as their primary function. Instead of being driven by vision and strategy, they have become about placating their internal constituencies above all else.

- Our politics is stuck in a racial paradigm where parties seem unable to talk coherently about solving the country's most pressing problems.

- An array of our constitutionally enshrined institutions were seriously compromised by state capture. As a result, there is a growing trust-deficit between the country's leadership and the public.

- The current leadership needs to take advantage of this unprecedented historical moment, which requires looking beyond the trap of ANC unity versus South African stability as a binary choice. The focus must be on the well-being of the people above all else.

As I was finishing this book, the country went to the polls for the 2019 general election. It was clear to me, looking at the outcome of the vote, that all was not well with our politics.

We seem, despite the vast investment in reconciliation during the Mandela years, to be stuck in a racial paradigm.

What is particularly concerning is the failure of parties to talk coherently about solving the country's most pressing problem: the need for rapidly accelerated inclusive economic growth that will provide jobs for the millions who find themselves without a stake in the establishment.

Instead, parties remained stuck in identity politics and opted to call each other out on race, adding fuel to the fire that is burning up valuable social cohesion.

It is worth taking a brief detour to look at exactly what happened in the election.

Lessons from the 2019 election

The 2019 general election perfectly illustrated the dysfunction at the heart of South Africa's politics. On the surface, it was a free and fair election, which was peacefully contested with the exception of a few incidents of protest on the day and a handful of polling stations that opened late.

But beneath the surface, it was a landmark election that underscored the growing irrelevance of the 1994 compact.

The 2019 election was notable for its low voter turnout. The final voter turnout number was 65%, with 17 671 616 votes cast. This is not the lowest turnout in numbers – fewer people voted in 1999 and in 2004. But when the increase in population and in the number of registered voters is taken in account, this

	1994	1999	2004	2009	2014	2019
Population	40 602 000	44 760 000	47 793 000	50 133 000	54 490 000	58 606 415
Voting age adults	22 500 000	25 300 000	30 209 415	33 184 188	36 494 109	39 778 969
Registered		18 172 751	20 674 923	23 181 997	25 388 082	26 756 649
Votes cast	19 533 498	15 977 142	15 612 671	17 680 729	18 402 497	17 436 144
Percentage turnout	100	88	76	76	72	65

Table 7.1: Voter turnout, 1994–2019

was the lowest percentage turnout since 1994, as Table 7.1 shows.

While the 1994 election – the first where all could vote – was exceptional, it is remarkable that two million fewer voters turned up 25 years later, despite an increase in the size of the adult population of more than 17 million.

In most societies this growing voter apathy would be put down to 'normalisation' with those accepting the status quo feeling secure enough not to bother to turn up to vote. But in South Africa there are other dynamics that must be considered. The first is the large number of illegal immigrants living in the society. Exactly how many is a bone of contention, but it runs into millions. On the other hand, illegal immigrants are less likely than South African residents to present themselves in census surveys on which Stats SA bases its population projections. There could, in fact, be millions more 'off-the-books' people added to South Africa's adult population.

The second dynamic is the coincidence between the high rate of youth exclusion from the economy (about 50% of the country's youth are unemployed) and the rise in extra-parliamentary politics, which is partly evident in the rapidly increasing number of 'service delivery' protests. There were even protests against voting in some parts of the country on election day.

These factors suggest that a large part of the potential voting population is politically engaged but is utterly disillusioned with parliamentary politics and chooses to use other means for political expression.

The temptation to wave this away ought to be resisted as it has implications for the legitimacy of the state and affects governance – cooperation with the police service or support for a local school, for example.

What the numbers demonstrate is a stark decline in the 'representivity' of the party that won the election when its electoral support is compared against registered voters and against the adult population[1] who might qualify to vote.

	1994	1999	2004	2009	2014	2019
ANC vote as proportion of on-day voters	62.6	66.4	69.7	65.9	62.1	57.5
ANC vote as proportion of registered voters	62.6	58.3	52.6	50.3	45.0	37.5
ANC vote as proportion of adult population	54.4	41.9	36.0	35.1	31.3	25.2

Table 7.2: ANC vote, 1994–2019

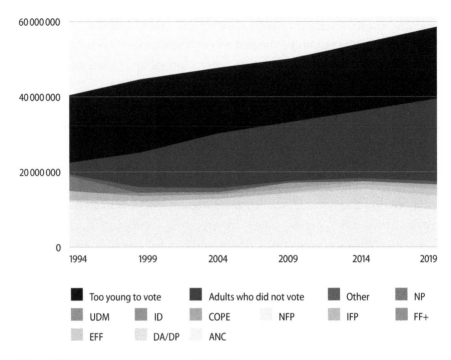

Figure 7.1: Voters versus non-voters, 1994–2019
(Source: IEC; Stats SA)

This shows that the ANC enjoys the electoral support of just 25.2% of adults of voting age, a number that begins to undermine the parliamentary system's legitimacy.

Understanding this statistical 'black hole' and its motivations ought to be the preoccupation of political researchers who wish to grapple with South Africa's governance weaknesses.

Figure 7.1 shows the magnitude of this black hole, which is expanding as fast as the universe of voters declines. This was the first election where the number of adults of voting age who did not vote exceeded the number who voted, and the second election in which the ANC vote was less than 50% of registered voters.

Figure 7.1 ought to be seen as a warning of the pace at which the legitimacy of parliamentary politics and of the state is declining among most of those who are governed.

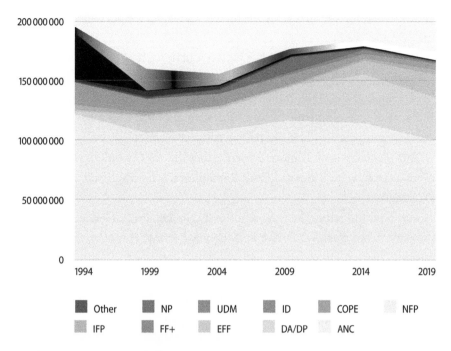

Figure 7.2: Voter support, 1994–2019
(Source: IEC; Stats SA)

The election was won by the ANC with 57.5% of the vote – down on 62.2% in the last election, with the Democratic Alliance (DA) in second place with 20.8% of the vote (22.2% in 2014) and the Economic Freedom Fighters (EFF) third with 10.79% of the vote (6.4% in 2014). In the provinces, the DA retained control of the Western Cape while the ANC retained control of all the other provinces, albeit with reduced majorities in many, especially in Gauteng and KwaZulu-Natal.

On the face of it, there was no change to governance nationally or in the provinces. But the result did nonetheless reveal some underlying trends.

The first is the decline in social cohesion. Both parties of the broad centre, the ANC and the DA, lost votes to populist political parties. This, especially in the case of the EFF, which nearly doubled its vote, suggests a trend away from the centre and towards a polarised contest over the country's destiny.

109

Figure 7.2 shows the shrinking of the DA and ANC support and the rise of the EFF and the FF+.

There was a notable divergence between national and provincial support for parties.

In Gauteng, the ANC polled 50.2% of the provincial vote compared to 53.2% of the national vote. In KwaZulu-Natal it polled 54.2% in the provincial vote compared with 55.5% for the national election.

This tactical voting is more evidence that the ANC would have declined more sharply were it not for Cyril Ramaphosa, who improved its national showing.

This ought to strengthen the argument that a change of leadership saved the party from electoral failure and further decline. However, it also feeds into the concerning over-personalisation of our politics.

What is abundantly clear if you look at voter (non-) participation and the rise of the EFF, and ignore the demographically contained FF+, is that all the pressure in the system is coming from the populist left.

Given that Ramaphosa's support comes from the left within the ANC (the unions and the South African Communist Party), this pressure could, in theory, push him in the direction of more radical rhetoric around the economy and land reform.

But, as Ramaphosa and the party leadership know, the ANC is now in an existential crisis. At the current rate, it may lose its majority in the next election.

The only hope of turning the tide for the ANC lies in economic revival and the creation of jobs at a fast pace, the achievement of which requires a growth-oriented stance and reforms that bolster the private sector as the public sector has run out of fiscal room to employ – perhaps even to sustain its current high rate of employment. I believe that Ramaphosa is acutely aware of these realities, and that more muddling along without a clearly expressed direction cannot be an option.

For the DA, the result was devastating as it represented the first reversal of fortune for the party in 25 years. It could be argued that it is a blessing in disguise, freeing the party from having to accommodate ethnic nationalists and finally allowing it to aggressively pursue the black middle-class vote on which it can begin to build stronger electoral support. But to accomplish this, it is going to have to find the ability to resonate more strongly with voters than it currently does.

The EFF's achievement, against a background of poor voter turnout, is not to be underestimated. Had the country polled higher, it would no doubt have done even better as it is the poor, marginalised and those without transport who were less likely to vote. The evidence is that voter turnout in townships, where the EFF is strongest, was much lower – possibly by as much as 7% – than in the suburbs.

For the EFF, the challenge is simple. It will grow if it is able to persuade young black voters to register and participate in parliamentary politics. This may be more difficult than it seems as the level of disillusionment is high.

The election was also notable for the high number of smaller parties that entered the fray and how they failed to ignite popular support. The failure of the Black First Land First movement (19 796 votes nationally) is particularly noteworthy. It demonstrates once and for all that the BLF has no traction with ordinary South Africans.

Commenting on the election result, the EFF's Dali Mpofu said that South Africa has now entered the era of coalition politics with the ANC unlikely to sustain its parliamentary majority in the next election. Based on current trends, and if the ANC is unable to reform, this could take place within two election cycles, but, be that as it may, Mpofu may be onto something.

On current trends, the ANC stands to lose its majority in at least Gauteng and KwaZulu-Natal, the country's two most populous provinces, at the next election, unless the ANC-led government can produce the jobs and growth that will revive hope in the party's leadership.

The bottom line is that the scene is set for a realignment of some kind. The ANC has already flirted with populist positions in a number of areas, including on land policy. This could have serious implications, including entrenching the ANC into a populist trajectory with potentially catastrophic ramifications for South Africa and the region.

There are various realignment options, but all are fraught with major dis-advantages for one or more of the potential partners, suggesting that there could be a great deal of uncertainty, brinkmanship and chaos in the event that the ANC loses its majority.

111

But, having said that, anything is possible. The DA and EFF are already governing Johannesburg with a great measure of consensus despite the vast chasm between them on the national stage.

Another option is of a 'government of national unity', but what is certain is that this election was the last hurrah of the 1994 political era and an uncertain future awaits.

The politics of power at all costs

There is a danger that the leaders of political parties have come to see the object of attaining and retaining power as their primary function. Instead of being driven by a vision and strategy, they have become about placating their internal constituencies above all else.

In such an environment, unseating the incumbent leader or seeing off challengers absorbs the attention of the leadership to the detriment of the country they are supposed to be serving.

Political life within the ANC has become about these internal power battles. The Jacob Zuma faction sought to unseat Thabo Mbeki. And then the Ramaphosa faction sought to unseat Zuma. It is highly likely that there is already a faction working on unseating Ramaphosa.

The danger becomes that political appointments to Cabinet and the upper echelons of the civil service will continue to be aimed at placating certain internal factions or wreaking revenge on others. In such an environment, it is not about the best-qualified or experienced person serving the nation, and the state's ability to serve the people is diminished.

New, disruptive ideas that are needed to seek a way out of our economic growth and jobs malaise are shelved in favour of shuffling political deckchairs.

All of this is exacerbated by another distracting tendency – the rise of the provincial strongman (the person is usually male) whose obvious failings must be ignored in favour of appeasement because they bring a block of votes to bear in national leadership elections.

These provincial barons run powerful local patronage networks and manage vast procurement budgets, which they use to keep themselves in power, once again relegating the task of effective governance to an afterthought.

All of this takes place under the cover of a false moral authority derived from being a 'liberation movement'. The ANC, in particular, has doggedly stuck to calling itself a liberation movement rather than a political party because this mythology allows it to assert moral leadership. Even when it fails, it will say that such failures are better than handing the country over to 'the enemy' – another political party.

While such claims to moral authority were no doubt valid during the fight against apartheid, they are inappropriate in an open democracy. When in government, ethics and morality are defined and managed by society through the Constitution and the rule of law and cannot be owned by one political formation.

The most cogent analysis of why corruption and cutting corners for financial enrichment took hold among former liberation fighters was made by Joel Netshitenzhe, who runs the Mapungubwe Institute for Strategic Reflection.

Written in 2012, his paper is notable for its forthright analysis of 'whether as cadres we have not become six-day sinners who on "Sundays" go for penance at rallies, branch and other meetings ... but revert to the sinner's default for the rest of the week!'[2]

Netshitenzhe argues that the exaggerated wealth of white South Africans accumulated during apartheid has spurred those new in power to seek the quick path to riches in a race to become part of the middle classes.

> Such lifestyles are based on a standard of living that is artificially high compared to today's global 'middle class', in terms for instance of assets, number of cars per household, domestic assistants, swimming pools, emulation of the European 'gentry' and so on. In pursuit of non-racial equality, the Black middle class and upper strata aspire to achieve that living standard of the metropolis; and many strive to do so in one fell swoop. Aggravating this is the global culture of short-termism in the conduct of business and material self-advancement.[3]

Without the historical assets of the rich whites they seek to emulate, 'they have to rely on massive debt and/or patronage. Having dipped their toes into that lifestyle but with no such historical assets as are available to the white middle and upper strata, some then try to acquire the resources by hook or by crook.'[4]

The effect of this cycle of rent-seeking is that political parties become less able to control their members who hold them hostage by threatening to reduce the party's access to local voters. Netshitenzhe argues:

> Within parties, intra-party patronage and corruption take root. The political centre is unable to correct the local mediators to mass constituencies and the foot soldiers on whom it relies to garner votes. In pursuit of numbers, a price is attached to a Conference delegate's vote. And to paraphrase a lecturer at a recent Gauteng political education workshop, a toxic leadership then begets toxic members, some of whom actually demand financial and other incentives to vote in particular ways.[5]

The ANC has been its own harshest critic and, in his report to the 2017 ANC conference, then secretary general, Gwede Mantashe, put it bluntly:

> Our movement has experienced a decline. The decline manifests itself in a multi-faceted manner across different areas such as: quality and quantity of membership; ideological outlook and policy articulation; efficiency and effectiveness of our structures; organisational discipline and the waning of our values and principles among leaders and members alike; cohesiveness and cohesion in the Alliance; electoral performance and ability to govern; and influence in the broader society.[6]

Mantashe went on to say: 'Fierce, even fatal, contestation, together with an almost endemic factionalism between and among comrades, dominates our structures, causing grievous divisions in the movement as a whole.'[7]

Just days before the 2017 ANC conference at Nasrec near Soweto, four ANC regions took the organisation to court over the outcome of provincial conferences.[8] The party's largest province, KwaZulu-Natal, had its 2015 provincial conference declared invalid by the provincial high court in September 2017. The North West, Northern Cape and Free State were also embroiled in legal battles.

Mantashe said there was a growing 'trust deficit' between the ANC and the public. 'Central to the crisis is the adverse effect of global capital accumulation of wealth for a minority elite, against impoverishment of the majority, and the seeming – if not perceived – collaboration of politics or the state.'[9]

The 'growing trust deficit' has manifested itself in a loss of voter support. In 2019, for the first time since democracy was introduced in 1994, the ANC's votes fell below 50% of those registered to vote, a wake-up call for the party faithful.

Stuck in the muddle

It is clear to me that we have entered a vicious cycle of political decline. The question is: why are we stuck in this paradigm, which has palpably failed to deliver inclusive growth and which has failed to deliver on the promise of a better life for all?

One answer is that our elections have validated this outcome by delivering more or less the same result over the 25 years of democracy. This has only been possible because the excluded and marginalised have opted out of voting in favour of extra-parliamentary politics due to disillusionment and apathy. The shrinking voter cohort (as a percentage of the adult population) has continued to reflect the wishes of those who struck the 1994 compact.

A second answer is that the ruling party now finds itself in a tricky catch-22.

It must choose between two outcomes: reform itself and risk imploding the party so that the country can chart a new growth-oriented course; or place the party first, even if this means economic failure for the country.

The consequences of being stuck, which appears to be the default course for now, are severe. A survey of our recent history bears this out.

There have been moments of coherence resulting in a few brief years of growth over 5% and even a budget surplus in the mid-2000s, but this has not been sustained because the underlying structural problems with the state, the economy and the labour market have not been addressed.

And, even in the 'few good years', questions of inclusivity, unemployment, inequality and other ills, which have resulted in considerable social discontent, often accompanied by violence, have not been addressed.

The mountain we have to climb is growing steeper by the day. It is not going to get easier. We now live in a world that is less positively disposed towards a country and economy like ours, than was the case 25 years ago. Even then, in international relations in the period of transition, with the collapse of the Soviet Union and its allied states, the new administration encountered an environment that was difficult and reluctant to invest or provide other forms of economic support. The new government took various measures to inspire confidence in investors, with some results.

In Part Two of this book I will make a range of proposals to take the country forward. There are hard choices that need to be made and pitfalls that must be avoided.

While I advance these with confidence that they deserve serious attention, the question is: who will take the lead in implementation? The proposals presuppose rational actors, taking forward the ideas with integrity, and placing the country above party politics.

The ruling ANC has been riven by patronage and corruption and has demonstrated contempt for legality and constitutionalism, leading the Constitutional Court, in a landmark judgment, to find the previous head of state, Jacob Zuma, had failed to carry out his constitutional obligations and breached his presidential oath of office.

In so doing, the court demonstrated that there was still institutional resilience in an all too frequently wilting state.

The removal of Zuma and his replacement by Ramaphosa as president of the ANC and then state president in 2018 engendered a measure of optimism in the business and investor community. This was partly because of Ramaphosa's background in business and understanding of the economy as well as his stated commitment, from early in his presidency, to eradicate corruption and ensure that the state would operate with integrity.

Some institutional weakness, much political weakness
In 1994, a momentous decision was taken to make South Africa a

constitutional state with an array of checks and balances on government. At the heart of this decision was that the Constitutional Court would be the final arbiter on disputes over law.

The Constitution itself was framed as an instrument to build a responsive, open and democratic society, impelled to heal the wounds of the past and to improve the living conditions of its citizens. The preamble read:

> We therefore, through our freely elected representatives, adopt this Constitution as the supreme law of the Republic so as to: Heal the divisions of the past and establish a society based on democratic values, social justice and fundamental human rights; Lay the foundations for a democratic and open society in which government is based on the will of the people and every citizen is equally protected by law; Improve the quality of life of all citizens and free the potential of each person; and Build a united and democratic South Africa able to take its rightful place as a sovereign state in the family of nations.[10]

The last ten years have put the Constitution and the independent institutions it summoned to life through a severe stress test. For much of the last decade, South Africans despaired as government – and private sector enablers – ignored the Constitution's imperatives and built a system in which sections of the powerful 'captured' the state and used it to enrich themselves.

It seemed, at times, that the Constitution was a noble document that would be honoured in the breach by the corrupt and even that South Africa would cease to be a country governed by the rule of law.

In fact, the stage was being set for an almighty showdown between the imperial Zuma Presidency and the Constitution. The battleground would be defined by the spending of some R250 million on refurbishments at Zuma's Nkandla homestead in KwaZulu-Natal.

The *Mail & Guardian* newspaper broke the story in December 2009 and it soon ballooned into a national crisis as the bill for renovations grew from R65 million to more than R250 million.

The matter was investigated by the Public Protector, Thuli Madonsela, whom Zuma had appointed to the position in the same year the scandal broke. Zuma clearly believed that Madonsela, then a soft-spoken ANC back-bencher, would be someone he could bully. He was sorely mistaken.

In March 2014, Madonsela issued her report 'Secure in Comfort' after several attempts by Zuma and some Cabinet ministers to delay it or undermine it by conducting their own investigations.

Established under Chapter Nine of the Constitution, the Public Protector's office has the power to issue rulings that carry legal weight. Madonsela found: 'It is difficult not to reach the conclusion that a licence to loot situation was created by government due to a lack of demand management by the organs of state involved.'[11]

She found that the renovations did not comply with government guidelines and concluded: 'The allegation that the excessive expenditure added substantial value to the President's private property at the expense of the state is substantiated.'[12] She found that Zuma had 'unduly benefited' and that he should pay a portion of the costs back to the state.

Instead of paying back the money, Zuma defied the Public Protector with the backing of the ANC benches in parliament, where Madonsela's report was not adopted. An executive cover-up was adopted instead.

The matter of whether Madonsela's rulings were binding found its way to the Constitutional Court. In a landmark ruling delivered by Chief Justice Mogoeng Mogoeng, Madonsela's powers were upheld and Zuma was ordered to pay back a portion of the money as she had ruled.

But the ruling went further.

Mogoeng used the opportunity to make a powerful statement about the limits of executive authority in a constitutional state. He did not mince his words: 'Public office-bearers ignore their constitutional obligations at their peril. This is so because constitutionalism, accountability and the rule of law constitute the sharp and mighty sword that stands ready to chop the ugly head of impunity off its stiffened neck.'[13]

Describing the Public Protector as 'one of the most invaluable constitutional gifts to our nation in the fight against corruption,'[14] he said: 'She is the embodiment of a biblical David, that the public is, who fights the most powerful and very well-resourced Goliath, that impropriety and corruption by government officials are. The Public Protector is one of the true crusaders and champions of anti-corruption and clean governance.'[15]

At the time of writing this book, the incumbent public protector, Busisiwe Mkhwebane, had had three court judgments against her for what one constitutional law expert described as 'at least some evidence that the Public Protector has an adventurous relationship with the truth and may have attempted deliberately to mislead the courts and the public to protect powerful individuals, and may, therefore, be guilty of misconduct'.[16] I certainly agree with this view that this fundamentally important office has been misused under the current public protector to fight factional political battles. It is precisely this cannibalisation of our sacrosanct constitutional institutions that needs to be opposed going forward.

Setting out the president's constitutional obligations, Mogoeng said:

> The President is the Head of State and Head of the national Executive. His is indeed the highest calling to the highest office in the land. He is the first citizen of this country and occupies a position indispensable for the effective governance of our democratic country. Only upon him has the constitutional obligation to uphold, defend and respect the Constitution as the supreme law of the Republic been expressly imposed.[17]

The Constitutional Court had shown that independent institutions and the Constitution itself could not be brought to heel by the executive.

However, an array of other institutions were seriously compromised by state capture. The prosecution service failed to halt state capture because of the appointment and elevation of a host of compromised individuals to its leadership structures. Those involved in state capture were never prosecuted or properly investigated and a range of others, some of whom were fighting state capture, became its targets instead.

Even as the country's independent institutions fought for their survival with varying degrees of success, its political institutions – its political parties and parliament – showed profound weakness and confusion, failing to stand up to powerful forces seeking to turn the state into a private money-dispensing machine. Shot through by factionalism and backbiting, they failed to offer a coherent direction for the country.

The state capture project was about diverting procurement to companies, real or imagined, or parties that would share the loot with politicians or their relatives. In its more sophisticated manifestations, this was about diverting the flow of cash from government departments and state-owned enterprises through third-party 'brokers' to skim off a percentage. When the procurement or financing amounts run into billions – or in some cases, tens of billions – this sort of skimming has a high yield.

Parliament, steered by a recalcitrant ANC majority, singularly failed to intercede to halt state capture.

Conclusion: Leadership, hard choices and justice

President Ramaphosa has assured international investors that his government is committed to rooting out corruption and prosecuting those responsible. He has already appointed some ministers and officials who are dedicated to this task.

But will Ramaphosa and the new leadership be able to pursue powerful individuals whose support is needed for the next election? If they are prosecuted, will it not endanger his already precarious national leadership, with the possibility that he will be removed? Hard decisions will have to be made and it could leave South Africa with a leader who fears taking some difficult decisions or one who will not take those decisions at all. On the other hand, if Ramaphosa is able to look beyond the binary, but umbilically linked choices, of ANC unity versus South African stability, and instead takes some courageous and disruptive decisions, he stands to benefit from the unprecedented historical moment he currently faces.

One thing is certain, if the difficult decisions are not taken now, the future looks bleak. Iron will is required to stare down those who want to destroy the country.

Part Two

Mapping Possible Ways Forward

8

Setting the Basis for a New Agenda

A vision which could provide the foundation for a new consensus and a
positive identification with society, has yet to be elaborated. — Frank Furedi

Chapter summary

- We need to build a new national consensus around a vision of shared
  growth to counter the divisive, cramped, reactionary and racial story that is
  currently defining our identity.

- South Africa's inherited asset and wealth inequality and its low-growth
  trajectory coexist in a vicious cycle, each reinforcing the other. This cycle
  must be disrupted.

- We need to change the structure and ownership patterns of the economy,
  but do so in a manner that does not compromise competitiveness or
  inhibit growth.

- We need a critical mass of the state, business, labour and civil society to be
  mobilised behind this agenda.

Our inheritance in 1994 was a black African majority – making up almost
80% of the population – with very little education and skills, no means or
access to wealth-generating assets, limited access to basic services, and no
history of legislated democracy, albeit with strong traditions of active democratic citizenry. Added to this, we inherited a state machinery built to exploit
and oppress, and serve the interest of a small white minority.

I think freedom caught us all by surprise, and we had to literally shift overnight from a politics of resistance to a politics of governance. Suddenly we had to manage a capitalist economy (even though we called it a mixed economy), build a democratic state from scratch, and try to reconcile enormous racial and political divides that continually threatened to take us into full-blown war.

Our journey has been remarkable when one considers how far we have come. The 1994 social bargain that was negotiated through the Convention for a Democratic South Africa and the drafting of the Constitution has largely brought peace, stability and dignity to South Africans. Desired levels of political and institutional stability were achieved, which have underpinned a sustained period of national and political reconciliation for the greater part of the past 25 years. Through our Constitutional provisions we built a robust and resilient system of public accountability.

The fiscal redistribution component of the bargain has brought significant social returns in reducing extreme poverty and vulnerability, and extending access to basic services for millions of citizens. I cannot think of any other country on the continent that has such an expansive system of fiscal redistribution, combining social grants, free education and health, housing, and subsidised basic services for the poor and indigent.

Despite these gains, the 1994 consensus is fast unravelling. Sustained low growth has reduced the fiscal income for redistribution. Inequality has not reduced. While the black share of income has increased, the black share of wealth in the economy has not really increased. Ownership of the economy remains extremely concentrated, and higher economic returns continue to accrue to those already endowed with capital and skills. Our 1994 dream of peace and shared prosperity is fast disappearing. What can be done to break this high-inequality trap?

How unequal is South Africa?

South Africa is a relatively rich country. In 2016, we had a GDP of R4.4 trillion at current prices, with 16.9 million households.[1] So, if our GDP were to be equally distributed among all households then each household would receive about R260 000 per year or R22 000 per month. Allowing 30% of

GDP for fixed investment and 20% for the provision of public goods[2] would still leave each household with R11 000 per month.

About 20% of households earn less than 10% of this amount (R11 000/month), and about two-thirds of all households earn less than half of this.

Only 8% of black African households have monthly expenditure of more than R10 000, while 63% of white households do.[3] Also, the wealthiest 10% of the population own 90–95% of all wealth.[4] (With figures like these, it is not surprising that many of our people cannot see beyond the 'skin thing'.)

South Africa is classified as an upper-middle income country, with real GDP per capita currently at US$5 916, up from US$4 652 in 2000.[5] Despite our uneven, sometimes stagnant growth in average income levels, there has been a moderate decline in poverty, from 40 per cent of the population in 1995, to 26 per cent in 2013, using the World Bank's US$2 a day poverty line. With a current population of almost 53 million, this equates to about 13.7 million people living in poverty in South Africa. However, at perhaps the more appropriate national poverty line, measured by Stats SA,[6] the poverty headcount ratio has, in fact, increased from 31 per cent in 1995 to a current level of 53.8 per cent. This headcount ratio is calculated using the upper-bound level of a newly rebased national poverty line, but even at the national lower-bound headcount poverty rate of 37 per cent, poverty has remained unacceptably high.

South Africa's inability to transfer growth, however moderate, into reducing poverty is unfortunately not surprising given the extremely unequal nature of our society. With a Gini coefficient of 0.59, our exceptionally high level of income inequality is arguably the most serious fact hindering our ability to inclusively grow the economy and reduce poverty. The exclusivity of South Africa's growth path is only further emphasised by an unemployment rate of over 27 per cent, and one that has averaged 23.7 per cent over the last two decades.

Why is South Africa so unequal?

Our patterns of inequality and underdevelopment are deeply rooted in our history, most notably the colonial wars of dispossession of the nineteenth century and the later apartheid system, which saw Africans violently removed from the land of their birth and their livelihoods and forced, through a range of legislative measures, to reside in the so-called native reserves.

In the understanding of analysts such as Harold Wolpe and Martin Legassick, this both freed up prime land for white occupation, forced Africans to work on white-owned mines and farms to survive, and reduced the costs of reproducing African labour power (in what became known as the cheap labour thesis). Within this apartheid capitalist system, some differentiation among and between the exploited classes was developed to co-opt and curtail resistance. This included some differentiation among black citizens (coloureds, Indians, Africans), the establishment of small black elites in the homelands, and the later creation of a small black middle class in the urban townships to serve as a buffer between the oppressors and the oppressed.

Since 1994, South Africa has implemented what is the largest welfare programme in Africa, with relatively higher rates of fiscal redistribution than countries such as Brazil, Chile, Colombia, Indonesia and Mexico.[7] We have also redistributed assets (primarily land), although not in a manner that has dented asset inequality, and we have adopted a range of regulatory measures aimed at addressing race inequality (affirmative action, preferential procurement, Broad-Based Black Economic Empowerment or BBBEE, among others).

But inequality remains. Research by Arden Finn, Murray Leibbrandt and Vimal Ranchhod shows that if your parents are poor, the chances of you being poor are about 90%.[8]

This is because inequality is rooted and reproduced in the concentrated structure of the economy, which we need to understand if we are to transform.

Historically, South Africa's highly unequal economy was built around the minerals-energy complex. In the mid-1980s, some 83% of Johannesburg Stock Exchange (JSE) shares were owned by four giant companies, all owned by white South Africans, which controlled economic activity in mining, finance, the industrial sector, agri-business and retail. This historical fact underlies our preoccupation with so-called white monopoly capital, and feeds racist narratives around black nationalism. This is a red herring. Yes, nine of the ten richest South Africans are still white men, but to say that the apartheid structure of capital has remained is historically inaccurate.

Our large conglomerates have unbundled and globalised. Anglo American, for example, now has a mostly mining focus and has shed holdings in other sectors. Primary share listings are held in foreign stock exchanges, with massive and growing interests elsewhere in the world (far surpassing their interests in South Africa). The reality is that much of our big capital is far more mobile than we think, which has enormous implications for how we engage capital to retain and expand fixed investment. Probably we need them more than they need us. I don't think this has quite sunk in.

A further consequence of the same liberalised capital controls that enabled our large conglomerates to export capital and list abroad is that private capital in our economy is now significantly foreign-owned. Just under 40% of JSE capitalisation and 50% of the JSE top 40 companies are foreign-owned. Foreign ownership also extends to government debt, with approximately 40% of our debt financed through foreign savings. This leaves us extremely vulnerable should our investment status get downgraded.

Consistent with global trends, capital in South Africa has also increasingly financialised since the 1980s. The finance, real estate and business services sector[9] now accounts for 20% of GDP, and a startling 53% of Pay As You Earn (PAYE) tax payments (the second largest sector PAYE payments contributor is government at 19%). This sector has been growing at twice the rate of the 'productive sectors', such as manufacturing. The financialisation of capital in South Africa has directly fuelled income inequality and has redirected capital away from productive investment, where low- and semi-skilled jobs could have been created.

How to break our low-growth and high-inequality trap

Policy debates around inequality seem to veer, in the main, between two competing approaches, neither of which is correct. The first, the trickle-down neo-orthodox position, suggests that economic growth will lead to inequality reduction. This has underlined the global growth model of 1980 to 2008 (often referred to by its critics as neoliberalism), based on liberalisation of trade and capital flows, financial sector deregulation, monetarism

127

and fiscal austerity. There is now growing recognition, even by the architects of this global growth model themselves – the International Monetary Fund – that this model has not generated inclusivity. Instead, it has become associated with rising inequality, deindustrialisation, stagnant household incomes and increased social discontent.

The second approach downplays the importance of economic growth. This approach has been heavily influenced by the Kuznets hypothesis, which holds that inequality increases with income in the early stages of development and only decreases in the later stages. In other words, the poor, because of their low levels of per capita income and education attainment, do not benefit from a growing economy. In its worst policy iteration, this has been interpreted to mean growth does not matter. Inclusivity should rather be addressed through legislation and regulation, no matter the impact on the economy (for example, the indigenisation policies of Zimbabwe).

This approach is wrong. Klaus Deininger and Lyn Squire's study of growth and inequality in 54 countries suggests rather that the relationship between growth and inequality is complex.[10] In some countries, growth has taken place with simultaneous inequality reduction (for example, a number of Southeast Asian countries), while in others growth has been associated with rising inequality (a number of commodity-exporting African and Middle East countries).

Evidence suggests that where redistribution happens in a shrinking economy, both the rich and poor are adversely affected. On the contrary, evidence from a number of countries shows that the redistribution of assets impacts most on the welfare of the poor when accompanied by increased aggregate investment. So, in contexts where aggregate investment is in decline, even where inequality may be reduced, levels of poverty will also likely increase (as a result of reduced fiscal redistribution, rising unemployment, etc.). Growth both expands the fiscal resources available for redistribution as well as expands the wealth and assets available for redistribution. Growth and inequality reduction cannot be decoupled.

And just as growth is good for inequality reduction, there is a developing consensus that inequality is bad for growth. This contradicts the orthodox view that there is always a trade-off between economic equality and economic efficiency.[11] Deininger and Squire's study is particularly revealing in its finding that there is a strong negative correlation between asset inequality (proxied by land ownership) and growth. In their study, only two of the 15 developing countries sampled with a Gini coefficient for the distribution of land in excess of 0.70 managed to grow at more than 2.5% on average over the 1960–92 period. Countries with lower levels of asset inequality were able to achieve sustained levels of higher growth. High levels of asset and wealth inequalities cause investment-reducing political and economic instability, and undercut the social consensus required to adjust in the face of major shocks.

Besides asset and wealth inequality, education inequality also constrains growth, depriving the labour market of the necessary skills and human capabilities. Also, the higher the levels of education inequality, the less likely growth will be inequality-reducing, with benefits disproportionately accruing to the better educated. This is precisely the trap within which South Africa is stuck. We are unable to compete in the low-skill, labour-intensive industries where low-income countries enjoy competitiveness, and we do not have the technological know-how and human capabilities to compete with high-income countries in more sophisticated industries and services. The result has been deindustrialisation and a growth slowdown as we have been unable to transition to higher-value activities and therefore growth.

Ultimately, long-run slowdowns and very low per capita growth play into a vicious cycle of rising inequality and declining growth. Poverty traps in the lower quintiles of the population reduce aggregate demand, and poor education outcomes limit the human capacity required for higher productivity growth. High levels of asset and wealth inequality cause investment-reducing political and economic instability as political elites compete with the poor and unemployed for diminishing fiscal resources. Social discontent increases, not only among the unemployed but also among the working and middle classes who see living standards decline, which in turn fuels the rise of anti-democratic populism.

Towards a new model of inclusive growth

To overcome our unequal economy, we have to (a) change the structure of the economy; and (b) change the ownership patterns of the economy, but in a manner that does not compromise competitiveness and growth.

Shared or inclusive growth is a relatively new concept and the debate on the appropriate definition and measurement is ongoing. Most proposals involve two or more components that are related to income, poverty, employment or distribution.

The definition by the United Nations Development Programme's International Policy Centre for Inclusive Growth states:

> Inclusive growth is both an outcome and a process. On the one hand, it ensures that everyone can participate in the growth process, both in terms of decision-making for organising the growth progression as well as in participating in the growth itself (and earning income). On the other hand, it goes some way towards ensuring that everyone equitably shares the benefits of growth. Inclusive growth implies participation and benefit sharing. Participation without benefit sharing will make growth unjust and sharing benefits without participation will make it a welfare outcome.[12]

The African Development Bank (AfDB) defines inclusive growth as 'economic growth that results in wider access to sustainable socioeconomic opportunities for a broader number of people, regions or countries, while protecting the vulnerable, all being done in an environment of fairness, equal justice, and political plurality.'[13] The AfDB emphasises the following features of inclusive growth:

- Rapid and sustained poverty reduction requires inclusive growth that allows people to contribute to and benefit from economic growth;
- Inclusive growth refers to both the pace and pattern of growth, which are considered to be interlinked, and must therefore be addressed together;
- The inclusive growth approach takes a longer-term perspective as the focus is on productive employment as the main instrument to increase incomes for excluded groups; and
- The ability of individuals to be productively employed depends on the opportunities to make full use of available resources as the economy evolves over time.

Therefore, inclusive – or shared – growth combines the increased participation of poor and marginalised people in the economy through employment and with increased sharing in the benefits of growth via rising incomes and economic participation, as well as increased benefits from social expenditure, including skills and education. The essence of inclusive growth is that poor people's income must grow faster than that of wealthier people, resulting in decreased inequality.

So, what are the core features of an inclusive growth agenda?

The obvious starting point is quality public education, which both increases economic growth potential and increases the employment prospects of the marginalised.

The other obvious starting point is fiscal redistribution, that is progressive taxation combined with state spending on grants, public services and social infrastructure, which is a proven method of reducing poverty and increasing inclusivity, and to date has significantly impacted on South Africa's human development index. But we have reached a tax ceiling, and urgently require revenue-generating growth to sustain social programmes for the poor and finance new fiscal instruments for innovation and economic restructuring.

Without this economic growth, significant spending cuts and fiscal reprioritisation will be necessary, including making hard choices between salaries for public servants and spending on the poor. This will bring political instability risks. Fiscal risks associated with the contingent liability risks of Eskom and other state-owned entities also require careful management in the short term to protect both sovereignty and pro-poor fiscal spending.

Investment is the feedstock that grows economies, and levels of investment are at an all-time low. The space for counter-cyclical state-led investment has been seriously limited by fiscal constraints, and the private sector (both domestic and foreign) has reduced levels of fixed investment in the face of rising costs of business, red tape and policy uncertainty. Addressing investment constraints at industry level and assembling a new investment value proposition deserve the highest level of political attention. New state capabilities need to be assembled to work with the private sector to grow and sustain the investment pipeline.

Growing fixed investment on a sustainable basis will, in turn, depend on whether we can diversify and restructure the economy towards higher value competitiveness, with the requisite technological, logistics and human capabilities to compete in higher-productivity industries. As a latecomer, we need to leapfrog competitors and let 'a thousand techno-parks bloom'. Key, too, will be enabling innovation and start-ups through venture capital financing, and relaxing skilled immigrant visa restrictions to reverse our tech brain drain.

A growing and diversified economy will provide the necessary condition for inclusivity, but must be accompanied by active measures to increase levels of economic participation of the historically excluded in prioritised value chains. This must move beyond the usual suspects of regulating inclusion (such as BBBEE) and focusing narrowly on state-sector markets (through preferential procurement). Positive discrimination and indigenisation policies have been less effective when the state is weak, when benefits are captured by elites and encourage patronage entitlements, or when the policies discourage private fixed investment and provoke capital flight or out-migration of skills.

Instead, the focus must be on practically addressing the actual productivity constraints faced by new entrant firms owned by the historically excluded. This includes (a) access to capital (through development finance institutions, venture capital funds, investment partnerships with established players), (b) access to technology (through innovation and technology parks, incubators, technology transfer incentives with established players); (c) access to efficient and cost-effective logistics and ICT connectivity (including free Wi-Fi); (d) access to cost-effective inputs (supplies, including technical skills); (e) access to ongoing business support and mentoring; and (f) access to markets (export support, offtakes, competition reform to dismantle cartels).

Importantly, these support measures cannot be random and generalised, but must be specifically tailored to opportunities in identified and prioritised sectors and industries. The established private sector and banks, which could act either as enablers or as barriers to entry, must be engaged and reoriented through a set of appropriate incentives and sanctions. This should be at the heart of industry-level compacts that need to be negotiated with state and non-state players.

Wage-led inequality reduction measures – for example, effected through the National Minimum Wage – are also important, but only when accompanied by rising productivity.

Jobs in the low-skills, low-productivity sectors will also be key to ensuring immediate and shared benefits of growth while the economy transitions towards higher productivity competitiveness, and the education and training system adequately prepares citizens for higher productivity employment. Transitional instruments (such as incentives and subsidies) to encourage low-skill employment during this transitional period (the next ten years) are vital to ensure industry competitiveness in the low- to mid-productivity sectors.

No inclusive growth without state reform

There will be no inclusive growth without urgently addressing state performance. Countries that have successfully restructured their economies, and transitioned out of low-growth, high-inequality traps have had high-performance states, built on professional bureaucracies and meritocracy. Policies and strategies that get approved at the level of the executive get implemented. The South African state is notorious for its coordination and coherence failures and weak policy execution. In our context, causes of state dysfunction include corruption, the politics of appointments (deployment), technical skills deficiencies, and the absence of consequence management. And we cannot escape the fact that many of the problems have their roots in intra-party dynamics. Any attempt to build a high-performance state must commence with dismantling the abusive patronage interests that have captured and repurposed the state for corrupt gain. Key here will be a revamped security cluster that impartially upholds the rule of law as prescribed in the Constitution.

Further addressing state dysfunction will require some degree of restructuring and rationalisation to derive efficiencies, avoid duplication and strengthen coordination. The local sphere of government, where an increasing number of municipalities are deemed unviable, needs to be rethought, and South Africa's metros must be better geared to contribute to the country's growth and investment targets. State-owned enterprises require urgent attention to address governance concerns, and need to be restructured towards competitiveness and efficiencies.

New state capabilities for economic restructuring must be developed, including the development and implementation of industry-level compacts that are able to broker trade-offs that achieve productivity gains, innovation, strengthened competitiveness and transformation outcomes. But economic restructuring requires long-term frameworks that extend beyond short-term political cycles, suggesting the need for new models of relatively autonomous institutions to drive economic development.

Importantly, while this economic restructuring agenda will require party political championship, it does require to be embedded in broader society and underwritten by a coalition of interests. This is necessary for securing the required trade-offs, as well as for sustaining accountability. Questions remain whether capable leadership across social formations exists, and building a leadership – especially among the youth – able to put national interest above self-interest is an important starting point.

Rethinking state and markets

Achieving inclusive growth necessitates a rethink of how we view the state and markets. History reveals that overly free market or state interventionist approaches have their weaknesses, leading to market failure and state failure respectively. International experience shows that countries that have successfully achieved sustainable and inclusive growth have moved beyond old paradigms and taken more nuanced and pragmatic approaches to the respective roles of the state and markets. What is required to move South Africa forward is closer collaboration between the state and the private sector around innovation and technology development, productivity enhancement, inclusivity and human capability development.

Orchestrating this shift may sound logical and achievable, but in reality there are still deep-rooted ideological divides across the state, business and labour. Most of us who were politically educated in the liberation movement were steeped in Cold War-type ideologies, in which capitalists were adversaries

– part of the ruling class that oppressed and exploited the struggling masses on whose behalf we fought. And our lived realities on farms and in factories and of those in the trade union movement supported this worldview.

We did not really have a plan for the economy when we took power and, truth be told, were more driven by idealistic notions of economic justice than the cut-and-thrust realities of economic growth and competitiveness. We were more interested in ensuring we had a comrade labour minister in the Government of National Unity (to dispense labour rights), than in assuming control of the economic portfolios (which we allowed the National Party ministers to head).

I cannot help but feel we have not moved beyond these old paradigms, and many of us are still living in Cold War-type politics. There is no doubt that unfettered capitalism, if left to its own devices, will reinforce historical patterns of wealth concentration and inequality. The system needs to be managed and cajoled to deracialise and deconcentrate ownership. And the business community – especially established wealth – must understand that things must change. But change has to be managed in a manner that enables the economy to generate the jobs and revenue we need as a nation. Despite our claim that ours is a mixed economy and our ongoing affinity with co-operatives, the reality is that our economy is driven primarily by private sector firms, which contribute roughly three-quarters of output and jobs. These firms compete for market share with other firms around the world, and I am not convinced that, as the governing party and state, we appreciate and enable their competitiveness. Often I think the exact opposite, probably driven by old thinking of capitalism as adversary. Even communist countries such as China and Vietnam have long grasped the contribution that capitalist firms make towards national prosperity, and have truly enabled their growth and sustainability. Their pragmatism and ability to transcend ideological stasis offer huge lessons for us in South Africa.

Conclusion

Globally, we are in a period of uncertainty with the rise of populism and economic nationalism. At home, unemployment is stubbornly high and growth is stagnant, threatening to limit government's existing fiscal redistribution programme. Inequality has not reduced. Inequality-reducing measures of government, including fiscal redistribution, regulatory interventions such as BBBEE, and asset redistribution (land reform) have had marginal impacts on inequality. This is because inequality is rooted in the structure and functioning of the economy, meaning that we can only really address inequality through economic restructuring. Growth (and related fiscal redistribution) without transforming the structure of the economy will not significantly reduce inequality.

Our future growth story is not about a choice between transformation and growth. Instead, we need growth with transformation. Growth without transformation will exacerbate inequality, lead to increasing social tensions and provide fertile ground for the rise of populism. Transformation without growth will be accompanied by disinvestment, rising unemployment, and less wealth and assets to redistribute. Decreased state revenue will lead to reduced fiscal redistribution (for example, on social welfare). Simply put, without growth, transformation will make us poorer; without transformation, growth will exacerbate inequality, which will make the growth itself unsustainable.

Inclusive growth will only be achieved if we are able to deconcentrate ownership and cartel behaviour (both in the private and state sectors), disincentivise rent-seeking and reorient the finance sector to incentivise financial flows to the productive sector, in particular firms that are investing and have competitive capabilities to grow and increase employment and exports.

At the centre of the new consensus for inclusive growth must be expanded redistribution that simultaneously grows investment, and supports growth and restructuring of the productive economy. BBBEE and land reform cannot simply be about ownership transfer, but must grow productive capacity (investment, output, jobs and exports).

Another key factor will be upscaled investment in human capability, as well as a range of innovative measures that address productivity constraints of firms and start-ups (access to technology, skills and costs of logistics). Firms operating in underdeveloped spatial areas (former Bantustans and townships) must be enabled to connect to productivity-enhancing inputs and networks. Productivity increases, over time, will also allow for higher wages, stimulating aggregate demand.

Such a consensus will not be easy to broker, given the vested interest in the current status quo. Visionary leadership capable of mobilising support across interests and sectors and managing spoilers is required to stand up. We have no choice.

9

A Conducive Environment for Investment and Business

To create wealth, high motivation and incentives are crucial to drive people to achieve, to take risks for profit, or there will be nothing to share.
— Lee Kuan Yew

Chapter summary

- Make it easier to do business: the administrative burden on business – particularly small businesses – needs to be reduced.

- Create an institution to promote investment: our Investment Development Agency should focus its activities on metrics of growth, jobs and the creation of a positive international profile.

- Build skills: only with a vast improvement in education will all children enjoy the same opportunities.

- Leverage Africa, access the world: moving beyond the rhetoric of summits on trade areas, South Africa should undertake to reduce barriers to intraregional trade, which will not only create greater prosperity but remove substantial friction and sources of corruption.

- Fight corruption: to assure the public of the government's commitment to restoring integrity and accountability, successful, high-profile prosecutions must be completed, independent institutions must be strengthened, and the governance of the South African Revenue Service and state-owned enterprises must be reformed.

In 2018, the new government under President Cyril Ramaphosa generated a surge of hope and goodwill, both within South Africa and around the world. Ramaphosa's message of a 'new dawn' resonated with the business community, which had long sought an end to stagnant growth and corruption in government.

To this end, in March of that year, Ramaphosa announced an ambitious five-year target of attracting US$100 billion in fresh fixed investment, which was aimed at creating a positive cycle for business and society.

Ramaphosa handed this unenviable task to four investment envoys. I was selected to be one of the envoys, along with Jacko Maree, Trevor Manuel and Phumzile Langeni. Over the course of 2018–19, we travelled extensively to countries including the United States, Hong Kong, the United Kingdom, Singapore, various European countries and some African countries.

Despite the anticipation of trying to turn the minds of investors, at perhaps South Africa's lowest point since 1994, we found these trips invigorating because of the frankness and depth with which investors engaged with us, which, in turn, created the space for us to talk openly about the undulations of South Africa's growth story, to which there is no quick fix. Unsurprisingly, the overriding concerns of investors during this time were the health of the state-owned enterprise sector, principally Eskom, the management of the public sector wage bill and the land question.

What struck us on these trips was that despite the fickleness of capital markets, there remained an underlying personal desire among investors for South Africa to succeed – there was perhaps slightly less flippancy about our country than there may have been about other emerging markets. But it was also obvious that this goodwill was not endless and we had to create the conditions for investment, and quickly. This would require structural and lasting improvements in state finances, predictability of policy and governance (through the protection of institutional independence), probity and the protection of private sector property rights.

I was also repeatedly reminded on these trips that the distance between the interests of business and investors, labour, society and the state was far closer than our ideological suspicions allowed us to believe.

I do not believe that any one of these stakeholders would disagree with the basic fact that we simply cannot build an inclusive, peaceful society without investment. Without investment, there can be no growth; without growth, there can be no job creation.

There is no way around this. For our new inclusive growth agenda to succeed, so must business. A conducive investment environment is not mutually exclusive of the imperative of popular welfare, premised on growth and job creation. Unless we approach this reality with practicality and urgency, there will be cataclysmic knock-on effects for peace and prosperity.

As detailed in Part One, our reality speaks for itself: South Africa's unemployment rate stands at 27% (or 38% if those who have stopped looking for work are included) – this has increased from a strict unemployment rate of 16% in 1995. In 2018, there were more service delivery protests than in any other year since 2005. In 2018, Africa received just 3% of the US$1.47 trillion in global foreign direct investment allocated that year. South Africa's share of this global store fell threefold in the preceding ten years, to less than 0.1%, before recovering to 0.6% (US$5.3 billion) in 2018. And South Africa's gross loan debt stood at R2.2 trillion in 2016/17, according to the National Treasury, which translated to about R40 000 per person living in the country. Servicing this level of debt accounted for 9.2% (or R146 billion) of general government expenditure – this was more than what was spent on health (R105 billion), tertiary education (R77 billion) and housing (R69 billion) during that period, according to Stats SA.[1]

Understanding South Africa's investment constraints

Despite this moribund state, South Africa's weak growth record does not reflect its true potential. There is a significant gap between the country's needs, its aspirations and its capacity.

Although we are the most developed economy in sub-Saharan Africa, South Africa has suffered slow and, at times, falling rates of economic growth, especially over the last decade, partly as a result of global economic conditions, but mostly because of political, policy and institutional deterioration.

The absence of a clear value proposition for investors has severely dampened business and consumer confidence, which has stagnated our economy.

Investment decisions rely on two crucial factors: transaction costs and production costs. Inefficiency, burdensome regulation, contradictory policies, crime and institutional instability have all raised transaction costs; while a shortage of skills, low productivity, debilitating regulations and expensive inputs have raised the cost of production.

One of South Africa's difficult idiosyncrasies is that we contain many worlds in one country. As such, we face the constraints of both a developed economy (onerous regulations, crowded market) and a developing one (low skills, state capacity and high joblessness).

Despite long periods since 1994 of sound and prudent macroeconomic management, state interventions did not deal adequately with these contrasting realities. Furthermore, the complexities of our ruling Tripartite Alliance, and differing views on the expression of transformation, have, over time, manifested in intensifying political factionalism and a commensurate lack of policy coherence.

Attempts to focus government policy through various policies (see Chapter 3) and programmes, such as the Nine-Point Plan, the National Development Plan and the New Growth Path, have failed on implementation. Growth and jobs have slipped down the priority list of many government departments because the focus has shifted to one where bureaucracy is seen as a mode of creating employment rather than one that is service-driven, meritocratic, attentive and effective. Indicative of this is the size of the public service, which has grown significantly, with the national wage bill now nearly double the average across emerging economies.

Unsurprisingly, the interests of South Africans – jobs, living costs, education – have become increasingly estranged from this policy world, which has manifested in the rise of illegal economic activity, more and more people being shut out of the formal economy, political populism and investor flight. Government is viewed neither as a friend nor a champion of business. There is too often an antagonistic or hostile attitude towards the private sector, in both policy and rhetoric.

Two examples, which we tend to shy away from confronting because they espouse so starkly the entanglements of our economy, are Broad-Based Black Economic Empowerment and land redistribution. These precepts are

141

perceived as a risk to capital, and exacerbate concerns about policy unpredictability and attractiveness. Yet, their importance in successfully dealing with the complexity of transformation in our economy is a non-negotiable responsibility of all stakeholders. It goes without saying that investment in our key sectors, agriculture and mining in particular, will remain tepid without reassurances of tenure rights and regime stability, but so, too, will social security, broad-based prosperity and the centrality of identity and dignity unless we do better at balancing the competing needs of our bifurcated economy. In essence, economic growth without transformation will reproduce and exacerbate inequalities, which in itself will make any growth unsustainable; and transformation without growth will lead to less investment, jobs and wealth to redistribute, which in itself will likewise trigger elite conflict, making any new economic growth consensus impossible to manage.

The lesson from successful cases everywhere is that it is impossible to separate trade, governance, bureaucracy, openness and efficiency, infrastructure and education from investment, inclusive growth and jobs.

The imperative now is not to rehash old dialogues about policy, or rake over ideological coals, but to catalyse action on a systemic, practical basis. South Africa needs a positive narrative of its future, with which investors, local and foreign, feel comfortable; but from which the competing class interests within South Africa feel less estranged.

Lessons from around the world

Countries that have made the journey successfully from commodity dependence, social fragility and poverty to diversification, social cohesion and sustained prosperity took four practical steps at the outset:

1) They united their people around a common vision for change;
2) They established an incorruptible and meritocratic public service;
3) They created a technically proficient and professionally managed investment development agency; and
4) They invested in their most important asset, their people, by developing an uncompromising, performance-based education system.

At the apex of all of these factors was single-minded, bold political leadership and citizens who were inspired to become active in their own development.

High-growth countries got their basics right first – by understanding what their weaknesses were, what their assets were, and then by developing policies and taking action based on these existing realities, rather than mere aspirations. They focused on lowering barriers and targeting those sectors with the greatest growth potential, while action and execution replaced any obsession with planning.

Consider two examples of success that have followed these guidelines: Singapore and Costa Rica. During the course of my work as an investment envoy, I visited Singapore and recount many of my observations below. I have engaged with key individuals, both current and former, who have built Costa Rica's investment environment.

Singapore's GDP per capita at over US$52 600 is more than 50 times what it was in 1960. It ranks at the top of all key Ease of Doing Business indicators, from the ease of starting a company to labour force and intellectual property rights protection.

Singapore's Economic Development Board has played a crucial role in this transformation. The board is a central investment promotion and innovation agency reporting to the Ministry of Trade and Investment, driven by market research in its key role of understanding the needs of today's businesses and the direction of those in the future. Self-labelled as 'pro-business', it is focused on improving the ease of doing business in Singapore, with the metrics of growth in jobs, fixed assets and business spending in that country. Enterprise Singapore, also under the Ministry of Trade and Industry, has the mission of strengthening Singaporean enterprises, tailoring its programmes for 200 000 businesses, both large and small. With 35 offices worldwide, including three in Africa, it assists start-ups with market access, employs specialists to transform existing businesses, conducts commercial matchmaking, and offers grants and loans to state-owned enterprises. Both these investment agencies are entirely protected from political interference.

Openness is a crucial dimension of the island's success. Singapore has concluded 22 free trade agreements, with its trade volumes 2.5 times its

GDP. Along with the ease of doing business, including ease of transportation, this has been used to attract multinationals to base their regional operations in the country. There are more than 7 000 multinationals on the island, two-thirds with their Asian headquarters there. Singapore does business with 40 000 other companies, of which around 50% are from elsewhere in Asia.

'Quality, standards and trust' are, according to Enterprise Singapore, the underlying values and ethos behind the success of the country's products and services. Close integration of government around a common purpose is another, explaining the corporate institutional practice of the government investment entities, including the likes of Temasek, the US$308-billion, commercially run government investment vehicle.

Similarly, the results from Costa Rica over the last three decades show what is possible when governments consistently listen to investors and focus on implementation.

In 1980, Costa Rica's exports comprised mainly coffee, fruit and beef. Today it exports 4 300 products to 150 countries, and is home to 300 hi-tech companies, including Intel and Amazon. Traditional exports have fallen from two-thirds of the total in the mid-1980s to under 15% by 2016. With just five million citizens, it has similarly revolutionised its tourism sector, with visitor numbers growing tenfold to three million over the same period, and the average stay doubling to 12 days.

Investors speak warmly of the reasons for being in Costa Rica: the quality of the workforce, with free mandatory education since 1869; openness, with 14 free trade agreements in force to access a market totalling 2.5 billion consumers; and political stability, given its 125 years of democracy. It was, like Singapore, deemed not enough for Costa Rican business to serve the domestic or even the regional market. Free trade offered the opportunity to produce, manufacture and provide services to the world.

The rule of law, effective government and sound macroeconomic fundamentals are taken as a given. But they are bolstered by extremely focused and energetic export and trade promotion bodies.

The initial Intel Corporation investment 20 years ago, which was the catalyst for much additional investment that followed, was the result of a deliberate government effort to attract the blue chip company. Costa Rica's real per capita income has gone up fivefold in the last 35 years, and the country ranks number one in education and health care in Latin America, and number two in terms of social progress.

Skills have been critical to Costa Rica's success, but people also require a reliable and trusted facilitator in government. CINDE was set up to promote investment, combining an endowment with private and public sector income, and was apolitical, with an independent board and consistent management between governments. Aftercare provision for investors is as important as helping those who first enter the Costa Rican market, given that the most powerful signal to future investors is the experience of existing ones.

In summary, in both of these cases, my observations are that success has required the following components:

Single-minded political leadership premised on consensus building: a major influence on the success of investment attraction strategies has been the commitment of the highest level of political authority to attracting investment. Officials had a story to tell that excited investors, and policy to match. Leadership was willing and able to spend its capital on managing the politics of policy choices, having built a national consensus around the centrality of growth and investment.

Target, but do not pick winners: as Costa Rica's former trade minister put it, 'If we had been picking winners, we would have picked everyone wrong.' Success also demands the discipline of getting out of those businesses that are proving unable to graduate from protectionism or subsidies.

Openness is key: export growth was prioritised over import substitution. This means that free trade areas and agreements are critical. While protectionism may be an entry-level ticket to industrialisation, this path is expensive and inefficient because it adds costs, punishes consumers and invites retaliation. It also encourages rent-seeking in less disciplined markets, which can threaten industrial transition.

Improve the ease of doing business: the overall focus of policy initiatives must be to improve the environment for doing business, by reducing costs and increasing incentives.

Listen to business: successful governments spent time listening and responding to the concerns of business and acting on their needs.

Ensure government proactivity: government has to display proactivity, follow-up and follow-through in engaging with the investor community, but also in creating a favourable regulatory and fiscal environment for investment.

Develop human capital: in the quest for labour force improvement, training institutions, universal health care and education systems were established. In the case of Costa Rica, for example, the president took the education minister along to Intel Corporation in his negotiations with the multinational company.

Actively seek investment: to further the pro-business investment agenda, institutions with a mandate to target, facilitate and support investors can assist if driven by comprehensive insight into companies and sectors to provide them with an advantage in their dealings and negotiations.

Support infrastructure: the provision of industrial parks, airports, freight facilities, energy, industrial land and port connectivity can positively shape investor decisions.

Enhance value chains: countries with matured markets have realised the importance of backward-forward linkages in sustaining investment inflows. Development of industrial clusters and enhancement of the service sector are among the strategies needed to achieve this.

Position as a strategic regional hub: to keep momentum amid the threat of investor relocation to nearby countries with lower labour costs, more mature economies repositioned as regional hubs to serve regional markets.

Implement zero tolerance for corruption: anti-corruption actions were led from the top, were swift if sure, and firm if fair.

Establish the context, set priorities: success demands an appreciation of the current rather than aspirational realities, but it also needs continuous evolution of policy as circumstances change.

An institution for investment

Investment promotion agencies in South Africa have failed thus far because the country has not been able to coherently, effectively and consistently articulate and implement its economic policy priorities. Moreover, coordination failures, a lack of accountability and overlapping mandates have hindered the implementation of policy. This confusion has been compounded by an overall lack of common purpose, reflecting a deep-seated lack of trust and cooperation, and the absence of a shared vision between business, labour and government.

Success at promoting South Africa as a destination for business and capital depends on two factors: the market to sell and the quality of the sales machine. To achieve this success, we need a modern, technically adept, innovative, lateral-thinking, responsive investment development agency, driven by a dynamic combination of skilled personnel, digital techniques and carefully nurtured personal relationships. The aim of the agency would be threefold:

1) To sustain economic growth and job opportunities in South Africa;
2) To enhance South Africa's reputation as a global centre for innovation, business and talent; and
3) To assist South African businesses to develop in international markets.

Our traditional investment promotion model has been relatively passive – a one-stop shop for arriving investors, offering a measure of handholding, facilitation and incentives. But we now need to move towards a new model, which should rely on sophisticated targeting of investors and research that shapes this effort, a high-functioning bureaucracy that not only offers a one-stop shop but actively seeks and engages with investors, and a range of policies and incentives to attract them. Crucially, it needs to remain flexible enough to solve a problem or make a national deal as each case demands.

Within a modern architecture, this approach to investment attraction combines policy and promotion, investment and development.

Such an investment development agency is best established as a statutory body, reporting to a relevant government ministry (the Department of Trade and Industry or the Presidency), but with a clear mandate and operational autonomy, governed by an independent board of directors selected from across the public sector, commerce and industry. Exceptional technical leadership and staff are a requirement for success, demanding remuneration commensurate with the private sector and freedom from government bureaucracy. Innovation, agility, responsiveness, standards and trust should be the agency's bywords.

Conclusion: Implementation and execution

South Africa needs to signal a commitment in action to the new dawn, and to harness the goodwill that Ramaphosa has generated. The focus must be on delivery, rather than paper, projects, platforms and summits. Its metrics must be measurable in terms of jobs, growth and international profile.

Economic policy has to be focused on expanding the ability of the economy to produce, ensuring sufficient infrastructure is in place to support faster growth. To do so, political leadership will have to brand the government and country as pro-business and pro-growth if we are to be successful in our aim of tackling poverty.

There are five policy traps that we must avoid as we navigate the path forward:

Populist rhetoric: there is a danger that frustration with slow growth and high unemployment will result in increasingly radical populist rhetoric as a means of cementing political support. The result has historically been uniform: economic decline leading to failure and, at best, a slow process of recovery.

Excessive state intervention: South Africa needs to improve its competitiveness. The state must allow sufficient room for the private sector to encourage innovation and dynamism. Everyone agrees that South Africa requires more competition. This applies across the board, to labour as well as private- and government-owned businesses.

Nationalism and pride: it is important to walk back on bad ideas. In the same way, South Africa should abandon the belief that we are unique, and that our solutions have to be entirely home-grown. Many others have confronted similar challenges, and their solutions can, in some circumstances, be adapted.

Politicisation over consensus: we should seek to emphasise excellence and delivery over dogma and ideology, and to pursue common goals in the interest of all South Africans.

Policy without execution: it is imperative to avoid the trap of vision without plans, plans without priorities and priorities without execution. Leadership and a capable state founded on meritocracy and performance are necessary to avoid this.

10

A Twenty-First-Century Economy

It is not the strongest of species that survives, nor the most intelligent that survives. It is the one that is the most adaptable to change.

— Charles Darwin

Chapter summary

- Champion labour-intensive productive sectors, including tourism, mining, manufacturing and agriculture.

- Expand infrastructure capacity and pursue intraregional trade opportunities.

- Revolutionise logistics and energy supply.

- Address the agro-industry and tech as value chains, from land to skills and capital.

Singapore is regularly cited as the beacon of global development from third to first world status, and deservedly so. But it is also an example that leaves some feeling defeated and, perhaps, frustrated. The development of every country is defined by the idiosyncrasies and complexities of their unique histories – these are least solved by binary comparisons. So, I cite my trip to Singapore advisedly, and on the advice of my various inspirational hosts in that country who were reticent about over-selling their success, a product both of their unaffected modesty as a nation, but also their caution against direct comparisons in the intricacies of nation-building.

Like Singapore, the struggle for survival is built into the DNA of our system in South Africa. But unlike Singapore, our focus in South Africa has too often been on the plan, rather than on what needs to be done and how to get it done. We stumble at the point of implementation. As I have written elsewhere in this book, I believe that the basic reason for this is that we lack a common vision: Who are we as a people? What do we want? What can we offer?

Part of Singapore's success was its early obsession with, firstly, making sure that the majority of the population felt a sense of belonging to the place, and secondly, making Singapore relevant to the world. This required absolute clarity of vision about what the country stood for.

During my visit there, I met with the inspirational Suppiah Dhanabalan, the former chairperson of Temasek and a high-profile political leader in the country during the 1980s and the early 1990s under prime ministers Lee Kuan Yew and Goh Chok Tong. At 81 years old, Dhanabalan is razor-sharp and unequivocal about getting the basics right as the key to success: 'We are able to be here today because we were open to doing the right thing even when the wind was blowing in a certain direction – for example at a point in our history, there was a prevailing anti-multinational corporation culture, but we decided to take the opposite stance. We knew that if we failed to succeed as part of the global economy, we would cease to exist as an independent nation. Our success has been by deliberate design, not luck – at all times we have kept a clear differentiation between our development mandate and our growth mandate, and our institutions are structured accordingly.'

On the contrary, he said, the overriding issue stopping Singaporean firms from investing in Africa, and in South Africa, is a 'lack of clarity around the opportunity' on offer.

South Africa's growth story

Narratives matter. Another stimulating discussion I had in Singapore was with Barry Desker, a veteran Singaporean diplomat and corporate executive who has been central to building the country's investment environment. 'South Africans need to have a narrative of where they've come from and where they're going,' he said.

Self-awareness must be the first step in our economic progression. We will not succeed on the back of plans and ideas, however ambitious, if we do not understand our DNA. This means knowing what we are good at, what we are not good at, and what our potential is based on this reality. Pragmatism must prevail.

Following the political and economic instability of the 1980s, the onset of democracy in 1994 propelled a relatively prosperous period as South Africa stabilised domestically and re-entered the global economy. Between the first quarter of 1995 and the third quarter of 2008, South Africa experienced 55 quarters of uninterrupted GDP growth – one of the longest periods of sustained economic growth in South Africa's history.

There were three distinct periods during this time: the first from 1995 to 1999 was characterised by volatility and a weak average annual growth rate of 2.58%.[1] In 1998, average income per capita declined compared to the previous year as a result of the Asian financial crisis. The second, the post-2000 period, was a time of relatively strong and sustained growth, largely a result of the commodity super-cycle, when per capita income increased by 3% per annum until 2007. The third period was marked by the onset of the global financial crisis in the final quarter of 2008, when per capita income growth turned negative for the first time since 1998, decreasing by 2.9% from the previous year.[2] Since 2009, growth has gradually deteriorated, with negative rates recorded in 2015 and 2016.[3] As a consequence of the financial crisis, we lost close to one million jobs, one of the largest declines in a sample of middle-income countries.

In absolute terms, real GDP per capita has increased modestly from US$5 617 in 1995 to US$7 504 in 2016 – an increase of US$1 887 over 21 years, or equivalently US$90 per year. Growth in per capita income has been largely positive, though unexceptional, over this period, apart from 1997–8 (Asian financial crisis), 2008–9 (financial recession) and 2015–16 (post-great recession). But perhaps most concerning is that real income stagnated between 2011 and 2016.

The net effect of our growth story is that despite a modest upward growth trend since 1994, our economy has failed to generate sufficient employment opportunities for a growing labour force. The result is our catastrophically high unemployment rate.

We need to understand why some sectors have done better than others, the consequences of this and how we can capitalise on this reality to grow.

Premature deindustrialisation

The South African economy falls into the well-studied phenomenon of 'premature deindustrialisation'. According to this phenomenon, emerging economies that fail to develop their manufacturing sector as they grow are likely to suffer from lower growth prospects later down the line, because manufacturing industries tend to be particularly conducive to productivity growth. Rather than following the broad linearity of agriculture, to manufacturing, to services, etc., since 1994 there has been a major structural shift in the South African economy towards more capital-intensive sectors – a change that has been more coincidental than intentional.

South Africa is now a services economy. Between 2001 and 2014, the size of the financial services sector increased by 29% – by far the biggest increase in any sector. Seventy per cent of GDP is now concentrated in only five sectors – trade, transport, financial services, government services and personal services.

By comparison, since 1994, mining's contribution to GDP has decreased from 15.5% to 8.1%; and agriculture and manufacturing are down by 28% and 13% respectively.

This is the antithesis of what happened with the East Asian model, where labour-absorbing, low-skilled manufacturing catalysed growth.

The fact that the South African economy is becoming increasingly reliant on the services sector would not necessarily be a bad thing. However, this has happened in conjunction with a shrinking tertiary (and to some extent secondary) sector, which is self-defeating given the structure of our economy. To date, no country has transitioned from middle- to high-income status without the presence of a vibrant manufacturing sector.

South Africa's leapfrog to a services-led economy is even more concerning given the reality of our skills base – most working-age individuals are in the low-productivity, low-skills space. Despite the growth of the services sector and the commensurate generation of high-productivity jobs, the sector will

153

not catalyse the large-scale structural transformation required to put South Africa onto a new growth path.

We must structurally transform

The phrase 'structural transformation', despite its stodginess, is quite simple and refers to the transfer of labour and other inputs to higher-productivity activity as a driver of economic development. Historically, most workers in pre-industrial Europe once pursued agricultural work. Later, the economy shifted to manufacturing jobs and then to the service sector and so on – marking evolutionary changes to the structure of an economy for growth.

Leading global economists Margaret McMillan and Dani Rodrik describe structural transformation as follows:

> One of the earliest and most central insights of the literature on economic development is that development entails structural change. The countries that manage to pull out of poverty and get richer are those that are able to diversify away from agriculture and other traditional products. As labour and other resources move from agriculture into modern economic activities, overall productivity rises and incomes expand. The speed with which this structural transformation takes place is the key factor that differentiates successful countries from unsuccessful ones.[4]

But structural transformation can be as growth-enhancing as it can be growth-reducing, depending on the reallocation of labour. In Asia for example, structural transformation has been growth-enhancing because labour has transferred from low- to higher-productivity sectors. The converse is the case for sub-Saharan Africa and Latin America because labour has been transferred from higher- to lower-productivity sectors and this has reduced growth rates. Ultimately, growth is about increasing productivity.

I, like many people interested in theories of economic development, follow Ricardo Hausmann's work closely. Hausmann, a former minister of planning in Venezuela and former chief economist of the Inter-American Development Bank, is now a director of the Center for International

Development at Harvard University and a professor of economics at the Harvard Kennedy School of Governance.

As an aside, not only do I have great respect for his work, but during the most difficult times in South Africa over the past decade, Hausmann has stood alongside us, always generous with his advice and expertise. In 2017, during a visit to our country, he eloquently described South Africa's democratic institutions – despite the fact that, in our view, many were teetering dangerously – as our 'extensive immune system'. He said: 'South Africans should cherish the immune system that they have and work to strengthen it. It is this immune system which will protect you from what is happening in Venezuela.' This sticks in my mind, perhaps for the olive branch it offered at the time, but also as a reminder that we are a remarkable nation, against all odds. We have the wherewithal to grow. But this will not come easily, unless we get our basics right first.

Economic complexity

Hausmann, together with two other leading global economists, César A. Hidalgo and Sebastián Bustos, has developed the concept of economic complexity. This is a measure of the knowledge in a society (measured by the notion of 'person bytes') as expressed in the products it makes. This is, in turn, closely linked to a country's level of development and is predictive of its future economic growth – that is, its potential to structurally change.

Economic complexity embodies the notion that different products require different capabilities in different ratios in order to make them competitive globally, and thus allow a country to export them. Capabilities can be thought of as the standard inputs in a production process, but they are so much more than that: capabilities range from having cold storage to having highly skilled phytosanitary officials in a government department; from owning a particular machine to knowing the recipe for Coca-Cola. Capabilities boil down to the ingredients that are used to build up a product, and, much like baking a cake, you need all these ingredients together to be able to produce the goods for the export market.

When analysing how a product is produced, one is essentially pulling out the capabilities that are required for the said product. For example, in order to grow and export grapes, a country would require, apart from the appropriate soil quality, capabilities in how to train and prune vines, the application of the correct manure and fertiliser, regular weeding, management of a secondary irrigation system, early detection and treatment of diseases, harvesting, packaging, warehousing, certification procedures for export, cold storage facilities, marketing, and final global distribution channels, among others. All of these capabilities are put together using a specific method – the knowledge of which is, in itself, another capability – in order to ensure the end product of a box of grapes being ready for export. In this basic one-product example, it is clear that countries need to develop capabilities in order to develop specific products and industries and thus turn firms and sectors into engines of growth and development. The process of building up capabilities in any product, whether it is boxes of oranges, pasteurised milk or iPads, is the process of building economic complexity.

The economic complexity of a country is calculated based on the 'diversity of exports a country produces and their ubiquity, or the number of the countries able to produce them … The complexity of a country's exports is found to highly predict current income levels, or where complexity exceeds expectations for a country's income level, the country is predicted to experience more rapid growth in the future.'[5]

The logic of this theory is that high-growth countries not only produce more output per worker, they also produce different and more complex products – the more complex an economy is, the more successful it is. For example, countries that produce goods such as chemicals and machinery (more complex products) are more successful than countries that produce rice, raw minerals and frozen fish (less complex products).

I understand the notion of economic complexity as the achievement of growth through exploiting the richness and complexity of an economy in reality: infrastructure, land, laws, machines, people, books and collective knowledge.

To advance, economies must combine their knowledge across large networks of people in order to generate a diverse mix of knowledge. Simpler economies have a narrow base of productive knowledge and therefore lower growth.

During the same visit to South Africa in 2017, Hausmann gave the following example to explain the logic of economic complexity. Speaking at an event organised by the Centre for Development and Enterprise in Johannesburg, he said: 'The key point to understand is that rich societies are not made up of geniuses, each of whom has more know-how than people in poor societies. What separates rich and poor societies is that in poor societies everyone knows more or less how to do the same things: to farm, hunt, fish, build, trade with neighbours. In rich countries, lots of people know nothing about any of these things, but collectively they know a great many different things. So a society has more know-how, not because it is a society of geniuses. It has more know-how, not because everybody knows more, but because everybody knows something different. When everyone knows different things, society as a whole has more collective know-how than the individual. This means that the growth of social know-how, of collective know-how, is related to the breadth of collective know-how, not how much each individual knows.'

Hausmann used the example of building a Boeing 787: 'Boeing, the company, with 165 000 employees makes less than 15% of the parts that go into this aeroplane; the rest are made by a vast range of firms all around the world. To make this aeroplane, you need all of these companies that span all of these countries to contribute their collective know-how. A turbine has nothing to do with landing gear, that has nothing to do with avionics or the toilets in the aeroplane or the seats or the fuselage. And that is before we even think about the accountants, lawyers, logistics experts and the sales force that Boeing needs. So, in order to make this thing, you have to bring together a vast network of humans that have to collaborate in production.'

Ultimately then, a country that can produce a larger variety of products – for example China, which produces products as diverse as clothing and robots – is going to find themselves further up the developmental ladder than a country that produces fewer, less complex products – for example, Senegal, which is focused mainly on fish and peanuts. Put simply, Japan is a more economically complex economy than Mauritius, which is in turn more complex than Kenya.

Lasting growth is, therefore, not about producing more of the same. Instead, it is about producing a diversity of products (and services) that do not exist, using techniques that do not exist. If a country remains stuck in capabilities and producing products that do not have alternative uses, this will naturally have negative implications for productivity and diversification and therefore economic development.[6]

This does present a chicken and egg problem and the inevitable questions arise: how do we accumulate new productive capabilities and produce new products that will catalyse our structural transformation? Hausmann and his fellow economists show that new capabilities are more easily accumulated if they are combined with others that already exist – in other words, don't reinvent the wheel. Countries develop when they move rationally from industries that already exist to others that require a similar set of capabilities, but are progressively more complex in nature.

The basic idea then, in this framework of product spaces and economic complexity, is to craft an economic development and thus industrial policy strategy that tries to move an economy from the product it is currently producing and possibly exporting to nearby products. For example, if you are growing cocoa, the product closest to the economy and its firms in the product space would probably be chocolate. If the economy exports diamonds, a jewellery industry could potentially be the next product to move into; steel into cutlery; oil into petroleum jelly, and so on. These next-step products start allowing countries to build their overall complexity and are termed frontier products – they are on the frontier of unlocking greater complexity and development, after all.

How complex is the South African economy

Some of South Africa's leading economists have done ground-breaking work to understand where the country's economic complexity is located in comparison to other developing nations.

Through their research, Professor Bhorat and colleagues from the

Development Policy Research Institute found that South Africa's economic complexity is located at the centre of a comparative group, composed of Brazil, Argentina, Colombia, Saudi Arabia and the United Arab Emirates.[7] The two Middle East countries are considerably wealthier than South Africa, but this is because of their oil reserves, as opposed to complexity advantages.

These economists also found that while South Africa is relatively more complex than almost all African countries, our productive structure remains peripheral and rooted in commodities, including mineral products, such as platinum, coal, gold, diamonds and other minerals, and agricultural commodities, such as raw sugarcane, wheat and corn.

In essence, South Africa has failed to undergo complexity-led structural transformation in the post-apartheid period. In fact, the diversity of South Africa's export portfolio has declined since 1994 from 244 to 211 products.[8]

Don't reinvent the wheel

South Africa's economic complexity cannot be separated from the ossification of our manufacturing sector.

Manufacturing sits at the heart of driving productivity and therefore economic development. All countries that are now classified as developed economies have transitioned from agriculture to manufacturing and so forth – the logic of structural transformation.

Bhorat and his team's research confirms that apart from some growth and diversification in machinery and chemicals, there has been an overall decline in South Africa's complexity-led structural transformation in the post-apartheid period.[9] This has impacted negatively on the South African economy's ability to generate employment for a growing labour force, particularly for women and youth.[10]

There are five likely reasons why South Africa has failed to keep pace with the structural transformation trajectory that other countries in our position have undergone.

Firstly, the global commodity boom during the early 2000s may have inadvertently prolonged our position as a commodity-dependent country. Secondly, the 2008/9 global financial crash, combined with domestic

ALL	Description
Rock wool	Slag, rock wool, mineral fibre and similar mineral wools
Vehicle parts	Parts and accessories (e.g., bumpers, safety seat belts, gear boxes, drive axles, exhaust pipes, radiators, suspension system)
Pig and poultry fat	Pig fat (including lard) and poultry fat
Lifting machinery	Lifting, handling, loading or unloading machinery (e.g., lifts, escalators, conveyors, hoists, elevators)
Traffic signals	Signalling, safety or traffic control equipment for railways, tramways, roads, inland waterways, parking facilities, port installations, airfields
Aldehydes	Aldehydes, whether or not with other oxygen function; cyclic polymers of aldehydes; paraformaldehyde
Other engines	Engines and motors (e.g., reaction engines, hydraulic power engines, pneumatic power engines)
Rubber sheets	Plates, sheets, strips, rods and profile shapes of vulcanised rubber other than hard rubber
Engine parts	Parts for engines (spark-ignition reciprocating or rotary internal combustion piston engines, diesel or semi-diesel engines)
Vinyl chloride polymers	Polymers of vinyl chloride or of other halogenated olefins, in primary forms
Large flat-rolled iron	Iron or non-alloy steel; flat-rolled products, width less than 600 mm, not clad, plated or coated
Nitrile compounds	Nitrile-function compounds
Refractory cements	Refractory cements, mortars, concretes and similar compositions
Fire extinguisher preparations	Preparations and charges for fire extinguishers; charged fire extinguishing
Other agricultural machinery	Agricultural, horticultural, forestry, poultry-keeping, bee-keeping machinery; poultry incubators and brooders
Dairy machinery	Milking machines and dairy machinery
Iron radiators	Radiators for central heating, not electrically heated and parts thereof, of iron or steel; air heaters
Harvesting machinery	Harvesting and threshing machinery, straw and fodder balers, grass or hay mowers; machines for cleaning, sorting or grading eggs, fruit or other agricultural produce
Large construction vehicles	Bulldozers, graders, levellers, scrapers, angle dozers, mechanical shovels, excavators, shovel loaders, tamping machines and road rollers, self-propelled
Prints	Engraving, prints and lithographs

Table 10.1: The top 20 possible frontier products

political instability and policy uncertainty, stymied our progress. Thirdly, South Africa is geographically remote, and entering global manufacturing value chains is difficult. Fourthly, our very poor schooling system has kept us trapped in a low-skilled, low-productivity spiral. Fifthly, we have suffered from policy uncertainty and a lack of vision.

Bhorat and his team make a compelling argument for boosting our economy out of its current path dependency by pinpointing products called 'frontier products'. Frontier products are more complex than South Africa's current export mix and provide potential for further diversification, but are near enough to our current product and knowledge space to make their development realistic. The researchers identified 164 frontier products, of which the top 20 are listed in Table 10.1.

While many of these products were surprising, when I understood them within the context of the economic complexity modelling, they make a persuasive case for where our manufacturing growth potential may be.

Firstly, these products are related to South Africa's current productive structure and to the primary sector activities that dominate South Africa's export structure. For example, dairy machinery, harvesting machinery and other agricultural machinery all relate to South Africa's relatively robust commercial agriculture sector. Similarly, large construction vehicles and lifting machinery are related to South Africa's mining sector, and vehicle parts are related to its automotive sector.

Secondly, it appears that the frontier products are related to one another. A number of the frontier products are likely to feature as inputs into the production of other frontier products. For example, pig and poultry fat is used in the production of sausages. Similarly, vinyl chloride polymers (plastic) and rubber sheets are used as inputs into motor vehicle parts. Engines and engine parts are used as inputs into the production of construction vehicles and agricultural machinery.

From a policy perspective, a key implication of this is that frontier products are an interconnected network of related products that can be targeted in a broad holistic manner.

Invest heavily in logistics capabilities: South Africa could become significantly more competitive by lowering the cost of transportation in and out of the country. For large firms integrated into global supply chains, speed to the customer is of paramount importance. It is necessary to gear infrastructure to the manufacturing, tourism and agricultural sectors, rather than only the mining sector. For example, smart ports could be linked with other smart city investments, and regional airport investments should be linked to road and rail planning, and to visa and aviation policies like open skies (the single African air transport market) for passengers and cargo. The costs of moving containers at South African ports must be halved, and the time it takes to do so should be reduced by 75% to match international benchmarks.

Embrace the Fourth Industrial Revolution: new technologies such as robotics, automation and 3D printing are revolutionising production around the world. To remain competitive, South Africa must transition to higher-value production. There are several positives from the new 4IR world, some of which offer advantages to developing countries. According to McKinsey & Company, for instance, 4IR is expected to create up to US$3.7 trillion in value to global manufacturing.[11] Training engineers and craftsmen to use these technologies are key, as is making sure that our labour costs do not mean mechanisation becomes the only solution for manufacturers.

Pursue regional integration: the shift towards regionalisation of production could benefit South Africa as an entry-point destination to African markets, building on our strengths around financial services and the knowledge economy. At another level, de-globalisation and trade wars could mean losing global market share, and we need to lessen global dependencies through building domestic and regional markets. Regional integration remains low, and we need more deliberately to pursue regional integration and support South African businesses as they move into regional markets. This requires fully operationalising the continental free trade area, ratifying the agreement that President Cyril Ramaphosa signed in July 2018. It also means strengthening the Southern African Development Community (SADC), facilitating greater freedom of movement for African citizens, especially those with needed skills, and relaxing our visa regime. While South Africa dominates regional trade in the SADC, we are operating at only a fraction of our potential. One reason for this is that we have developed a contradictory set of policies, favouring protection in some sectors while seeking to foster exports and outward foreign direct investment in others. We must do more to spur intraregional trade volumes in both goods and services by simplifying and streamlining our trade policies. Above all else, we must use technology to remove obstacles to trade at our borders, especially high-volume border posts such as Beit Bridge in Limpopo.

Cherish our strengths: Mining, tourism and agriculture

In addition to catalysing our economy into the twenty-first century, we must also build on our exiting economic strengths.Two of our greatest national strengths, the mining and the agriculture sectors, have risen off the back of our deepest historical wounds – race-based economic exploitation. We cannot forget this, but we also need to choose whether we allow ideology and point-scoring to paralyse our future development of these centuries-old sectors. I believe that now more than ever, we need to act on our opportunities and opt for innovation, vision and leadership. We do not have to ask for permission to progress, but nor will we succeed if we keep looking back.

The economy needs to create jobs for millions of unemployed South Africans, many of whom are young and low-skilled but willing to work. We need to achieve this while upgrading skills and knowledge to build a different economy for the future. The best way to do this is to do what we know best: focus on our mineral and natural resource endowments, our sophisticated financial and business services sector, our proximity to fast-growing African markets, our high-quality universities, our modern, productive agricultural sector, our world-class tourism sector, and our people who resist failure. The country possesses companies that are global leaders across many sectors from services to construction.

Make the most out of mining

It is a tragedy of our post-1994 development that our mining sector has stumbled to the extent that it has, despite various commodity booms. South Africa ranks only fourth among African countries on the Mining Investment Attractiveness Index, which combines an assessment of the government

163

policy framework with resource potential. Ghana, Mali and Botswana are judged the top three investment destinations on the continent.

Most concerning is the fact that South Africa is ranked a low 13 out of 15 African countries and a remarkably poor 74 worldwide on the policy perception component of the index, below even highly unstable countries such as the Democratic Republic of Congo. This suggests that government policy has served to actively discourage investment in the sector.

To put the sectoral crisis into perspective, more is currently spent on exploration in Nicaragua than in South Africa. Gold production is decreasing annually despite rich reserves, while the sector has shed more than 70 000 jobs in the past five years (in addition to nearly a million over the last 25 years) in the absence of any substantial new investment.[12]

Three quick and relatively achievable measures are needed to reignite investor confidence in the mining sector:

Firstly, fix energy supply: at 60% of national consumption, mining and manufacturing combined are the dominant consumers of electricity in the country.[13] Promoting the use of renewables and small-scale embedded power at household level can go a long way towards energy security for these productive sectors. At present, the peak capacity of residential photovoltaic systems in South Africa is just 10 megawatts, compared to over 1 gigawatt in the United Kingdom. Countries as diverse as Bangladesh, India and the United States offer households a tax rebate for solar power and feed-in tariffs to encourage installation, relieving excess demand on the grid and encouraging a significant new industry to emerge. In this regard, while I was writing this book, former energy minister Jeff Radebe announced he had written to NERSA, instructing it to get the ball rolling on small projects that generate between one and 10 megawatts. If this gets approval, it would mean that farmers, big and small industries and mining operations can apply to feed energy back into the grid. While encouraging embedded power, utility-scale power must transition to cheaper and more sustainable renewable energy production through wind, solar and other forms and through a gradual extension of the independent power producer procurement programme. In this regard, the recent Integrated Resource Plan must be implemented.

Secondly, adopt clear and consistent signalling: fixed capital investment (of the kind that we want) requires long-term returns and, therefore, long-term policy commitments. Investment in mining (as well as other industries such as agriculture and manufacturing) will be especially constrained until certainty prevails regarding how transformation objectives will be met. Populist statements do not help, especially when emanating from leaders of the governing party.

Thirdly, demonstrate a commitment to transformation without compromising investment and employment: we need to link the deliberations on transformation (such as the Mining Charter) to broader engagements around an aggressive strategy for growth based on attracting fresh investment. An agreement on where to go with the Charter could, for example, be followed by incentives for new exploration and an easing of licensing restrictions, as well as the establishment of new mining training centres to supplement the existing schools of mining engineering at Wits and Pretoria universities.

Tourism's enormous potential to drive jobs and growth

Tourism is often misunderstood and underrated, both as an intrinsic sector with its own potential and as a lever for economic growth. Its multifaceted nature makes it harder to appreciate and quantify as a sector.

Tourism is an export sector – an export service – that brings in high-spending overseas and African air tourists. Tourism is also an apex sector; most of tourism is a final good (final service) and it has a long and deep supply chain. It stimulates economic activity in manufacturing: buses, cars, linen and towels, crockery and cutlery, soaps and shampoos, cleaning materials, kitchenware; and it stimulates agriculture. Tourism stimulates demand in manufacturing and agriculture, as well as in other services and tertiary sectors (finance, marketing, wholesaling and logistics, fuel wholesale and retail). Almost one additional rand of value is added to the rest of the economy for each rand of tourism direct spend.

South Africa is a beautiful country. Our cities and sights have garnered many a global award, including most beautiful country in the world. We are usually in the top few on any such rankings and we are underweight in many areas of tourism compared to our similar peers, so we have huge growth potential.

165

The tourism private sector has honed a growth strategy. They have crunched the numbers and looked carefully at growth market opportunities, especially India and China – the biggest and fastest-growing outbound markets. With the right public-private partnership approach and strategic focus we can double the sector by reaching around 21 million foreign tourist arrivals by 2030.

Tourism growth is good growth. Not only does it bring in foreign exchange and stimulate other sectors, but it is an employment-intense industry. While tourism must embrace the digital and shared economies, it will never stop being a people-intensive industry and a high employer. It employs people across the skills level and geographically across the country, often in rural areas. It is a high employer of women (up to 70%) and youth (up to 60%).

Tourism is generally considered a jobs multiplier, creating jobs both directly and indirectly as money spent by tourists circulates through the economy. Currently, 1.53 million jobs are supported by tourism: some 726 000 direct and more than half, some 800 000, through the multiplier effect. The growth target of 21 million arrivals in 2030 will support about two million more jobs in total throughout our economy.

It is an industry in which you can still enter unskilled at the bottom and make it to the top. There are many stories of cleaners, rangers, bar staff and the like making it to lodge owner, hotel general manager, restaurant owner, etc. Motivated people can advance with no formal qualifications.

Tourism is also an industry that facilitates, and indeed needs, myriad small and medium-sized enterprises (SMEs).

What does South Africa need to do to realise this tourism potential?

The first imperative is to fast-track a world-class online eVisa system. It must handle capacity, be easy to use, documentation requirements must not be onerous and the turn-around should be quick, using AI algorithms, not human review. And it must have interfaces in multiple languages, especially Mandarin. Other low-income countries such as Ethiopia and Vietnam manage an eVisa system like this – why can't we?

We should recognise other visas, such as the United States, Schengen, Australia and the United Kingdom – as do numerous other countries. This will open up South Africa for many Indian, Chinese, Nigerian and other visa-requiring markets overnight.

As has been modelled successfully in the Western Cape, we need a national air access route development programme to woo the airlines.

We need a public-private partnership to address crime with tourism safety officers or tourism police. A nationwide implementation of the Department of Tourism's monitoring programme and the industry's tourism safety initiative needs to be ramped up.

We need China-ready, India-ready and Africa-ready destination development and marketing, with refocused smart marketing strategies for these markets. The aspirational destinations for Africans should not be London and Paris; they should be Johannesburg and Cape Town. This needs to be done with a new operationalised public-private partnership where South African Tourism works closely with industry to draw on its coalface expertise and synergise marketing activities.

Product development could be stimulated with resort Industrial Development Zone (IDZ) nodes located strategically close to coastal or inland attractions and to townships where they can stimulate employment and the supply chain. Think of Sun City, which was effectively an IDZ and is now estimated to support some 10 000 jobs. This is not a unique approach: Cancún in Mexico, for instance, did not exist in 1970 – it was entirely stimulated by public investment and incentives.

Grow agriculture

The success of commercial farmers over the past 25 years is despite, not because of, government. South Africa has lost competitiveness in primary agriculture and in the secondary agro-industry. Levels of state support for farming are a pittance compared to other developing economies, not to mention the dearth of policy certainty and trust in government. The sector has the potential to employ a million people;[14] yet current employment stands at about 850 000. Growth in agricultural value must be aligned with the goal of creating and protecting jobs.

Setting aside the racialised nature of agricultural support under apartheid, even small and unproductive farmers survived through massive government support programmes in the form of various subsidies, exploitative labour practices (enabled through legislation) and centralised marketing. Critically, each farming district was also offered expansive technical extension services.[15]

Since the end of apartheid, these support measures have fallen away, coupled with a brain drain from state institutions responsible for the management of agriculture.

Our biggest asset in agriculture is not only land, but human capital. South Africa has abundant supplies of unskilled labour. Meanwhile, very few farmers have the capability to farm competitively. 'Farmers are born, not made,' Mohammad Karaan, former dean of the Faculty of AgriSciences at Stellenbosch University, said in a discussion. The average farmer in South Africa is aged 62,[16] and with the decline of agricultural colleges there simply are not enough skilled – or passionate – farmers to replace them.

Furthermore, the existing productivity of farm employees, despite our high wages, is dismal by international standards. The minimum wage in the apple industry of South Tyrol in Italy, for example, is ten times higher than in South Africa, but their productivity is ten times what it is here. Greater efficiency and new technology further threaten existing jobs.

Turning South Africa's agriculture potential into practice will demand a range of integrated actions, not just capable farmers. Gideon Schreuder, the founder and proprietor of one of South Africa's largest agricultural equipment manufacturers, said in a discussion, 'to get farming right, you need not just better farming, but also a full back-up system of companies doing seed, chemicals, fertilisers, equipment and logistics, among other things, along with government policy that makes it sufficiently attractive.'

Best practices exist, for example from the Chinese experience where 237 million people were lifted out of poverty through agriculture, mainly because of state extension services and the harnessing of local markets. Similarly, the 'green revolution' achieved in the Cerrado region of Brazil in the last two decades was the result of tax incentives for agro-processing, together with active support for out-grower schemes and cooperatives.

Reversing our agricultural decline requires urgent steps. At all times, growth in agricultural value must be aligned with the goal of creating and protecting jobs:

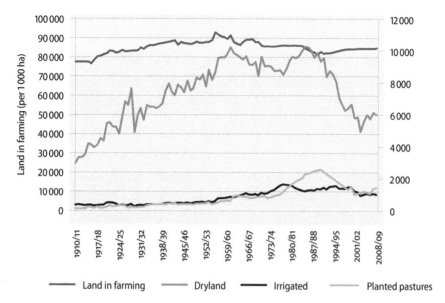

Figure 10.1: Land use in South Africa

(Source: AgriSA)

- Support knowledge production: agriculture must be a sector based on innovation and modernisation. To this end, government must invest heavily in research and development to produce new seed varieties and efficient techniques. Research should also go into the development and promotion of new end-products. This extends to the training of agricultural scientists and farmers through agricultural colleges.

- Support farmers: extension services must focus on high-value, high-productivity and high-labour agriculture. The National Development Plan identifies the crops that meet these criteria. There is large potential for the expansion of irrigation, soil improvements and making processing methods more efficient. Most of these services can be outsourced to the private sector.

- Partner with the private sector: the financing of an agricultural expansion together with land redistribution will require substantial investment over the next few years, which is unlikely to come from government alone.

- Policy certainty: the potential returns from high-value agriculture are not enough to attract investment. A stable policy climate and clear directives from government on the importance of the sector for jobs and growth are required, including getting the land question right. Successful land reform must go beyond the transfer of land. This is discussed in more detail in Chapter 16.

■ Respond to climate change: South Africa is a water-scarce country. We can become more productive with less water through smart irrigation, cropland nutrient management and innovation, such as vertical or hydroponic farming. Paradoxically, these technologies also hold the key to increasing employment because they increase the productivity of a unit of land. Currently, less than 10% of South Africa's land under cultivation is irrigated.

11

We Need a Legitimate and Capable State

It is the responsibility of the … government to enforce its own laws against the oligarchy; freedom is lost not when the state is too strong but when it is too weak. — Francis Fukuyama

Chapter summary

- South Africa's civil service has been expanded but with no commensurate increase in productivity. The result has been poor service delivery and growing patronage, which has fuelled populism.

- We must choose between a large, unproductive public sector that is funded by increasing debt but does not deliver on a scale commensurate with its size, or a smaller, efficient, professional public service that is productive and less costly, and ultimately delivers for South Africans across the inequality divide on a sustainable basis.

- The key to a smaller, more skilled civil service is to depoliticise appointments and base them on merit so that top skills can be attracted.

- There is consensus among development scholars from around the world that one of the basic conditions for growth and development is what in South Africa we must come to call a 'capable state'.

The question of 'state formation' used to be widely debated by South Africans, but this is no longer the case. Perhaps this is due to policy confusion, perhaps it is because of the great distraction that state capture has become.

The reality is that we must start making some tough choices about how we are governed. The country needs a new national agenda that has the support of a broad range of constituencies, including, but also beyond, the ruling party.

This vision needs to speak to how the country should be governed from economic orientation through to inoculation against corruption. To achieve this, the country needs leadership that society can identify with and which does not include those who have manifestly attempted to divert resources to enrich themselves or their cronies.

This will not be possible without a reformist leader at the helm of the country. But responsibility for change cannot be that of a few individuals either; it must be the responsibility of every progressive South African.

This needs to start with a reform of political parties and the political culture of factionalism, the gateway through which those with malign agendas seek to exert influence. It must also start with a remobilised civil society, consistently focused on protecting, advancing and building our democratic institutions, not just coalescing at moments of crisis.

We must return to the country's core values of democracy, consultation, listening to the people and directing government energy at service provision.

The ANC does not have the luxury of choosing another path. The growing revolt among disillusioned citizens who are rejecting formal politics and elections in favour of the streets or apathy is reaching a critical change. The ANC's sliding electoral support suggests that if it does not seriously reform, it will soon be a minority party, possibly governing through a coalition.

A reformist leadership, together with the active backing of society, will have to turn the state away from patronage and poor delivery and direct public resources at creating an environment in which the economy can grow, tax revenues can improve, debt can be reduced and the delivery of government services can be accelerated.

A number of choices will have to be made, none of them easy.

Disentangling party and state

Ultimately, progress will not be achieved without disentangling party and state. Over the first 25 years of democracy, the ruling party has entrenched itself as the primary decisionmaker on employment and deployment, policy and even its implementation, often without having the technical wherewithal to assess the impact of such decisions.

The problems besetting Eskom, for example, have their origin in the decision to cut down its engineering capacity due to a policy change made in the late 1990s. When this decision was later reversed, this capacity could not simply be wished back into existence and the result was a critical lack of capacity to oversee the building of Medupi and Kusile power stations, which have suffered from technical weaknesses and cost overruns.

The reality is that positions in government bureaucracy require technical competence. Some 25 years into democracy, we have to shift our focus from the 'transformation imperative' of political deployment – which was imperative at a point in time, but has now expired – to build a technically competent public service that is largely representative of the country's demographic make-up. In those exceptional cases where the pool of skills is not diverse enough, the skilled should be hired.

We must choose between a large, unproductive public sector that is funded by increasing debt but does not deliver on a scale commensurate with its size, or a smaller, efficient, professional public service that is productive and less costly, and ultimately delivers for South Africans across the inequality divide on an ongoing and sustainable basis.

Government must improve its efficiency and reduce wasteful expenditure to support, rather than distort, the market. Reducing the size of the Cabinet and quickly finalising and implementing a review of the public service – with a view to reducing its size, streamlining its functions, and preventing institutional overlaps – will provide evidence to the public that the state is serious about improving service delivery and creating a modern bureaucracy. President Ramaphosa has already signalled his intention in this regard with the initial reduction in the size of his Cabinet. We must end the expansion of government and its wage bill, which would result in unsustainable debt for future generations and divert necessary resources from expensive budget items such as tertiary education.

The argument against cutting down the size of the civil service is that this is the battle cry of 'libertarians', who want the state's role in public life to diminish so that private capital can get on with the business of accumulating wealth.

This is a red herring. The size of the state has nothing to do with its effectiveness, which derives from the quality of its leadership and the productivity of its civil service. South Africa's civil service has been expanded but with no commensurate increase in productivity. The result has been poor service delivery, which has fuelled a growing popular uprising.

In addition, it is now abundantly clear that the country can no longer afford the civil service it has. As a greater and greater proportion of the budget is dedicated to paying workers, so the money available for capital spending on infrastructure and maintenance declines, leading to a deterioration of infrastructure.

Those in favour of retaining – even expanding – the state are ignoring the fact that we have been through a period of the disestablishment of the state, weakening oversight in departments and resulting in leadership serving ulterior motives and not the people.

The finance minister Tito Mboweni pointed out in 2018 that eight out of every ten rand spent by government went to paying salaries.[1] Figures from the 2015/16 financial year showed that the average civil servant earned R328 104 a year – three times as much as the R104 028 earned by the average private sector employee.

The average employee in the basic education department earned more than half a million rand in 2016. There have since been above-inflation increases.

There is no reason why a smaller, more skilled civil service would not be more effective. The key to such a service is to depoliticise appointments and base them on merit so that top skills can be attracted. Salaries need to be in line with the equivalent position in the private sector and salary increases need to be capped. If this is not done, the civil service and the bloated state-owned enterprises (SOEs) will sink the country's balance sheet.

Take the politics out of appointments

The former president, Kgalema Motlanthe, has rightly advocated for a meritocratic public service where appointments are made based on a rigorous recruitment, interviewing and selection process underlined by ethics, morality and state-building. This is wholly contrary to the existing practice where appointments are made by party grandees and are based more on extending political influence and patronage networks than getting the job done.

The result has been a lack of productivity accompanied by a higher wage bill. It even became popular to deride 'technocrats' in the civil service as if it were somehow wrong to possess a high level of technical skill when what was needed was political loyalty to the ruling party.

The decision to appoint unqualified persons to positions of responsibility in the civil service was initially justified as a mechanism to make the service – which was dominated by whites – more representative of the general population. This imperative no longer exists. Twenty-five years into democracy it is possible to have a representative civil service that is peopled by qualified, skilled and experienced people who can raise productivity and bring professionalism to bear.

A further result of our politicised civil service is that it fell victim to manipulation by patronage networks.

It ought to be abundantly clear that there will be no faith in either the civil service or the criminal justice system until the high-profile politicians and public servants who have been corrupted are prosecuted and jailed. In a country where some say that as much as a third of public procurement has been siphoned off by the corrupt, no lower standard is acceptable. Until this happens, scepticism will exist over the state's real intentions and the belief that the corrupt are still governing will continue to take hold.

Cleaning up civil service corruption can only occur if a powerful and institutionally independent prosecution service is given the resources to prosecute all instances from the very highest level to the lowest. There are encouraging signs that Cyril Ramaphosa wants to do this with the newly appointed prosecution chief, Shamila Batohi.

'The NDPP [National Director of Public Prosecutions] must ensure that the NPA [National Prosecuting Authority] exercises its functions without fear, favour or prejudice and should not be beholden to any vested interests, whether in politics, in business or elsewhere,' he said on her appointment.[2]

Batohi has since appointed Hermione Cronje to head an Investigative

Directorate within the prosecution service, which will pursue cases of graft and corruption.

Batohi described her decision to take up the job as 'jumping into a shark tank', so she is under no illusion about the task she faces. 'We in the NPA have important work to do, which includes devoting our efforts to holding account-able those who have corrupted our institutions, who have betrayed the public good and the values of our constitution for private gain – especially those in the most privileged positions in [the] government and corporate power.'[3]

If these promises are lived up to, there is hope that the tide of graft may be turned. But this will not occur if those pulling the strings of corruption remain in office in the upper echelons of government. At the time of writing, I was concerned, for example, by the composition of some new members of parliament and the chairs of the various portfolio committees, many of whom had clearly been placed in their positions based on political factional-ism rather than competence.

The Constitution's Chapter Nine institutions, such as the public protector and the auditor-general, were put in place to act as watchdogs should the state not live up to the constitutional promise of improving the lives of the marginalised.

Institutions, such as the Constitutional Court and the public protector under Thuli Madonsela, have played an important role in checking the abuse of power.

Chapter Nine institutions need to be strengthened and their independ-ence jealously guarded so that they do not become weaponised in factional battles.

Government's planning and evaluation processes need to be set above party politics and directed at serving the greater good. The planning func-tion needs to be bolstered and outcomes properly implemented.

The decision to break Eskom up into three entities to make its costs more transparent and to find ways of bolstering generation capacity outside Eskom was taken in the late 1990s, but was never implemented, except for the stipulation that Eskom must reduce its generation capacity. The plan was abandoned and the result was the blackout period of 2007 and 2008.

This break-up plan was revived once more in much less favourable circumstances in 2019, and already there appears to be heavy political con-testation over how this plan will be implemented.

We must avoid a band-aid approach to fixing the problems with SOEs – we need to rethink their roles, their place in the economy and their financial sustainability.

This is not a privatisation debate but one about making these entities functional and sustainable (see Chapter 12).

The government-linked companies of Singapore played a key role in driv-ing their inclusive growth programme. But this happened in a context in which these companies operated in a corruption-free environment, where meritocratic appointments were made, and where bottom-line results mattered. This is a very different scenario from what we have, with SOEs currently buckling under R500 billion treasury guarantees – an enormous contingent liability risk for government.

Reform public procurement

The reform of the system of public procurement in South Africa in the 1990s was driven by two main imperatives: to overcome the inefficiency of the existing system and to incentivise the emergence of black-owned small and medium-sized enterprises.

In particular, there was a turn away from the centralised State Tender Board to a decentralised model. Procurement points proliferated across gov-ernment and the state.

It is difficult to know how many procurement points there are today as this number changes regularly. For example, in the Eastern Cape there are over 5 000 schools – a legacy of the Bantustan period. In the 1990s, procurement for school furniture and school textbooks was a provincial responsibility. In the 2000s and in response to weaknesses in the provincial government itself, this responsibility was devolved to many schools themselves. Suddenly, there were thousands of procurement points for school furniture and for school textbooks.

Decentralisation, together with management discretion in depart-ments and entities and low and often non-existent oversight, has massively increased the opportunities for irregular spending and for corruption.

Procurement officers are frequently junior staff and supply-chain management is often treated as an afterthought. The truth, however, is that many government departments, especially municipalities, rely on service providers more than they do on their own capacity. Procurement, in other words, is what they do.

When they get it wrong, it has devastating consequences for service delivery.

The establishment of the Office of the Chief Procurement Officer was an attempt to bring greater transparency and accountability to the system. Yet, the Office is handicapped by the failure to pass enabling legislation. It is also understaffed and under-resourced.

Beyond the Office, however, we need to rethink the way that public procurement happens in South Africa. It is currently failing to improve efficiency in government or advancing economic transformation.

Conclusion: Ensuring strong and enduring institutions

It is now well known that societies with strong and enduring institutions are also the ones that have created wealth primarily through investment-led innovation and productivity gains.

There is consensus among development scholars from around the world that one of the basic conditions of growth and development is what in South Africa we must come to call a 'capable state'. In other words, the ability of the state to raise taxes, to administer social grants, to carry out economic and industrial planning, to generate and distribute electricity, to build classrooms and to educate children, to treat the sick, to recruit, train and deploy effective police officers. All of this requires autonomous, stable and professional administrations.

Developmental states around the world know this and actively promote institution-building as a core strategic goal. Where wealth is created primarily through rent-seeking, institutions will always be under threat. While inclusive institutions must restructure the economy towards shared and sustained prosperity, elite interests controlling rents actively prevent the necessary innovation and institutional change.

In South Africa's case, while our state executive institutions show strong signs of weakness and corrupt capture, our legal and democratic system still displays signs of life and with robustness, as do our main development finance institutions and the Reserve Bank.

We also need to give greater thought to checks and balances in the appointment process of key institution heads (the Hawks, the NPA, the South African Revenue Service, etc.) to avoid abuse. The Constitution currently gives too much prerogative to the president to make key appointments – a power that is easily overlooked in times of 'good leadership', but, as the Jacob Zuma years demonstrated, it can be catastrophic when the opposite applies. President Ramaphosa set in motion a progressive precedent in this regard through the panel appointment process he implemented for the NPA and SARS appointments.

We must collectively protect our democratic institutions – our Constitution, judiciary, media, civil society, academia, Reserve Bank, etc. It is these institutions and traditions of democratic accountability that differentiate us from a Venezuela or Zimbabwe, and it is what ultimately safeguards us from absolute capture and collapse. We need a process of renewal going forward where we find a structured way to learn from other countries that have either solved such problems or are in a similar situation. We cannot afford self-deception that the leadership change of 2017 and the positive 'new dawn' that followed are the solution to our crisis. As this book has detailed, South Africa's crisis is much deeper and wider and requires rigour and dedication to understand it, confront it and implement change. There can be no heroes and short-term, shiny solutions – the heroism will be in those South Africans who put their shoulder to the wheel for the national interest, sweeping aside the rampant culture of individualism that has come to define our politics.

12

State-Owned Enterprises Must Become Smart Growth Enablers

It is safe to say, if decisions are being made elsewhere – which determine the future of institutions and impact on the country, we should all be very afraid. — Pravin Gordhan

Chapter summary

- Fix Eskom by separating the power utility into three entities and expanding the Renewable Energy Independent Power Producer Procurement Programme.

- Redefine the role of SOEs to provide public goods while generating revenue rather than draining resources from the budget.

- Improve governance and accountability by depoliticising executive and board appointments, and centralising oversight of SOEs in a new, highly skilled unit.

- Focus on strategic companies and make a few SOEs globally competitive, rather than spreading the state thinly across many failing entities.

In my experience, the discussion about how to fix state-owned enterprises (SOEs) has been centred on a binary choice: whether or not to privatise. This debate, which ignores the reality of extensive private involvement in the SOE supply chain, has had a crippling effect on policy formulation.

Over the past eight or so years, this debate has become even more senseless because how do you even begin to debate privatisation in the context where the state is weak and threatened by corruption?

Having said this, however, we are now at a point where we no longer have the luxury of long debates: unless we make tough choices, and quickly implement these, our SOEs will collapse our country. On the present debt trajectory, South Africa faces a round of ratings downgrades that will give it junk status with all major lenders, increasing the cost of capital and further draining the national fiscus as larger and larger repayments have to be made. The only logical end to this is the loss of our sovereignty because South Africa will be forced to approach international financial institutions, such as the International Monetary Fund, for a bailout, which will be conditional on us handing over our fiscal management.

In simple terms, the International Monetary Fund will impose what are called 'structural adjustments' – harsh economic reforms that will involve a major reduction in the size of government's expenditure bill, mainly by cutting jobs and probably our welfare budget. The National Treasury will cede much of its decision-making over budget allocations to the lender, leaving us in the hands of powers beyond our control.

It is no exaggeration to claim that the dire state of many of South Africa's most important SOEs represents an imminent systemic and sovereign threat to the country's economy and our development agenda.

Equally, it is easy to glance at the balance sheets of major SOEs such as Eskom and SAA, or to read reports of corrupt procurement on a grand scale, and to despair.

But despair is not an option. While the challenges facing SOEs are steep, there are pragmatic and feasible actions that we can take to restore them to profitability and effectiveness. To address this crisis and ensure that SOEs are serving the people – and not merely providing a conduit for corrupt officials to enrich themselves – we need to take four urgent steps towards reform.

One: Fix Eskom

The ongoing crisis at Eskom is among the most urgent and politically charged issues facing South Africa today. Chronic underinvestment, policy uncertainty, corruption and mismanagement have taken the utility to the brink, and with it, our economy. Eskom's debt is almost R500 billion, and its own estimates suggest that it will need a further R160 billion to complete existing capital projects.

It would be convenient to relegate the fate of Eskom to within the confines of the utility – to turn our backs on the mess and move on. But this would be akin to removing a person's heart from their body and hoping for the best – the utility's embeddedness in our economy means that the repercussions of its decline could kill the country. Eskom still generates about 95% of South Africa's electricity, making the utility, for now, too big to fail. If Eskom collapses, our entire electricity system goes down and, with it, in one way or another, our livelihoods.

The historical conflation of Eskom with South Africa's energy future also needs to change – they are not one and the same. This requires a combination of short-term, rapid response interventions, not as an end in themselves, but to create the space for the audacious changes needed to secure our energy future (so that it is not only reliant on Eskom). If we do not take a long-term view of reforming the utility so that it is fit for the future, we will have stabilised Eskom only for it to unravel again later with catastrophic consequences.

President Cyril Ramaphosa has already taken an important initial step towards the short-term stabilisation of Eskom by appointing a capable and independent board, competent executives and a highly qualified advisory task team staffed by energy sector experts.

Failing by design; redesigning for success

In its current form, Eskom has a monopoly on all three stages of the energy supply – generation, transmission and distribution.

A vertically integrated power company with monopoly power is uncommon in the world today. With its archaic, slow-moving and unaccountable structures, Eskom is an anachronism. The size and complexity of this single entity have made it almost impossible to be well governed and prevented it from keeping step with international developments. The Eskom monopoly has led to devastating inefficiencies and cost inflation, forgone investment and a lack of transparency and accountability, which has placed it at the centre of the state capture saga. It has actively blocked the entrance of new players into the sector, leaving South Africa behind as other African countries experiment with new technologies to improve access and develop new energy sources.

Apart from the governance and management challenges at Eskom, the power sector in general has changed profoundly over the past five years. It will change even more radically over the next decade. Electricity sale volumes are lower than a decade ago, future growth is uncertain, and solar and wind energy are now cheaper than Eskom's. We have yet to anticipate the inevitable changes that disruptive technologies will have on the sector.

So, what is to be done?

For a start, Eskom must be broken up, as recommended by the Presidential Eskom Sustainability Task Team. This is important for several reasons.

Firstly, Eskom's control of both generation and transmission creates a conflict of interest because independent power producers (IPPs) have to feed into an Eskom-controlled national grid, while competing with Eskom's own generation arm. In order to facilitate the entry of private companies into generation, and thereby both introduce dynamism into the sector and relieve the financial burden of the state, a properly independent grid company is a necessary condition.

Secondly, separating the three functions – generation, transmission and distribution – will make it easier to raise private capital, particularly because Eskom's highly indebted generation unit would no longer weigh down its transmission and distribution functions.

Thirdly, this structure would allow Eskom to alienate non-core assets, and to sell its older power stations to private operators which are better able to maintain, refurbish and manage them. The capital raised through this streamlining process could be channelled towards critical construction projects, while independent producers could offer energy to the grid at competitive rates.

Breaking up Eskom is a necessary first step towards comprehensive reform and will signal credible commitment to transformation in the sector. How we proceed thereafter will determine what can be achieved in the future, with binary economic and political consequences. In this regard, major legislation solidifying our long-term vision must be developed through appropriate processes.

Lessons from our own and other developing country experiences call for the path of least regret, a strategy that reduces the risks and costs of structural change. In South Africa, this could be to use the existing Eskom Holdings structure to establish a subsidiary that will house transmission and system operations, a company with an expert board, appointed not only for their knowledge and experience but for their leadership and commitment to good governance. This board would steward the state-owned grid company, and drive the migration of relevant people, systems, assets and debt into the new entity. Only once this is done will this subsidiary be separated to become independent of Eskom, accountable to government and the people.

Eskom reform will also only take us so far. We need a major shift towards renewable energy sources that are radically diversified and operated by private suppliers. This would represent a tectonic shift in the energy landscape, not merely a tinkering with financial instruments and legal structures, and would require the completion of further rounds of the Renewable Energy Independent Power Producer Procurement Programme envisioned by the Integrated Resource Plan.

Compare, for example, the four rounds of the programme completed thus far with the progress of the Medupi coal power plant. Medupi is owned entirely by Eskom and built using capital procured from lenders, without any equity funding. When the project was launched in 2007, its targeted completion date was 2014 – it is now expected to be fully operational by 2021, seven years late. Its eventual cost will total over R200 billion (including interest costs), more than double the original estimate. Of those units that have already been built, operational and design errors are ubiquitous, resulting in an energy availability factor of only 70% (in other words, they do not work one-third of the time). Medupi's levelised cost of electricity, a measure which calculates the cost of electricity produced by the plant during the course of its lifetime, will be R1.05 per kilowatt – and may rise to R1.17 if costs continue to escalate. Experts suggest that given foreseeable tariff increases, the plant will operate at a loss overall.[1]

184

By contrast, renewable energy IPPs are built by private sector firms, and are typically funded through 75% debt and at least 25% equity. Most importantly, they are subject to a competitive bidding process, which is conducted in rounds with specific megawatt targets that can be divided among several successful bidders. Bidders must present a complete financial model to support their proposal, and the cheapest and highest-quality bids are selected. The process has been transparent and well governed, and most projects undertaken so far have been completed on schedule and within cost estimates. Not only are IPPs better managed and constructed to specification, their output in the latest rounds has become significantly cheaper – it is estimated that the cost of offshore wind in round 4, for example, is just R0.66 per kilowatt. Given the rapidly reducing cost of solar and wind technology generally, it is expected that future rounds will yield energy at even cheaper rates.[2] In short, encouraging the participation of private developers and equity investors – and focusing on cheap and efficient renewable energy sources – makes all the difference.

Furthermore, procurement need not be limited to IPPs. New players could include municipalities, community-owned projects and small, medium and large companies investing in energy generation. In this way, the energy system could be democratised over time.

To privatise or not to privatise

We also need to get real about private participation in the energy industry – and, for that matter, the SOE sector in general. The simple truth is that the majority of capital expenditure in Eskom, and most of the other SOEs, is private-sector driven through a myriad of private contractors, but without these companies sharing the risk. This makes the 'to privatise or not to privatise' debate futile and one from which we need to move forward. Private sector participation is seminal to the energy sector, but this must be on a balanced and equally beneficial basis. The private sector must be invited to become a full player, but this also means sharing the capital risk. The solution does not have to be binary.

Singapore, for example, has a highly effective working model of state capitalism, which debunks the global standard view that fully privatised enterprises are more efficient than state-owned companies. Isabel Sim, in her analysis of Singapore's government-linked companies (GLCs), shows how Singapore's GLCs perform better and more efficiently than private companies. She attributes this to four success factors.[3] Firstly, the GLCs operate with a very strong corporate governance culture, which limits short-term political interference. Secondly, the GLCs operate within a zero-tolerance corruption environment, with Transparency International ranking Singapore as one of the least corrupt economies globally. Thirdly, the GLCs are meritocratic and are characterised by high levels of technical capacity and professionalism. Fourthly, there is a primary focus on bottom-line performance and competitiveness.

Ultimately, while moving on from outdated debates and accepting that models of privatisation are now a non-negotiable, we cannot lose sight of the fact that in doing so, we need to tread carefully, mindful of the impact of job losses, escalating costs for consumers, and – as experience elsewhere has demonstrated – the potential for significant corruption in the battle to control Eskom's assets. The key will be to introduce private competition and streamline Eskom's mammoth operations, while retaining state involvement in the sector and ensuring that the sale of any assets is conducted rigorously and independently.

Two: Redefine the role of SOEs

The Polokwane Conference of the ANC called for a review of the performance of SOEs and a reassessment of their role in economic and social development. As a result, in 2010, President Jacob Zuma established a Presidential Review Committee on State-Owned Enterprises to address the question of 'whether SOEs are responding appropriately to the developmental state agenda.'[4] The Committee's final report, issued in 2013, made 31 recommendations – most of which were vague enough to be acceptable to every constituency – and placed SOEs at the centre of the state's development strategies. Perhaps strategically, the report made no mention of privatisation (although it did raise the possibility of 'consolidation', 'streamlining', and 'a reduction in the number of SOEs') and barely referred to the widespread corruption, which was already evident by then.

The overriding emphasis in the report was on the political agenda of building a 'developmental state'. In the final draft, the report noted:

> South Africa aspires to be a developmental state ... SOEs are expected to assist the state in addressing issues of social and economic transformation and in bridging the gap between rich and poor, black and white, rural and urban and other divisions in our society. If the country is to attain improved quality of life ... the state must preside over viable, efficient, effective and competitive SOEs.[5]

The report envisioned the contribution of SOEs to development in at least three ways: (1) through providing services to the poor and extending the country's economic infrastructure; (2) by using massive procurement budgets to benefit local and black-owned businesses; and (3) by advancing transformation through hiring and training. Critically, however, the report noted that to achieve these goals, SOEs would need to be efficiently managed and adopt an aggressive transformation mandate.

The problem with this strategic orientation is twofold, and indeed lies at the heart of state capture and the failure of SOEs to contribute meaningfully to the economy. First, multiple and conflicting objectives complicate the management and oversight of SOEs and create a frequent tension between profitability and social mandates. A 2018 World Bank evaluation explains: 'SOEs typically have both commercial objectives and broader public policy objectives, but balancing these goals can be difficult and lead to negative effects on efficiency and performance.'[6] SOEs are expected to generate profits and be financially self-sufficient, while also carrying out ambitious public investments and meeting social targets.

Of course, this dual role is integral to the structure of SOEs. There would be no reason for their existence if they did not serve a policy purpose, and if they did not operate as commercial entities, they could simply be absorbed into the functions of line departments. The problem, however, is a lack of clear delineation between these mandates. The government, as the owner and main shareholder of SOEs, usually fails to provide direction about how different objectives should be prioritised, and how social projects should be funded or weighed against profitability concerns. Expectations of profitability and development goals need to be specified, quantified and monitored separately – and profitability should be explicitly prioritised. If major public investments are made by SOEs, the mechanisms by which these costs will be recouped must equally be specified. Will a 'user pays' principle apply, will a project be cross-subsidised by other revenue streams, will direct support from the national budget be required, will the private sector participate jointly in the funding and the risk? In short, how will the SOE carry out its mandate *while remaining profitable*, and not merely divert government's resources away from other expenditures? In order to maintain the profitability of SOEs, tariffs must be cost-reflective and services that are provided for free or at a discount must be costed and funded explicitly by the state.

The second problem with the developmental state orientation is the vulnerability to exploitation, manipulation and corruption of preferential hiring and procurement. The requirement that SOEs should use procurement to benefit local and black-owned businesses has regularly been used as a smokescreen to facilitate corrupt tenderpreneurship, which is anti-developmental by its nature. For example, the infamous forced sale of Glencore's coal operations to the Gupta-owned Tegeta Mineral Resources was ostensibly designed to benefit smaller and black-owned companies in Eskom's supply chain. However, the result was vastly more expensive coal, and of a quality so low that it crippled the functioning of vital power stations. Part of the reason why SOEs across the board, from Eskom to SAA and the SABC, have seen their profits collapse and their costs balloon out of control is the practice of engaging in uncompetitive and unmeritocratic procurement to secure expensive, low-quality inputs and services.

How do we overcome this? The failed Zuma experiment on infrastructure with Eskom and Transnet led to poor delivery funded by crippling borrowing.

The point of SOEs is to operate as successful and profitable commercial enterprises, allowing them to invest some of their earnings in public goods and to reduce the cost of direct services to citizens. The point is not for them to make a loss, or to take on unsustainable levels of debt in pursuit of apparent public policy goals. Equally, their objective should be to provide infrastructure and services of the highest possible quality at the lowest possible cost – not to benefit a few tenderpreneurs in their supply chain.

The government needs to redefine the mandate of SOEs to emphasise their revenue-generating potential, including clear funding arrangements to introduce more efficiency and reduce debt, and their vital role in expanding strategic economic infrastructure and service delivery.

It should go without saying that the value of effective services and working, modern infrastructure will be far greater to the economy, and to the crucial project of transformation, than that of enriching a handful of politically connected millionaires.

Three: Improve governance and accountability

The quality of governance and accountability at our SOEs will override the adequacy and sustainability of even the best plans, the most sophisticated financing models and the most progressive objectives. New rules and standards will be meaningless if they are lost in a complex web of existing governance arrangements, and they will never be enforced if boards and management are not properly appointed.

These problems plague SOE governance under the current policy regime: First, overlapping and often conflicting legislation and regulations, which create ambiguity and confusion; second, fragmented oversight between different ministries and departments, and a lack of strong centralised control of the government's shareholder function; and third, most worryingly, a pattern of politicised appointments and, consequently, incompetent and inexperienced boards and executives unable to lead large and complex organisations.

SOEs are currently governed by the Public Financial Management Act, the Companies Act, founding legislation that establishes individual companies, and a plethora of regulations issued by the National Treasury, the King Code IV, national ministries and even municipalities. This leaves the respective roles and mandates of government and SOE boards unclear, creates conflicting and unaligned processes for board appointments and remuneration decisions, and makes inadequate provision for compliance and accountability. The result is lax governance and oversight. For example, a survey of water boards owned by the Ministry of Water and Sanitation conducted by the Presidential Review Committee found that '10 percent of [shareholder compacts] were not signed off by the board and minister; 65% were signed by the board but not the minister; and only 25% were signed by both'.[7] The World Bank assessment highlights the effect of regulatory confusion on appointments:

> In contrast to good practice, the existing legal framework for board appointments in South Africa is scattered across various documents and there is no single legislation or policy in place, leading to confusion and conflicts in the process. In many cases, the founding legislation of an SOE gives the executive authority the power to appoint and dismiss the board and CEO. Meanwhile, the Protocol on Corporate Governance for the Public Sector states that the board should appoint one of its members, preferably an independent non-executive director, as chair, which may conflict with the founding legislation. An SOE's articles of association may also codify the appointment and recruitment process. And for listed SOEs and SOEs with other shareholders, JSE requirements and the King Code also carry weight.[8]

In order to streamline and strengthen oversight and control of SOEs, a new single piece of legislation is needed, which should bring together all existing regulations in a coherent document. Beyond simply resolving overlaps and contradictions, however, this legislation should establish a new central authority to pool the shareholder responsibilities of the state and exercise active oversight. This model would both enable consistency in monitoring and accountability and separate the shareholder functions of the state from its policy and regulatory functions. The new agency could take responsibility for more than the nine SOEs in the Department of Public Enterprises' current portfolio, bolstered by additional resources and highly competent staff from the private sector. It would centralise and standardise appointment and remuneration procedures, and reduce their ad hoc and highly politicised nature.

This model has already worked in countries such as Singapore, which established a separate company – Temasek Holdings – to serve as the central ownership and monitoring agency for SOEs. When Singapore became independent in 1965, the government owned or took stakes in companies in a vast array of industries, from defence to telecommunications and air transport. In 1974, the government created Temasek as a commercial holding company to take over all of the assets that had been managed by the national government. From its initial portfolio of US$354 million, in companies ranging from a bird park to a detergent manufacturer, it now controls a combined portfolio of US$308 billion and has offices around the world. The Ministry of Finance remains its sole shareholder, and its board is appointed by the president of Singapore, whose approval is also required if Temasek draws on its cash reserves. But the company is run like any other commercial entity, is managed by professional staff and pays dividends to its shareholder. The key success of the Singapore model has been to vest active oversight and management functions in a single independent entity – rather than distributing these across government departments – and to separate the policy and regulatory mandates of government from the demands of running a profitable company.

The need for vastly improved accountability and governance has already been recognised by the South African government. The National Development Plan, for example, includes the following exhortation:

> Accountability in state-owned enterprises has been blurred through a complex, unclear appointment process and, at times, undue political interference. We recommend clarifying lines of accountability by developing public-interest mandates that set out how each state-owned enterprise serves the public interest, ensuring appointment processes are meritocratic and transparent, and improving coordination between the policy and shareholder departments.[9]

By far the most urgent task in reforming SOEs is to fix the appointment process for boards and executives. SOEs will only become profitable if they are run by independent, experienced and highly competent professionals with proven integrity. These officials, in turn, must be carefully monitored and held accountable by government. But for this to happen, oversight of SOEs must be centralised and tightened, and kept separate from political control and policy functions. Only if governance is drastically improved will investors and lenders trust SOEs enough to secure their funding and survival.

Four: Focus on strategic companies

Every rand allocated by the national government to SOEs could have been spent elsewhere. This opportunity cost is frequently overlooked in analyses of the effectiveness of SOEs and the burden of sustaining them. When we consider channelling more money into indebted companies and capital projects, we should ask not only whether we can afford it but whether the same money spent elsewhere could achieve a higher social return. In recent years, the answer to this question has been a resounding 'yes' in almost every case. In the 2015/16 financial year, the overall return on equity of SOEs for government as their main shareholder was a paltry 0.8%, while in other years their return has been negative.

If SOEs are efficient and well run, they can contribute in unique ways to economic growth and pro-poor policies. Indeed, they are at the heart of the developmental state model as it has been pursued by countries such as China and South Korea. Conversely, if they are corrupt or mismanaged, they will actively prevent South Africa from expanding its economy and providing services to its citizens.

The simple fact is that the South African government does not have the capacity to actively and effectively manage the entire current portfolio of SOEs. Its financial and human resources are stretched thin, and it is not able to operate a diverse range of large and highly complex companies at maximum efficiency. If we try to do too much, we end up doing nothing at all.

In order to place SOEs at the forefront of the developmental state agenda, we will have to focus selectively on the few strategic companies that can be globally competitive, and those which are essential to the objectives of the state. The remaining companies that have failed to prove their profitability and cannot be salvaged are not worth investing public money into, which could otherwise be going to the poor.

In order to reduce the extreme burden that SOEs currently place on the state, and to free up funds for social spending, the government must perform an independent review of all SOEs and consider all financing options in each case. These options must include the following:

- Recapitalisation and continued state ownership;
- Strategic equity partnerships to introduce private shareholders;
- Partial or full listing on the Johannesburg Stock Exchange;
- Absorption of functions into government departments; and
- Phased divestment and exit.

In some cases, non-performing SOEs may be partially privatised. In other cases, SOEs may be listed on the stock exchange to raise capital. It is likely that several of those SOEs that are most expensive to maintain will have to be relinquished by the state entirely.

Perhaps the most glaring case requiring urgent consideration is that of the airline, SAA. Is it to be permanently funded as a tourism loss-leader or should private capital be asked to share the risk with the state and turn it into a profitable business?

It cannot continue on its current flight path – continuously promising to become profitable and continuously failing to do so, requiring ad hoc bail-outs in the multiple billions that hurt the national budget.

These decisions will have to be taken on a case-by-case basis, and without regard for short-term political imperatives or powerful constituencies. The strategy chosen for each SOE must depend on its financial condition, its strategic national importance, its contribution to the provision of public goods and its future potential. Most crucial of all will be to avoid policy dogmatism: either in favour of privatisation as an ideological goal or against any privatisation at all. Pragmatism must be placed above expediency and doctrine.

Importantly, those SOEs that the state retains ownership of must be properly capitalised and positioned to succeed. At the root of many failures in the past two decades is the fact that SOEs were not sufficiently capitalised when they were corporatised. Either an SOE must be properly invested in and committed to by the state, or it must be relinquished. Anything in-between is a waste of our resources because SOEs that receive ongoing support from the state despite being uncompetitive, inefficient or monopolistic will crowd out private-sector competition and stifle dynamism in the economy.

Conclusion: Addressing suffocating monopolies

The structure of the economy that we inherited in 1994 was highly uncompetitive and racially skewed, with the majority of South Africans entirely excluded. Excessive state intervention shaped the economy into a distorted, uncompetitive form, much of which persists today. To create space for new black-owned businesses to thrive, the stifling effect of large monopolies must end.

By focusing on the few SOEs that work, capitalising them properly and meritocratically staffing them, we can create global champions that expand our infrastructure, create jobs and grow our revenue. At the same time, by changing the funding models of unprofitable SOEs, we can ease the burden of debt and channel money back into productive assets. Doing so will require political courage and long-term commitment.

13

Transform Our Labour Market and Reap Our Youth Dividend

The children of any nation are its future. A country that does not value its youth and children does not deserve its future. — Oliver Tambo

Chapter summary

- Bar administrators from being members of the teachers' union to prevent the usurpation of government authority over education.

- New incentives (for example, tax allowances) are needed to radically increase the uptake of learnerships and apprenticeships.

- Roll out substantial wage subsidies and productivity-enhancing measures as an incentive for the private sector to increase youth employment.

- Ensuring performance contracts for teachers would be a step in the right direction. This will, however, take time. A short-term opportunity exists to create BBBEE credits possibly using tax incentives to encourage apprenticeships, complementing and invigorating the government's Youth Employment Service programme.

In the opening to this book, I made the point that we need to put jobs at the centre of economic policy while we restructure towards higher-productivity competitiveness.

We talk all the time about job creation being a key priority. Yet, our unemployment levels are among the highest in the world, the structure of our economy perpetuates the fault lines of our history, and, most inexcusably,

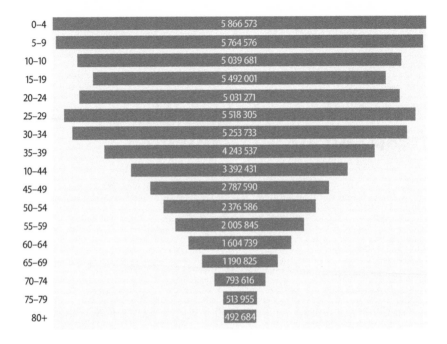

0–4	5 866 573
5–9	5 764 576
10–10	5 039 681
15–19	5 492 001
20–24	5 031 271
25–29	5 518 305
30–34	5 253 733
35–39	4 243 537
10–44	3 392 431
45–49	2 787 590
50–54	2 376 586
55–59	2 005 845
60–64	1 604 739
65–69	1 190 825
70–74	793 616
75–79	513 955
80+	492 684

Figure 13.1: South African population, mid-2017

(Source: Stats SA)

our youth dividend has become a youth burden because we have failed to create the space for our young people to innovate, take risks, catalyse entrepreneurism and stimulate productivity and demand. The impact of this failure can be seen at all levels – in the economy, in politics and in society.

There is a grave danger that unless there is a rapid improvement in the employment prospects of the youth, the dividend will turn into a disaster.

Already the youth are disengaging from political life and turning to anti-social behaviour as well as extra-parliamentary protest movements to vent their anger. The question is: where are jobs going to come from?

Growth in our labour-intensive industries – agriculture and manufacturing, which in theory should absorb large numbers of under-skilled people – has largely been absent. South Africa's growth has instead been capital-intensive, led by the services sector. This is incommensurate with our low-skilled, low-productivity young labour profile.

The consequence is that South Africa's labour market remains one of the most unequal in the world, as I detail in Chapter 8.

Our failure to create jobs is a combination of ineffective or incorrect policy and interventions, including competing goals between employment creation and worker protection; our broken education and skills system; the structure of our economy; our failure to grow the informal economy; and our failure to create an environment conducive to entrepreneurialism and small and medium business growth. In all of these areas, we require new long-term policy measures, preceded by transitional packages, including subsidies and incentives, to encourage labour-intensive inclusive growth. These innovations and their risks require robust discussion among employers, government, labour unions and youth formations.

Fix our education and skills system

There is a substantial body of literature confirming that quality education is a critical enabler of economic growth. Education as an investment in human capital is a surprisingly recent formulation, dating from the 1960s. Human capital theory, and later (from the 1980s) endogenous growth theory, explored the relationships between investments in education and economic growth, including the importance of quality education for technological change, innovation, entrepreneurship and research and development. The importance of technology in driving economic growth has increasingly been recognised, and as a consequence the focus on the quality of educational investments has increased.

Total macroeconomic returns to investments in quality education are greater than private returns (through higher employment earnings), which, in turn, are higher than average returns on other forms of investment. Total returns to education investments can be greater than private returns because of positive spillovers of education.

Another important aspect of education investment relates to the cumulative nature of knowledge. For example, investments in secondary education will be lower if the quality of primary education is low because students will lack the basic cognitive skills (such as reading and numeracy) to progress.

There is also a strong relationship between educational outcomes and class/inequality. Globally, richer people tend to have achieved higher educational outcomes. Poorer people tend to have lower educational outcomes. Educational outcomes and economic (class) outcomes reinforce each other over time, producing an intergenerational social reproduction. That is, class divisions and economic inequality are both a partial cause and a partial effect of unequal educational outcomes.

The intergenerational reproduction of inequality is transmitted mainly through the inheritance of wealth and unequal education. Unequal education impacts on economic outcomes through the mediation of labour markets. With the increasing importance of human capital and skills in labour markets, educational outcomes become relatively more important in influencing income inequality.

Thomas Piketty's *Capital in the Twenty-First Century* examines the relationship between education and social inequality.[1] For example, he looks at the intergenerational correlation of education and earned income for several countries. The United States has the highest correlation, while Scandinavia has the lowest. The United Kingdom, France and Germany are in the middle.

This intergenerational correlation of education and earned income is related to the concept of social mobility. The higher the correlation, then the lower the rate of social mobility.

Public investments in education are fiscally redistributive only if they yield quality education outcomes and increased social mobility. Private investments in education can enable growth in the longer term but will have less impact on inequality. Indeed, private investments can simply reproduce existing inequalities.

To this effect, I propose six actions to address the education crisis.

Action 1: A new social compact to address the crisis
Education is frequently touted as a route out of poverty towards development. However, children's socio-economic status plays a significant part in the educational outcomes they achieve, and thus influences the direction their education route takes. For this reason, we cannot disengage education from social structures, and education must be seen as the shared responsibility of

198

families, communities, schools and the education authorities.

The collective leadership in education needs to articulate a common vision and action-based set of priorities for the sector, and begin to mobilise all stakeholders and role-players around this. Tensions between national and provincial government, as well as recurring conflicts between government and teachers' unions, distract leadership attention away from the burning issues of school dysfunctionality. New levels of cooperation are needed, which, in turn, will require compromises among and between role-players and interested parties. Hardliners who put narrow interests above the interests of the sector as a whole must be dealt with.

The role of the Education Policy Units at various universities is crucial for this new social compact. The continual contestation around the interpretation of policies must not be usurped by political expediency, and must be firmly rooted in sound academic discourse. This will overcome the issues of uneven participation and other constraints in policy formulation, and it will free up the public service to deliver on policies.

The social compact to transform education must be fortified by a well-mobilised civil society that will hold government and schools to account. Reminiscent of the National Education Crisis Committee of the 1980s, a social movement anchored around improving school functionality needs to be mobilised to avoid an elite-driven social compact. Communities need to be rallied to take more interest in the performance of their schools, and hold them to account in terms of the 'Triple T' (Teachers, Text and Time) foundations of a good school.

The South African Schools Act of 1996 set out to decentralise decision-making. It further introduced school governing bodies as mechanisms for parents' democratic participation in schools. The Act provides for an active role for parents in appointments, deciding on school policy and oversight of financial management. The capacity of school governing bodies must urgently be built to enhance their role in school management as a key component of the new social compact.

Action 2: Teacher development and support

One of the biggest failings in the education system to date has been in the area of teacher development. Collectively, we have completely failed to develop the kinds of teachers needed to revolutionise education in the country and provinces. Going forward, a clear teacher development and support plan is needed to deal with the enormous capacity backlogs and the haphazard and uncoordinated approach to teacher development and teacher support. Tertiary institutions must be centrally involved in the development and execution of this plan, and must be held more accountable for the quality and orientation of teachers.

The focus of teacher development initiatives must be better targeted. A key source of support to teachers in understanding and implementing curricula and content changes in their classrooms lies with the education district offices. Subject advisers and education development officers based in the district offices are expected to provide district-level connections between national and provincial education structures through to schools and classrooms. The extremely high vacancy rate in the education district offices renders this intended support link academic. Recruitment and deployment of suitable support-providers is a critical component of transforming education.

Action 3: Accountability and discipline

A social compact on paper is worth nothing. Well-developed and supported teachers will have no impact if they are not unambiguously committed to transforming education. New levels of accountability from all role-players are required to turn around the education crisis in the country and provinces.

Political expediency and narrow interests must not be allowed to undermine hard choices that have to be made to develop fully functional schools. Effective school management and leadership are key factors in ensuring effective schooling.

These hard choices relate to a range of issues, including improving performance and dealing with non-performers, both in schools and government; assessing school and teacher performance through formal and independent audits, the reports of which should be publicly accessible; establishing a new institutional vehicle for school and teacher performance assessment; holding stakeholders to account for their role in the education turnaround compact; and undertaking the necessary human resource restructuring and financial resource reallocations.

The common thread through all of these interventions is accountability and discipline. Alone, these interventions are insufficient to improve education. A new mindset, a new attitude is required from all role-players to effect education transformation, with communities and schools playing the central role of ensuring that other role-players deliver on their distinct responsibilities.

Action 4: School functionality

School functionality is the consequence of efforts to convert human resources (administrators, educators, learners and parents) and material resources (facilities, equipment, textbooks, stationery) into meaningful educational and learning outcomes.

The extent to which school functionality can be demonstrated is dependent on the presence or absence of the core components of schooling: teaching, learning, management and parental support. Attention must therefore be given to developing programmes that address, among other priorities, the distribution and management of resources (to and in schools); time management on the part of all role-players; teacher work ethic, planning of lessons, assessments and extra-curricular activities; curriculum coverage; the regularity, quality and accuracy of assessment and feedback to learners; and parents' involvement in the education of their children.

Action 5: Access and equity

Access and equity are in many ways the desired end points of education transformation. The Constitution, under the Bill of Rights, enshrines the right to education. Until every child is able to enjoy this right in an equitable manner, our democratic transition will not be complete. Our failure in this regard will condemn our children to poverty and underdevelopment.

The introduction of non-fee-charging schools has assisted parents, but this has not changed the entrenched pattern of resource disparity between schools, which manifests in failure at the most basic delivery nodes, including learner support material, scholar transport, school nutrition programmes and underspending on school infrastructure.

Ultimately, for as long as our education system remains inequitable, our economic growth prospects will be obstructed, reproducing social relations of inequality and deprivation. This, in turn, will threaten social cohesion and political stability.

None of the ideas put forward in this book are new; in fact, they echo our existing policy framework for education and training. What is required, though, to put these ideas into action is for all stakeholders to put their sectional interests aside and develop a broader vision for the sector. They must endeavour to see beyond their blind spots.

For the plan to work, communities and schools must take centre stage: education transformation cannot be about securing jobs for bureaucrats and teachers. Education transformation must be about tangible changes in the conduct of teachers, the content of their teaching and the consistency with which resources are available. Communities and schools are where these changes must be monitored, and where the success of this plan will be evident.

The education crisis is, above all, a crisis of accountability – of teachers, of principals, of officials, of political leadership. The absence of a clear vision for education transformation, the inability to cohere the necessary critical mass of role-players and stakeholders, and the lack of sustained and consistent policy focus all indicate leadership problems in the sector.

These leadership challenges have been compounded by the high turnover of political and administrative heads, as well as the existence of corrupt cliques that act as gatekeepers to change and transformation. Also exacerbating the crisis is the deteriorating relationship between teacher unions and government, and the impact this is having on school functionality and performance. Clearly, any improvements in educator performance and school functionality will centre on making teachers and principals more accountable – to learners, to parents and to communities. This will require a new role for unions, and new strategic partnerships to be mobilised in the sector (for example, with school governing bodies). Ultimately, we need to assert the independence of a professional public sector that focuses on delivery in its purest sense, and a robust civil society that holds the public sector accountable.

Action 6: Translate education to work

The pace of the transition from school to work must improve, and policies to this effect must be designed and implemented. Germany has had relative success in youth employment because of its training system, which prepares the youth for the labour market and entrepreneurial activities through experiential on-the-job training. Commitment to experiential learning is one reason why the Chinese have accelerated learning within their firms and ensured skills transfer (and technology transfer) from multinationals investing in China.

There are three propositions worth remembering if this challenge is to be tackled in South Africa:

- Good-quality education is both a development goal itself and a central driver of socio-economic renewal and transformation.
- A good-quality education system is essential for long-term economic growth and the long-term reduction of poverty and inequality.
- Good-quality education also underpins a healthy society of a functioning democracy, good governance, strong institutions, social cohesion, shared values and good infrastructure.

Note the two qualifiers in these statements: education is only beneficial if it is of good quality and education is a long-term investment.

During my trip to Singapore in May 2018, the country's senior minister, coordinating minister for social policies and adviser to the prime minister on economic policies, Tharman Shanmugaratnam, noted that institutionalisation of a 'performance culture' across government, support for small and medium-sized businesses, the reduction of governance 'system' costs, and the 'enhancement of openness' through free trade agreements were all essential attributes in building that country. But the 'bedrock', he noted, was Singapore's education system.[2]

To create an ethos of performance, the government 'moved educators around continuously as an organising principle to enable the spread of success and isolation of failure, never permitting entrenchment in one place. Every principal moved after five to six years. This created a performance ethic in the key arena of action, the school, and not the ministry.'

Singapore is ranked as the top education system in Asia, and number seven worldwide by the Economist Intelligence Unit,[3] behind Finland, Switzerland, New Zealand, Sweden, Canada and the Netherlands, and level with Germany, and ahead of the next-placed France and the United Kingdom in the top ten.[4] South Africa was in 33rd place among the 50 countries surveyed, in the company of Brazil, Kazakhstan, Peru and Argentina.

'Education has been absolutely central to facilitating social mobility in Singapore,' said Shanmugaratnam. 'Our pinnacle is regarded as our public schools, not the private system. Indeed, public schooling is mandatory at the primary level. Admission is not based on the parents' means but on geography, which stems from our social housing policy, which aimed to mix people up. Also, our metrics are not limited to exams alone, but are rather focused on demonstrating the individuals' abilities. We have found that this performance-based ethic motivates parents, linking parents with the teachers, motivating them.' This is also backed up by the rewards. 'We pay teachers the same as other professionals in the civil service, which keeps them highly motivated and well rewarded,' he said.

Refocus our policy

We have had some policy successes with regard to employment creation, particularly on the demand side. We don't need to reinvent the wheel, but we need to apply pragmatism and action to what we already have in place.

The Employment Tax Incentive, now extended to 2020, has been a huge success. Simulations should be run on the scheme to explore if more employment generation for young people can be realised through, for example:

- Extending the full value of the subsidy for an additional year;
- Creating a new specific dispensation for small and medium-sized enterprises (SMEs); and
- Placing an additional subsidy premium on specific, labour-intensive sectors.

The Industrial Policy Action Plan should be specifically reoriented (and phased in over a few years) to shift the subsidy towards more labour-intensive, export-oriented manufacturers.

Packages of sector-growth solutions need to be offered to key sectors, wherein the cost and other constraints are identified (for example, wages, electricity, legislation and tariffs) and agreements are structured to resolve these problems. This should be at the heart of sector-level compacts, together with how sectors can be more inclusive.

Wage subsidies, for example, can be offered to counter competition in those markets and products where local wages may be too high. This would place less of a burden on firms and unions to negotiate lower-wage agreements. This is examined further in Chapter 16 in the discussion of the failing industries of Buffalo City and its surrounds.

In other sectors where the National Minimum Wage is binding, and likely to result in firms closing (for example, furniture), tariffs could be increased to allow for firms to adjust to the new higher-cost structures brought about through the National Minimum Wage. This should be negotiated through sector- and industry-level compacts and it requires quick and responsive policy to be effective.

Harness our informal economy

South Africa has one of the smallest shares of informal-sector employment in a sample of comparator countries: 18% in South Africa, far less than half the global average.

We need a clear strategy to grow the informal sector. Currently, the informal sector is, at best, viewed as a sector to be formalised, and, at worst, as one to be removed from the economy altogether. Most government business and financial support is targeted exclusively at formally registered enterprises. Yet, globally we know that it is the informal sector that provides the first portal of entry into work for the poor and marginalised. South Africa's historical legacy and current policy paradigm have resulted in an economy which, by emerging market standards, has the smallest share of workers in the informal sector. A key demand-side set of initiatives is required to ease the burden of operating and owning an informal-sector firm. These range from local government regulatory changes (giving these firms access to the consumer market) and improvements in storage facilities to skills train-ing and better crime prevention in localities of operation. As mundane as these interventions sound, a much more strategic view of the informal sec-tor remains a key missing policy cog in our attempt to realise a significant reduction in aggregate unemployment levels in the country.

Create an environment conducive to entrepreneurism and SMMEs

Government dispenses finance for small enterprises through the Small Enterprise Finance Agency, a subsidiary of the Industrial Development Corporation. Through direct and wholesale lending, the loans are capped at a maximum of R5 million to small enterprises and cooperatives.

The Small Enterprise Finance Agency offers bridging loans, asset finance and what it calls 'structured financial solutions'. In Welkom in the Free State, 26 youths each received a loan of R80 000 to start businesses operated out of containers in an initiative supported by Coca-Cola.

This and several other similar initiatives no doubt mean a lot to those who get access to the financing, but government has not really moved the needle when it comes to creating enterprises on a scale that seriously dents unem-ployment – for youth and otherwise.

On the next level, there is a long list of venture capital outfits that offer finance to more advanced small enterprises. A list on the website Ventureburn includes Justin Stanford's 4Di Capital, which has hundreds of millions in finance to support 'early and growth stage' start-ups, including some involved in hi-tech fields such as drones.

Such companies – the most successful are sometimes described as 'uni-corns' – require a rapid injection of much more capital if they are to take the next big leap. Stanford said in an interview in July 2017: 'There is still no cul-ture of IPOs [Initial Public Offerings] as an exit for startups in SA. I don't see this as likely to change in the near term. As it currently stands the structure of our stock exchanges and the typical participants in those markets don't really encourage this type of activity. There isn't much interest from the buy side, and the rules and regulations are more geared for well established companies.'[5]

But not all small businesses can use these funding networks because they are informal. Banks are not well aligned to the informal sector, in which more than 1.5 million South Africans run small businesses, and which do not meet registration requirements.

A workshop organised by Finmark observed that 'many of the "survival-ist" and small businesses were thought to operate informally which naturally cuts them off from most SME support programs and formal credit. Policy makers must craft innovative ways of incentivising formalisation of these businesses without burdening them with cumbersome red tape and tax liabilities.'[6]

Another way to seriously address access to entrepreneurial finance or capital to improve the quality of life for low-income earners is by getting the big banks to actively expand their offering to the unbanked.

Between one-third and a quarter of South Africans of bankable age have no bank account at all.[7] The Banking Association of South Africa puts the number at 12 million people or 23.5% of the population.[8]

According to the association, 'Growing evidence suggests financial sector development has a knock-on effect that promotes pro-poor growth and reduces inequality, by mobilising savings and investing in productive growth and reducing costs associated with information, contracting and transactions, which contribute to high growth and lower poverty.'[9]

The financial exclusion of millions of South Africans means that they live on the margins, never able to raise finance to improve their assets, such as their homes should they hold title to them, or to boost their small trading operations and skill-based enterprises.

According to the World Economic Forum, financial inclusion – defined as the adoption, usage and sustainability of financial services – faces 'numerous challenges in South Africa'.[10]

The Boston Consulting Group carried out research into the state of financial inclusion in 2017, and found that this was limited by perceptions of high fees. The fee structure of South African banks is up to four times higher than in countries such as Germany, Australia and even India. As a result, only 24% of account holders make more than three monthly transactions, such as withdrawals, deposits or card swipes. More than 60% of all purchases are paid for in cash.

There appears to be a trust deficit with the formal banks. Low-income earners – some 40% of them – are involved in informal stokvel-style schemes, where a group of friends or neighbours band together to fund each other. 'Community-based organizations such as these still provide the flexibility and support structure that is perceived as lacking in the banking industry,' claims the World Economic Forum.[11] There is serious money involved. As one sensational headline put it: 'South Africans will save so much through stokvels this year that they could buy Pick n Pay in cash and still have R10 billion left over.'[12]

If this money were to be held – at transaction fees that made them feel comfortable they weren't being ripped off – by major financial institutions, it could be leveraged to release a lot more capital to those wanting to lift themselves off the street and into a modest shopfront.

But mistrust in banks' motives, which 'is rooted in fears of exploitation' and is exacerbated by widespread financial illiteracy, stands in the way.[13] Concerns about fraud also explain the preference for cash over digital technology.

There are substantial barriers to using banks, not least the need for rates accounts and payslips, and approvals can take a long time for a low-income segment that often needs money immediately. Rather, this segment turns to family or loan sharks.

Conclusion

The current position of youth in the economy and the labour market presents significant risks to social and political stability. Having such high numbers of youth who are not in employment, education or training is a challenge that requires our urgent and unwavering attention.

Our extremely high youth unemployment is mainly a result of structural weaknesses in the economy (low growth and the capital-intensive and skill-intensive bias), and partly an unintended consequence of policy choices we have made, as well as our suboptimal education and training outcomes. This objective situation of high youth unemployment is, in turn, encouraging levels of instinctive discontent in the form of sporadic, militant and even violent protests, which are not linked to a broader transformation agenda.

High levels of unemployment and low levels of optimism about the future also fuel anti-social behaviour (crime, drugs, unsafe sex), which further reinforces vulnerability.

Hard policy choices are needed to break this vicious cycle, especially to combat youth unemployment and fix our education and training system. More of the same will not help. With such huge challenges and so much at stake, we should be more prepared to venture into new policy terrains and choices – experiment with new instruments, and if successful, run at scale.

We must also acknowledge we have been somewhat limited in harnessing the energy (and militancy) of youth. The youth are there to agitate and remind us that access to power is not the endgame. As leadership, we must use the power that has been bestowed upon us to transform society. And this is never easy because there will always be powerful interests vested in the current status quo. This is the broader struggle into which the youth must become more integrated.

14

It Is Time to Release Our Tech Potential

The development of ICT policy is the intersection of politics, economics, engineering, science (physical and chemical) and sociology. — Andile Ngcaba

Chapter summary

- Enable cheap broadband access for citizens by resolving regulatory, competitive and political barriers that keep prices high.

- Improve education, training and skills, as well as the elementary infrastructure and the systems that enable its full use.

- Develop a start-up culture through funding, incubation, investment in research and development and other necessary support to entrepreneurs.

- Overhaul the patent system to increase competitiveness and prevent precious intellectual property from relocating abroad.

The Fourth Industrial Revolution (4IR) could, if the dire predictions prove correct, cost up to a third of current British manufacturing jobs in the next 20 years, and perhaps as many as half of those in the United States. Employment of the poor and most vulnerable in both developed and developing worlds is apparently in greatest danger of being displaced by robots.

At the same time, income inequality in the developed world has reached levels not seen since the Great Depression. Automation, coupled with outsourcing, has had a downward pressure on labour earnings. In the three decades following the end of the Second World War, for example, hourly wages of the average US worker rose 91%, in line with productivity growth of 97%. Yet, from 1973 until 2013, hourly compensation of a typical worker rose just 9% against a productivity rise of 74%. In part, this is due to an increase in outsourcing to cheaper labour markets. A typical 'production and non-supervisory worker' in the US private sector, representing half of the workforce, earned US$767 per week (measured in real terms) in 1973. Four decades later, a similar worker earned US$664, a decline of 13%.[1]

It is not all bad news. While we focus on the losers in manufacturing, many others have prospered. The combination of trade, technology and liberalisation has especially empowered East Asia. This has led to a radical reduction in extreme poverty, from half of the global population in the 1960s to under 10% today. Asia makes almost half of the world's goods, today led by China, which in 1990 produced less than 3% of worldwide manufacturing output by value. Now China's global share of manufactured goods is nearly one-quarter.

There are several positives from the new 4IR world, some of which offer particular advantages for developing countries.

Technology affects all aspects of our lives. It is as much as a sector in itself (with the largest companies in the world today being tech companies with mostly intangible assets) as it supports and improves all other sectors, from health to finance, agriculture to governance.

If we can succeed in unlocking these improvements, we have nothing to fear from technology or the 4IR. A minimum, necessary but insufficient condition for a digital revolution in South Africa is affordable internet access.

Internet access as a silver bullet?

Mobile and internet access has been the ultimate source of technological leapfrogging in Africa. It is an avenue by which to bypass our infrastructural challenges. As Precious Lunga, a Zimbabwean neuroscientist and tech entrepreneur, put it, 'There are places where there's still no running water, but you can stream a music video.'[2]

This statement captures the complexity of the leapfrogging narrative. South Africa, with its more than 37 million unique mobile subscribers and 68% penetration rate (the highest in Africa), has severe challenges to address. But there is also immense potential for growth.

There are many challenges for the telecommunications sector – notably high data costs, uneven infrastructure and regulatory uncertainty – which can be overcome with the right set of policies and the necessary political will. The opportunities that will arise as a result provide the case for why they ought to be overcome.

Smartphone adoption on the African continent is projected to increase from 34% to 67% between 2017 and 2025, while mobile connectivity is expected to rise to 87% (from just 38% in 2017).[3] Whether this growth will materialise depends heavily on infrastructure improvements, such as the new South Atlantic Cable System, operational since September 2018, pro-viding the fastest-ever data connection between Africa and the Americas.[4] Infrastructure investments might prevent occurrences such as Mauritania's 48-hour internet outage in April 2018, due to a problem on the African Coast to Europe (ACE) submarine data cable, which affected nine other countries along Africa's West Coast.[5]

Intermittent and slow internet access is detrimental to any twenty-first-century economy, particularly to financial trading. South Africa is still a long way behind the rest of the world when it comes to broadband provision, rely-ing heavily on wireless to cover its vast spaces, sacrificing connection speed. South Africa has the third fastest internet in Africa (behind Madagascar and Kenya), but ranks only 76th in the world, according to the Worldwide Broadband Speed League 2018.[6]

Another current limit to access is the high cost of connectivity, which works as an exclusionary force.

In its long-awaited report on its Data Services Market Enquiry released in April 2019, the Competition Commission confirmed that South Africa's data prices are too high compared to international benchmarking.[7] It ruled that South Africa's data pricing is 'anti-poor' and lacks transparency. While the Commission acknowledged that a lack of spectrum (which government has failed to release to internet providers) increases operating costs, it noted that operators are unlikely to drop their prices unless there are competitive pressures to do so.

All of this is true, but the deliberation on data costs is more complex and requires deeper debate among all players – government, industry and consumers. South Africa is known to have the highest data cost among Africa's largest economies, at US$14 per gigabyte, but compared to other comparative, middle-income countries in this regard (namely Turkey, Egypt, Saudi Arabia and Mexico) our costs are competitive. This obviously is still not good enough for an economy with the inequality levels that we have in South Africa, but, in addition to spectrum, data costs are also affected by the topography of a country, the proportion of the population that is urban, a country's economic characteristics, the quality of service of 2G, 3G and 4G and whether 5G has been introduced; the availability and maintenance of fixed-line infrastructure that connects mobile base stations with the rest of the network, including the number of base stations per square kilometre; and the proportion of prepaid versus contract customers (an indicator of income).

Telecommunications companies in South Africa are currently conducting trials with the view of rolling out 5G technology towards the end of 2019. But they are coming up against the high costs as a result of the above combination of factors. In theory, South African mobile operators are ready to develop 4G networks and deploy 5G services, but because of the current constraints 3G is likely to be the prevailing technology over the next three years.

Technology always presents a moving target, as Lethabo Motsoaledi, tech entrepreneur and founder of an artificial intelligence start-up, puts it: 'Today we are trying to provide cheap broadband access. But soon Amazon will give everyone free internet through low-orbit satellites.'[8] (If Facebook or Google don't beat them to it.) We should be anticipating what the next challenge will be and trying to solve it.

Given fairly priced and fast internet access, the chances of reaping the benefits of technology – including a reduction of friction, greater productivity, lower marginal costs, improved transparency and governance, faster growth, safer cities and transport, and better education outcomes – are all the greater.[9]

Harnessing the advantages of tech

There are several major potential advantages in digital technology. These accrue across industries and sectors, encompassing efficiency in government, boosting productivity, financialisation and social inclusion.

The first of these is in improving the efficiency and effectiveness of government, both in the provision of social services and in government administration.

Technology could help expedite regulation and administration, including licence, visa and permit applications, along with tax returns.

There are already positive examples, including the payment of welfare through smart cards in South Africa. Nearly half of South African households receive a form of social welfare grant. Since 1996, the number of social welfare recipients has grown from 2.4 million to over 16 million.[10] In another area, big improvements in infrastructure provision are possible by utilising predictive data techniques to understand the impact of decisions and new construction techniques.

High-speed internet could bypass the inefficiencies of government and the challenges of geography in the distribution of education, electricity and health care. Already, technology has revolutionised university access by offering cheap (or free) courses online. For example, GetSmarter pioneered an online learning experience, focusing on 'industry-relevant' skills to professionals working in financial technology and big data.[11] Started in 2008 and growing to a staff of 70 in 2013 and more than 500 at the time of its sale to the Nasdaq-listed education giant 2U for R1.4 billion in 2017, GetSmarter has enrolled 100 000 students in 145 countries, including 35 000 in South Africa. Its co-founder, Sam Paddock, believes that technology can particularly assist in developing and homogenising curricula, and in ensuring certification standards. 'Technology,' he says, 'should be used to optimise the time spent with the student' over devising courses and fighting with bureaucracy.[12]

Technology also offers unprecedented opportunities to reskill people and matchmake job seekers with the jobs available. Cape Town-based OfferZen, for example, matches job openings with software engineers and programmers, many of them previously unemployed and subsequently upskilled.

Likewise in health care, there is enormous untapped potential for improving delivery efficiency. In the United Kingdom, for example, the National Health Service has partnered with private company Babylon to provide online medical consultations or 'digital first primary care', to relieve the pressure on clinics, while making it easier for patients to access a medical professional's advice. A similar service in South Africa could make great strides in rural health-care access.

The spread of communications could also assist in improving transparency and democracy. Blockchain technology and digital record keeping limit the opportunities for corruption, while digital voting systems can streamline elections and prevent ballot fraud. Technology also aids citizen democracy, to which there is a generational and likely political dimension: young people are the ones most likely to be early adopters of technology.[13] This is not lost on some governments in Africa, which have clamped down on the use of online media promoting good governance and expressing dissent, and have shut down social media during elections.[14]

The second major advantage is the boosting of output in productive sectors. This could potentially create a slew of new jobs – through improving competitiveness by better connecting Africa to global markets, capital and knowledge.[15]

In agriculture, for example, information on weather patterns, seed and fertiliser use or market information could radically ramp up production, perhaps even ensuring the continent could feed itself. On connecting smallholder farmers with advice, to the markets and to each other, Bill Gates has noted that this should enable farmers to get a slice of the US$40 billion in annual African food imports. 'Something is not functioning properly,' he writes, 'when half of the continent's labour produces food, and the continent still buys its food from somewhere else!' There is, he says, an 'information disconnect', which 'stems from the fact that agricultural markets, like banks, exist on a formal plane, whereas smallholders exist on an informal one. So farmers and markets cannot communicate effectively.'[16] Technology is rapidly changing this through apps such as South Africa's Khula, which allows farmers to list their produce and track real-time inventory levels.

Staying with agriculture, technology, such as land surveying and satellite imagery, makes it possible to monitor the health of crops and soil

215

remotely, and addresses information asymmetries between markets and producers to limit price speculation. It also allows for 'precision agriculture' through irrigation, weed control and harvesting, which increases output per hectare – a labour-saving mechanism. Hydroponic and vertical farming are two excellent examples of this that have not been harnessed on any grand scale in South Africa, but which could allow crop farming in urban areas.

In manufacturing, 3D printing gives everyone the opportunity to be an entrepreneur, even at a household level. Notwithstanding the potential job losses from labour-replacing technology, such as robotics, these present a way out of demeaning jobs in factory production lines into other industries where humans are irreplaceable and jobs are more dignified, such as old-age care and tourism.

Thirdly, technology will continue to drive financialisation and financial inclusion, as it has done on a grand scale in countries such as Kenya (with M-Pesa) and Nigeria (with 9pay and others). Financial inclusion through financial technology is not limited to money transfer, but has expanded into services such as insurance and credit with great success.

Finally, the development of technology as a sector in itself presents major opportunities for job and value creation, and the solving of even more of the types of challenges noted above. All we need to do is create the necessary conditions for tech start-ups to thrive, and entrepreneurs will do the rest.

The facts speak for themselves: the mobile industry is projected to contribute US$150 billion, or nearly 8% of GDP, across sub-Saharan Africa by 2022, up from US$110 billion in 2017.[17] New market entrants such as Rain in South Africa, promising a faster 5G network,[18] show the power of disruptors in the sector.

In addition to considerable potential markets, the telecoms sector in Africa is entering into collaboration and competition with a number of other sectors, such as media, finance and retail, promising large returns. Already, merger and acquisitions transactions in the tech and telecoms sector in Africa and the Middle East are estimated to be worth US$5.9 billion in 2018 (up from just US$1.2 billion in 2017).[19]

The internet is a vital tool for financial inclusion in Africa. Sub-Saharan

Africa has 140 mobile money services in 39 countries, representing over half of the 277 total services globally.[20] Telecommunication companies (or Telcos) are already competing with the finance sector by providing credit and insurance by leveraging their access to customers' spending data. Meanwhile, banks are growing increasingly dependent on internet service providers for access to clients.

Tech entrepreneurship provides massive potential dividends, given the appropriate infrastructure and business environment. The internet is revolutionising agriculture in Africa by giving smallholder farmers access to markets and finance. In the health sector, much of the internet's potential remains untapped, with limited use of smart devices or remote diagnostics to date. But with sub-Saharan Africa carrying 24% of the global disease burden with just 2% of doctors, this is sure to change.[21]

Media (music, videos, news and advertising) is the single most popular use of mobile devices worldwide. With smartphone adoption expected to double by 2025, this market will increase substantially. Already, digital income accounts for 50% of global music industry revenues.[22] Universal Music announced in early November 2018 that it would license its catalogue to Boomplay, Africa's fastest-growing music-streaming platform,[23] predicted to reach a 40-million user base by December.[24]

Along with digital marketing and customer engagement, e-commerce presents the proverbial next frontier in digital growth. While Africa's mail, road and rail infrastructure might not currently welcome deliveries, this is bound to change with drone delivery, now used by JD.com in China.[25] Amazon has been slow to enter the African market, leaving room for others to become Africa's largest internet player.[26]

How to foster a tech industry

To unlock these benefits, we must create a start-up culture that encourages entrepreneurship by making funding and mentorship available, allowing easy and convenient registration and administration, and internationally transferable Internet Protocol (IP). Entrepreneurs currently need permission to transfer IP offshore,[27] which means that South Africa loses out on valuable talent and IP as many start-ups decide to register abroad from the outset.

First and foremost, we must understand what start-up culture is. Start-ups are very different from small, medium and micro-sized enterprises by their nature, and should not be subject to the same requirements for funding. Indeed, our financial institutions still prefer funding bricks and mortar, as they have not yet developed a model for funding risky start-ups.

The Cape Town experience shows how successful start-ups grow under the right conditions. Cape Town is regarded as South Africa's tech hub. 'Cape Town's tech,' says its former Finance MEC Alan Winde proudly, 'is bigger than Lagos and Nairobi put together.'[28] Hence the moniker Silicon Cape.

Amazon and Yoco are among those companies that have contributed to the 5 000 tech jobs in the city. They have quite different origins: one a global logistics and tech giant, the other a small start-up, which has rolled out a point-of-sale card reader designed for small and medium-sized enterprises.

Amazon, which today employs 3 000 in the city (of 566 000 worldwide in 2019), was originally attracted to Cape Town in 2004 through a local computer services company, Elastic Compute. Its Business Process Outsourcing business presence followed. Cape Town's combination of location, accents, political stability, along with the predictability, stability and global reach of its telecoms network, all made it an attractive base for eight hours of Amazon's 24/7/365 'follow-the-sun' service operations.

Yoco, by comparison, was started in 2012 by four under-30s who saw the need for a technology merchant aggregator between the merchants and the customer, in a country where 75% of adults possessed a debit card, yet just 5–6% of merchants accepted such a card.

The name Yoco was employed since the company wanted something 'fresh and original' – eventually being named after a dog of one of the founders, 'which had the added advantage of a unique URL,' according to CFO Bradley Wattrus.[29] But the remainder of the challenges the founders had to overcome were more familiar.

The first was to ensure market access, given that South Africa was bank- rather than regulator-led in this regard. A second task was, following the acquisition of its licence in 2013, to raise a first round of US$500 000 in capital, which was eventually sourced from family and friends. To date, following six rounds, and with 37 000 merchants using their devices, Yoco has raised US$20 million. Fundraising, admits one of the founding quartet, Wattrus, was 'definitely a formidable challenge'. But so, too, was red tape, especially at the Department of Trade and Industry. 'You have a conversation, which leads to another conversation, which leads to another,' he says, 'and then to due diligence, and all this is too long for a tech company with a two- to three-month runway.' A second challenge concerns the lack of engineers in South Africa, 'where just 3 000 of 12 000 registered engineers are at a suitable level. We need structured training programmes,' he suggests, 'at our universities, and to permit a more open visa policy.' He strongly suggests that 'South Africa should be looking to create the conditions whereby our engineers are not happy to be exported to Seattle, and where we should be enticing other African technicians to an African hub.'[30]

Amazon similarly notes that a 'nexus' of web developers would make South Africa a more attractive market for hi-tech, along with assuaging concerns about water provision, general infrastructure, including electricity, and crime dynamics.

If we accept the reality of change in the relationship between technology and jobs, and if we can open up further opportunities, these experiences show that we can create new and more jobs in new sectors. South Africa's immediate value proposition in the tech sector is in the application of skills plus technology in a global market.

The fixes

A few years ago, bandwidth would have been cited as the largest issue facing technology companies. With fibre, this is no longer the case. Rather, pricing and market access are now more problematic, as is the availability of skills.

If the impact of the internet in areas such as health, education and democracy over the past 20 years is any indication of its potential for disruption and growth in the future, it can be a tremendously powerful catalyst for change, overcoming the weaknesses of government services. Even if it does not solve all our problems – from access to information and accountability to unemployment and poverty – simply attempting to improve the efficiency of the telecoms sector will deliver massive dividends. Limits to internet access are essentially limits to growth.

Technology is going to be a great disruptor. The impact of online services and retail on traditional stores, from touch screen purchasing and payment and automated food preparation, will likely increase the pressure on jobs. The introduction of robotics into retail stores is likely to have the same effect. In agriculture, the US experience has been negative for jobs. At the start of the twentieth century, nearly half of US workers were employed in agriculture; by the 2000s, this fraction had fallen to just 2%.

But at the same time, data collection and technology together could create jobs that we have not even dreamt of. And the more things change, the more some things will stay the same, including in the services sector, such as tourism, while fresh efficiencies in government could free up human and financial capital for better and more productive use elsewhere.

Five key actions stand out for South Africa to turn the 4IR into a positive reality and reap the benefits outlined above.

The first is to resolve regulatory and political barriers to enable cheap broadband access for citizens, using the allocation of spectrum as a tool for more competitive pricing.

A second action is to improve education, training and skills, and the elementary infrastructure and the systems that enable its full use. This includes expanding access in schools to internet, computers and training in coding.

Third, we must foster a start-up culture by providing incubation, support and funding opportunities for upcoming tech entrepreneurs.

Fourth, we must reform and relax our IP laws to make it possible for entrepreneurs to take their IP abroad.

And finally, we need to open up to create an environment that encourages foreign and local entrepreneurs to invest their time and money, through better policy, improved visa access and the ability to remit funding. Technology can turn this from a slow, friction-bound process into a smooth, hassle-free one. That is, if government wants to do so.

This is not the first time that manufacturing has faced challenges of technology. The ability of business to survive as an automator rather than being automated will, as before, hinge on the manner of the entrepreneurial response and the way in which governments, too, engage on the regulatory front.

Conclusion: The job for government

Today's entrepreneurs require patient capital, which is scarce. The banks do not want to lend you money for such long-term investments, and private equity investors want to double their money and get out in three years.

The difference between success and failure in today's business world is not likely to be found in levels of government support, however. It is about finding niche areas of competitiveness. It will be underpinned by sound engineering and business logic. It will depend not on the arrival of a big idea, but rather something that is evolutionary rather than revolutionary.

Governments could do more, in part by attempting less. They could help more through research grants and by structuring more patient capital.

But nothing will happen without those willing to take risk for reward, the entrepreneurs. Smart, motivated, competitive people, intent on leaving a legacy and able to work around obdurate regulations, still make the difference.

15

Rural Development Must Look to the Future, Not the Past

It was there in the hills and valleys of Qunu; in the rolling hills of KwaDlangezwa; in the Genadendal settlement; and along the Gariep, the Lekoa and the Luvuvhu rivers, that we first understood that we are not free. — Nelson Mandela

Chapter summary

- Secure property rights for smallholder farmers and those in shared landholding schemes.

- Get redistribution right to ensure the security of property rights, which are crucial for all parts of our economy.

- Diversify rural economies. Untapped opportunities exist in tourism, light manufacturing and technology through upskilling, to mention a few.

- Address the homelands landholding question. The sensitivities around this issue cannot prevent us from securing the position of some 17 million insecure landholders and residents in rural areas.

More than 25 years after apartheid, land remains the single most divisive and volatile issue in South Africa. The land question bears the full weight of our history, from colonial conquest to apartheid and structural inequality. It is an expression of the complexity of that history and the uncertainty of the present. Researcher Christian Lund thus captures the biggest issue of our times: 'It is never merely a question of land, but a question of property, and social and political relationships in a very broad sense. Struggles about property are as much about the scope and constitution of authority as about access to resources.'[1]

The land debate is a proxy for reparations, unresolved historical issues and pervasive inequality as well as landlessness, poverty and exclusion. Land underpins every aspect of our society – identity, belonging, marginalisation, gender and inheritance, birth right, custom, exclusion, community, agriculture, well-being, spatial design, citizenship, ownership and much more. Unsurprisingly, Section 25 of the Constitution was the last to be agreed on during negotiations because of the inherent tension between history and the future, between individual freedoms to hold property and the public interest to address historical injustice and dispossession. Failure to address this fundamental issue means that the promise of the Constitution has not been fulfilled for the majority of South Africans. This failure cuts across all aspects provided for in Section 25: land redistribution, land restitution and tenure security.

The often loud and heated debate about 'expropriation without compensation' clouds the complex issues South Africa needs to deal with. Who has received land transfers? How have patterns of land ownership changed? How has this benefited the prospects of rural communities? Has land reform contributed to poverty eradication and removal of extreme inequality? How are the tenure and ownership rights of recipients of transferred land strengthened? What assistance is given to those who have acquired land?

If we are to build the present and the future on a solid basis, we must peel back the layers that cloud this conversation and address the fundamental structural issues it reveals. This chapter contributes to the debate by focusing on agriculture and the creation of a thriving sector that is globally competitive, but where opportunities are extended to all. We need to examine all our options – expropriation, subsidies, extension services, better access to markets, improved technology and more productive partnerships – and ask ourselves how we can best achieve our goals. What do we want to achieve? How do we get there?

Despite assertions to the contrary, the Constitution is not the reason

223

for slow land redistribution. The Constitution empowers the state to take 'reasonable measures' to ensure 'access to land on an equitable basis', for 'expropriation with compensation', and for a 'just and equitable' process of acquiring and distributing land. The major problem is not the Constitution, but the policy choices made by government, incompetence and lack of political will. These problems will arise even if the Constitution were to be amended.

To see effective change and meaningful transfer of land, South Africans must revisit some of the assumptions that underpin land distribution and spatial design. Lack of clear understanding of policies and practices affects the well-being and status of people who live in these communities and has contributed to increasing poverty and marginalisation. It contributes to the breakdown of family life, community and the ability of people to provide for themselves. Therefore, the debate about land must be part of a larger conversation about the kind of South Africa we want. How do we create economic inclusion and participation for those who live in rural communities? How do we ensure that all laws that are passed, including laws pertaining to the status of traditional leadership, governance and rights, contribute to the development of one law for one nation which protects the rights of all citizens equally?

Looking at these issues with the benefit of understanding my largely rural home province, the Eastern Cape, it is evident that we have not taken extra care to undo the legacy of apartheid geography.

Following the scrapping of apartheid-era legislation, parliament passed the Traditional Leadership and Governance Framework Act of 2003 (TLGFA). Contrary to what it was supposed to achieve, the TLGFA reintroduced apartheid spatial design and logic. It entrenched the boundaries that were created by the Bantu Authorities Act of 1951.

In 25 years, South Africa has failed to unravel the apartheid spatial design and logic. Even in legislative and public policy processes aimed at undoing that legacy, it is produced, albeit unconsciously most of the time, because it feels familiar and logical. Until we revisit the underpinning assumptions of South African geography, we will not succeed in creating new areas of economic development that address the well-being of all South Africans.

Revisiting the spatial logic we inherited from the apartheid era is as important as understanding the centrality of land in our national DNA.

I have discovered that there are many examples that illustrate how complex our challenges are and it is worth looking at them closely when we try to cut a new path forward.

One such example is Grabouw, less than an hour from Cape Town, but a world away in terms of the rural-urban divide.

When approximately 100 farmers and two packing facilities are responsible for the bulk of economic activity in a town of over 100 000 people, the need for diversification is urgent.

A deep dive into this Overberg town reveals a complex web of social ills and political interests in the face of nearly explosive population growth. Migrants arrive in large numbers in search of jobs that do not exist and join informal settlements that until recently had not existed, going by names as hostile as 'Iraq', 'Marikana', 'Lost City' and 'Siyanyanzela' (meaning 'We take by force').

During the initial farming settlement during the seventeenth, eighteenth and nineteenth centuries and post-1994, intensification phases of farming in Grabouw have been enormously successful by any measure. Today, South Africa accounts for 1.02% of world apple production, or 918 000 metric tonnes, from 700 commercial farmers working nearly 25 000 hectares.[2] Roughly one-quarter of this occurs in the Grabouw valley, some 250 000 tonnes, valued at almost R2 billion per year. Since China accounts for half of world production of 64 million tonnes, but exports very little,[3] South Africa enjoys disproportional importance in the global apple export market, accounting for over 5% of the total of 7.5 million tonnes, bringing in nearly US$400 million annually. Nationally, the apple industry supports 27 297 workers and 109 187 dependants.[4]

While there is a growing tourism market in the valley of Grabouw and Elgin, based on passing traffic and day trips from Cape Town, the third aspect of the area's growth (alongside agriculture and tourism) has so far largely been missing: economic inclusion.

Local government has failed, on a colossal scale, to distribute tangible benefits to the poor and unemployed. Although the municipality had a

225

plan drawn up by an outside consultant at considerable expense in the early 2000s, it has delivered nothing. This fuels public disquiet.

The second half of 2018 saw police step in to contain at least five violent protests, according to the local station commander. In 2016, service delivery protests resulted in both the fire department and the traffic department being burnt to the ground. Each protest sees burning tyres obstructing the N2 – a major national road carrying about 22 000 cars and trucks per day past Grabouw, running from Cape Town to other cities such as Port Elizabeth, East London and Durban. The marginalised majority have had it – with poverty, unemployment and failing government.

A lack of government capacity also explains why the pace at which RDP houses are built is unlikely to ever catch up with the pace at which informal dwellings pop up. Recipients spend in the best cases five years, and in the worst cases 20 years, on a waiting list. The same goes for schools: a brand-new school accommodating about 2 000 isiXhosa-speaking students was opened in 2018. Construction on another school (currently housed in a derelict building) is set to begin in 2019. But at nearly 30% of the population, there are an estimated 4 500 isiXhosa-speaking children of school-going age now living in Grabouw and its surrounds.

In part, too, the area's problems are down to the lack of jobs, reflecting not just a failure to diversify but also a rapid increase in the number of people. The population has increased from 21 000 in the 2001 census to some 30 000 ten years later, and 80 000 in 2017, although word on the street is that it is closer to 100 000.

As the shacks creep higher up the hillside along the highway, they move nearer to the water catchment area of the Steenbras Dam, which irrigates the valley's lucrative pear and apple farms – the primary source of income in the area. This presents not only flood risks to these dwellings, but also water contamination risks to export fruit. 'Just one water scandal could shut down the entire valley,' says one farmer in a discussion. At just 100 members, the Elgin Grabouw Vyeboom Villiersdorp Agricultural Association represents the bulk of all major producers in the area.

Farmers are in no small way responsible for the annual influx of seasonal workers from the Eastern Cape. Migrant workers allegedly work for less than locals are willing to, and stay long after the season is over, often settling permanently. Farmers claim that bringing in labour from outside is the only way to get through the peak harvesting season, despite the scores of unskilled workers in town.

Linking Grabouw and Zwelitsha

Grabouw's predicament is not unique. In fact, it is in a decidedly better state than most rural or agriculture-based towns. The unfortunate outcome of urbanisation has not been the exodus of people from these towns, but the outflux of wealth. What remains is a hopeless cycle of unemployment, grant dependency, teenage pregnancy, poor schooling, domestic violence and drug and alcohol abuse.

As the N2 joins Grabouw to the Eastern Cape, the second half of this story unfolds nearly 1 000 kilometres away, in the rural villages and townships surrounding Buffalo City, such as Zwelitsha and Mdantsane.

From the 1890s through 1913 (when the Natives Land Act was promulgated), black peasant farming in the Eastern Cape was thriving. Black farmers had a lucrative system of selling their produce not just in the surrounds, but as far as the mines in the interior, which bought maize to feed their workers. These early farmer-entrepreneurs owned ox-pulled wagons and equipment and made a decent living off the land.

This system was progressively undermined through legislation, such as the Glen Grey Act, which forced rural farmers off their lands and into gold and diamond mines. The Natives Land Act decreed that Africans were to own only 7% of the available arable land, and prohibited the holding or selling of land as individuals, creating a distorted form of communal tenure. Artificial land shortages emerged, which made it even more difficult for black farmers to sustain themselves.

Fast-forward to the active support of white farmers by government throughout the apartheid years and a picture of preordained or non-accidental inequality emerges.

The telling of this part of our history, though essential, does not intend to detract from the successes of commercial farmers in the Grabouw area and elsewhere. Many of them became successful after the end of apartheid, when new international markets were opened and some of the distortions from preceding eras of state support were removed. But this chapter is not about them – it is about the need for a rural development and reform agenda to address past inequalities and build vibrant, diverse rural economies.

In line with the new inclusive growth agenda (set out in Chapter 8), the imperative for rural communities is simple: create jobs and change ownership patterns without compromising competitiveness and growth.

Neither fiscal nor asset redistribution has succeeded in bringing structural change to these areas. While social grants have aided poverty alleviation, without jobs there is virtually no upward mobility out of poverty and deprivation. The National Development Plan promised one million new jobs from agriculture. Yet, rural areas face unprecedented levels of unemployment as margins from agriculture become smaller and labour becomes more mechanised.

Meanwhile land reform, the main form of asset redistribution tackled by the post-apartheid government, has failed dismally, with only 5% of white-owned land redistributed to black landowners in 25 years.

As set out in the preface to this book, the post-apartheid consensus between parties has rapidly eroded; so, too, in agriculture. Established wealth – the white commercial farmers – have retreated inward, refrained from investing for fear of political change and not taken part at the scale necessary for redistribution programmes. Meanwhile, the new elite, those who have benefited from early land reform programmes, such as the Proactive Land Acquisition Strategy, have grown frustrated with the lack of new opportunities and the lack of accessory support to emerging farmers, in particular.

Those employed in agriculture, and those unemployed in agricultural areas, have become stuck in cycles of poverty, with minimum wage increases and social transfers doing nearly nothing to elevate their positions. Without growth in other sectors of the rural economy, and with dismal education opportunities and lack of jobs, they have grown ever more desperate.

Reconciling these parties in a new consensus is now a matter of urgency. One area where a new consensus for cooperation is sorely needed is land reform.

Land reform in numbers

In March 2018, the former rural development and land reform minister, Maite Nkoana-Mashabane, conceded that despite some R76 billion having been spent by government on land reform and restitution since 1994, only 4% of land was in the hands of private black landowners. While this figure is highly contested (AgriSA puts the number closer to 27%), the fact remains that, despite immense amounts having been spent, the positive effects of land reform remain limited, if immeasurable.

One of the reasons for the failure of land reform over the last two decades was perhaps that it has tried to do too much for too many, and done so without the needed nuance and focus. The different programmes encompassing land restitution, redistribution and tenure reform, while all important, have sought to serve such diverse groups as those deprived of land unlawfully between 1913 and 1994; those living under customary law systems or on communal land; and upcoming farmers or entrepreneurs looking to enter the sector.

The state has also flip-flopped in its approach, first transferring unconditional ownership in the early programmes, and in recent years only leasehold. As a result, some 25% of South Africa's surface area of 122 million hectares – 31 million hectares – is held by the state.[5]

State land ownership and administration of land reform have also buckled under corruption – one of the reasons for the R76-billion price tag noted above – as a report by the Special Investigating Unit uncovered in early 2018.[6] The report recommended that 42 people, many of them government officials, ought to be prosecuted for malpractice on some 145 farms that were targeted for land reform between 2011 and 2017. This includes transfers to beneficiaries that were not entitled to them, and inflated land prices with side-payments to government officials. Also tellingly, perhaps, government spends R10 billion annually on land reform, of which R7 billion is spent on some 2 500 staff.

Transferring an additional 18 million hectares of land to black owners (as required to reach the National Development Plan's target of 30%) will cost the state an estimated R330 billion, if farms are to be kept in production.[7] This amount is unlikely to come from government. The critical question is, therefore, how can the private sector be drawn in?

The debate around expropriation without compensation has left the private sector and particularly established white farmers reeling, and has discouraged, rather than encouraged, any partnerships or collaborative approaches to land and wealth redistribution. It is essential that white farmers, black emerging farmers and government sit at the same table, as a more equitable distribution of land and wealth is in everyone's interest.

One way of ensuring cooperation is by forming new industry compacts, for example by offering guarantees against expropriation without compensation (or for partial expropriation at a fixed percentage, for example 15% of landholding) for those farmers who willingly transfer land by entering into redistribution programmes with farmworkers or other BEE partners, based on set criteria.

In addition, we need to turn to other forms of collateral besides only land, as this is limiting. Indeed, land itself is now a minority item on the balance sheet of successful commercial farmers, alongside capital equipment and investment. The destruction of land values resulting from expropriation without compensation makes it dually important to seek other forms of collateral. New forms of financing can lead to creative ways of merging state resources with the private sector and pulling in existing financing institutions, such as the Land Bank and other development banks. This includes using the allocation of water rights more efficiently to help BEE partners to bring something to the table.

For land reform to succeed, it must be able to fail: the strategy should be to give land access and ownership to as many smallholder farmers as possible. We need to lose the 'one-shot' approach to land reform, where we put all our hope on a single beneficiary and criticise the entire programme when that one hope fails. Farming requires a multifaceted and crop-specific skill set, developed over many seasons and through difficult conditions. Even under favourable circumstances, agriculture is always a long-term, capital-intensive investment. Expecting emerging farmers to be successful within the first few years is like expecting a start-up to turn a profit immediately.

We need creative disruption in the area of land reform.

The question of smallholders

Contrary to popular belief, farmland in South Africa has not become concentrated in fewer hands. There are today 57 000 VAT-registered farmers, the same number as in 1993.

This brings us to the not so small matter of smallholder farmers. More than one million South African households are engaged in agricultural production, the vast majority (about 99%) of which do so as a secondary source of food and income, supplementing the remittances and grants on which they live. The small minority of those who manage to farm relatively successfully and produce surpluses for the market are severely constrained by tenure rights, lack of infrastructure and technology, and access to markets.

Considering the dismal record of land reform to date, helping smallholder farmers is a redistributive means of improving land use, increasing production and alleviating poverty. Yet, the conversation has largely been avoided due to the sensitivities surrounding traditional leaders in former homeland areas. The case of the Ingonyama Trust refers: the Trust, with its sole trustee being King Goodwill Zwelithini, owns 2.8 million hectares of tribal land, amounting to 30% of the land surface of KwaZulu-Natal.

The trust has been collecting rents from landholders with virtually no secure tenure – a transgression for which it has been taken to court by the Legal Resources Centre. What is more, the Trust concludes contracts with mining companies without properly consulting residents and claims royalties as its own revenue, evicting residents and holders of communal rights off their ancestral land and leaving water and soil pollution in its wake.

An action plan for rural landholding and former homelands needs to deal very clearly with altering the existing rural tenure system. People have access to land, but are not able to fully utilise it because they do not count as landowners.

The first intuitive step is therefore to secure property rights. Farmers in collective landholding schemes, such as communal property associations, at one stage a favoured land reform strategy, and those who were given land on a lease rather than title, have virtually no way of accessing credit and financing their activities under the current dispensation.

Policies to support smallholder and small-scale farming households (the

231

majority of which are female-headed) include essential extension services, access to plant material and breeding stock, and access to markets. Take BKB and the National Wool Growers' Association's wool-breeding programme for example: by giving smallholder sheep farmers access to better genetic material, they have managed to improve wool quality and yield to the benefit of all involved. Between 1998 and 2014, smallholder wool production in South Africa increased from 220 000 kilograms to 3.8 million kilograms, largely thanks to the intervention. But this was not down to genetic improvement alone: farmers were also given access to better shearing infrastructure and wool training classes, and a guaranteed market for their wool.

A by-product of insecure title in these areas is that there has been no integrated plan for economic development outside of agriculture, mining and social transfers. These areas hold immense potential in tourism, for example, which could be developed.

Conclusion: Balancing excess and dearth

The future of rural communities depends on our ability to think beyond the limiting scope we are used to. Currently, there is no law that provides for rights and ownership of land by rural-based citizens, almost 17 million South Africans. The Communal Land Act of 2004 was ruled unconstitutional. There is a vacuum that the law must fill. Secondly, redistribution of rural land must be done as a matter of urgency. For this to work, we need to look at ways of ensuring that rural land is utilised effectively for the benefit of people who live there, with secure rights. Changing land ownership patterns and strengthening people's right to land in rural communities is the only way to decongest places like the informal settlements in Grabouw. We must think of ways to decentralise the agri-economy, which utilises rural land to benefit poor people. Creating agri-economy in rural areas is not impossible, as we have seen with a number of initiatives that benefit a handful. The challenge is to develop meaningful and sustainable industries that serve communities rather than a few connected individuals.

Simple asset redistribution without growing investment and productivity might reduce inequality but will also increase unemployment and poverty.

We must rather focus on creating new wealth and assets in which the previously dispossessed have a growing share. As it is, commercial farming is already threatened by social unrest, which manifests as labour insecurity and populist land rhetoric. Agriculture must undoubtedly be transformed, but within this transformation there is an important trade-off: the speed of transformation against the disruption to the food production system. The Zimbabwean example shows the cost of hasty transformation, while the slow pace of redistribution, restitution and transformation in South Africa has resulted in growing frustration. Pressure on the system is building.

The National Development Plan envisions 'vibrant and inclusive rural communities'. Beginning with this goal in mind, we should endeavour to transform places like Grabouw through diversification into smaller industry, agro-processing, sustainable smallholder farming and tourism.

The reinvigoration of South Africa's rural economy requires a new spirit of cooperation between farmers, workers and local authorities to see to it that land use is optimised and that the conditions in which workers live are acceptable. Rural local authorities need to start re-imagining their towns and villages as crucial parts of the agricultural development story. The goal should be a greater stake for the community in farming and an improvement in productivity to justify improving wages.

16

Thinking Globally and Acting Locally

A 'New Urban Deal' for South Africa's Towns and Cities

The crisis of urbanism is all the more concretely a social and political one, even though today no force born of traditional politics is any longer capable of dealing with it. — Tom McDonough

Chapter summary

- Addressing the apartheid spatial form of our cities must be at the centre of the new urban deal. Densification and making land available for human settlement close to economic opportunities must be enabled and resourced.

- Create industrial zones for the twenty-first century with tax incentives, preferential electricity tariffs and capex support. Investment promotion agencies for all major metros must be set up to make it easier for business to thrive and create jobs.

- Get the basics right with reliable electricity provision, waste management, reduction of red tape, and quality roads and transport systems.

- A prerequisite for a new urban deal is dislodging the capture of the local state by political-business networks.

Most South Africans now live in cities. In 1900, the urban population comprised just 17%, or a million people, of a population of six million. By 1960, this had increased to 47% and by 1994, at the time of the country's transition to democratic government, 54%.[1]

Apartheid was central in keeping black South Africans out of cities. Black South Africans were forcibly removed from urban land and relocated to 'dumping sites' in the Bantustans, or in townships on the periphery of our cities. Urbanisation was tightly controlled to ensure just enough black labourers were allowed to live in cities as required by white-owned factories and homes situated 20 kilometres or more from where black people lived. If we didn't have a pass, we were fined, beaten or jailed. We had no property ownership rights, and the areas where we were forced to live had no services and amenities.

But we made these areas our own, and subverted the spaces meant to dehumanise and control us. Those long train rides from our townships to our places of employment in the industrial areas or the leafy suburbs became our spaces where we politically educated our people and actively recruited for our underground structures. We had our own governance structures in place, anchored around street committees. It was us – active black citizens – who made sure criminals knew their place and schools functioned in our communities. I often lament the fact that we demobilised so willingly after democracy, handing over these responsibilities to a local state that still struggles to find its purpose and continues to disappoint us.

Influenced by the business think tank the Urban Foundation, the 1980s saw some significant policy shifts in the apartheid state's approach to urbanisation, most notably the scrapping of influx control in 1986. Business was battling labour volatility and market shrinkage from sanctions, and required a politically stable and growing market of middle-class black consumers. The apartheid state saw a propertied black middle class as a buffer in their new 'winning hearts and minds' campaign, designed to isolate anti-apartheid activists in their own communities. We did not buy this, and were not prepared to accept urban citizenship without political citizenship. Our demands for political freedom in the late 1980s were met with armed forces deployed to our townships – the infamous last state of emergency. The urban spaces in which we lived and prayed became 'David and Goliath' war zones of school kids with stones facing down tanks and Buffels.

The rest, as they say, is history. Today, nearly two-thirds of South Africans, some 37 million people, live in cities. By 2050, some 80% of the country's population will be living in cities. Most of these city-dwellers will be under the age of 40. In the right circumstances, with enabling conditions of connectivity and densification, these could be sites of great industry, offering economies of scale in the delivery of infrastructure and services, and the congregation of capital, technology and skills.

It is cities and city regions that are driving the economies of India and China. Our cities are still small in comparison, but we can see where things are going. Mumbai, with its population of 15 million, has a population density of 30 000 per square kilometre. Johannesburg, our largest and most dense city, has a population of 5 million, and a density of 3 000 per square kilometre.

But the urban dividend can quickly turn into an urban nightmare, as evidenced by the so-called slum cities of South America.

Two factors are key to deriving a positive urban dividend:

1) Urbanisation must be properly planned and governed; and
2) Urbanisation must be underpinned by a growing and inclusive economy.

Urban planning and governance

The urban spaces we inherited in 1994 had been custom-designed to separate us, to subjugate us and to control us. Twenty-five years into democracy, our cities remain a study in contrasts, perhaps nowhere more than in Cape Town. Drawn by the backdrop of opulent coastal mansions, pristine beaches and 'old' wealth, visitors arriving at Cape Town International Airport are often shocked to pass through miles of squalid squatter camps where basic sanitation and electricity remain elusive luxuries. A reminder of the injustices of apartheid, the city's wealth inequality is mirrored by spatial divisions. The poor and gang-ridden suburbs of the Cape Flats and the townships spread interminably away from the heart of the city, with the consequence that the people who live in those areas have a long way to travel to their places of work. The violent crime rates in such places are the highest in South Africa, while Cape Town houses nearly 400 informal settlements where 20% of the population lives.

Still, the city remains an attractive destination for migrants from all over the country and the continent. The result has been massive pressure on housing, basic service delivery and public transport systems, and, more than anything, jobs. The population has increased by 65% since the 1996 census, or 3.1% annually, to 4.3 million.

Urban planning efforts post-1994 have mostly focused on addressing these apartheid service deficits and spatial patterns. The track record to date across South Africa's cities is discussed below. Generally, there has been steady improvement in service access, especially with respect to water, sanitation and electricity. But as the example of housing provides, these deficits are moving, and in some respects unattainable, targets.

The government has noted that the delivery of subsidised accommodation has 'declined steadily and at times sharply over the past decade', from a peak of 235 000 houses and serviced sites in 2006/7, to fewer than 175 000 houses, sites and subsidised rentals in 2016/17.[2]

In this environment, more households have been forced to resort to the unsubsidised market, mostly in urban backyards and informal settlements. In 2016, for example, 2.2 million households, or 13%, were living in such informal residences, with poor access to basic services such as water, sanitation and electricity. In South African metropolitan areas, the number of households in informal dwellings rose from some 970 000 to 1.25 million between 2001 and 2016, while migration resulted in 210 000 new urban households each year. A declining proportion of Cape Town's population occupy formal housing in 2016 compared with 2000.

It seems highly unlikely that the government can supply subsidised housing delivery to address historical deficits and the needs of the ever-increasing migrants from depressed rural areas.

Meeting the current subsidised housing demand was estimated to cost some R641 billion in 2018. Clearly, a fresh approach to human settlement planning is required; one that accepts that planned and serviced informal settlements are going to be with us for some time to come. Land availability close to urban centres and employment nodes is key, both for RDP housing, planned informal settlements and gap market housing. This imperative is well highlighted in the government's Integrated Urban Development

Framework. But implementation has lagged.

Property prices have pushed low-income and subsidised housing to the urban edge, mirroring the apartheid spatial form. Most black citizens still make the 25-kilometre trip to work, at least those fortunate to have a job.

City planners have not helped, failing to make use of the potential for connectivity offered by high-density accommodation. Our cities have expanded by sprawling and not through increased density of the sort seen in Hillbrow or Sea Point, for example, stretching out and not up. To densify, cities must better utilise government land on the urban edge. This applies equally to city, provincial and national land. Provincial and national departments must be more responsive to city spatial planning priorities. And cities need to better articulate their long-term land-use intentions, while guarding against unscrupulous speculation. The Spatial Planning and Land Use Management Act of 2013 was meant to resolve land administration bottlenecks, but has been slow in getting off the ground in many of our metros and secondary cities.

Land bottlenecks are retarding not only densification, but also growth and jobs. There is no reason for prime back-of-port industrial land in East London to still house a military base and a prison. This land should have long been given to the East London Industrial Development Zone (IDZ), for example, to attract a second automotive original equipment manufacturer, making Buffalo City a genuine automotive export hub.

While poor residents still live far away from place of work, public transport becomes key. Again, we have not fared very well here. Poor citizens spend upwards of 20% of income on transport, crowding out expenditure on food, health and education. The much-acclaimed Bus Rapid Transit systems have been some way short of effective, their main value seemingly being to feed local patronage networks. Gautrain has been a success, but more for taking vehicles off the highways and road network, than providing a transport solution to poorer citizens. The Passenger Rail Agency of South Africa has largely failed to take commuter rail to the next level. And while the taxi industry may have been successful from an access and small, medium and micro-sized enterprise development perspective, it does not provide cheap, safe transport options for the poor. Perhaps the closest thing to a 'silver bullet' for transport will be to shift the mandate (and funding) for commuter rail from the national government to cities. This would allow cities like Cape Town, eThekwini and others to build truly integrated transport systems for the first time.

The devolution of greater powers to local government – within the policy and regulatory frameworks set at national level – will resolve many of the intergovernmental blockages and could bring huge efficiency gains. Not least, it could end those constant and wasteful meetings that have become an end in themselves. Working as a public entity CEO and later as a political representative at provincial and national levels, I was alarmed at the time and cost implications of calling lengthy intergovernmental meetings involving large numbers of senior national officials, and representatives from provinces and municipalities (all of whom would have to fly to Pretoria and be accommodated). This intensified when I joined the National Treasury, and I was able to put rands and cents to these exercises. Sadly, these meetings tended to resolve very few issues and were more about the process than the outcome – what I came to call 'governing by consensus'; not consensus among stakeholders but consensus within government itself. I remain astounded why we need such consensus among public officials, when we have clear policy that must be executed.

But devolving powers to local government must be commensurate with governance and technical capacity. Key will be to ensure that policy implementation is insulated from narrow politics, as well as the burgeoning of local organised criminal networks that are circling state budgets in ways not dissimilar to what we have observed at the national level over the past decade.

Just as with our state-owned enterprises, capacity and systems that prevent looting in municipalities have been hollowed out. Our cities have not been immune to these tendencies. The closeness of business interests and political factions has also been at the heart of the intense contestation for leadership positions at local level. Unlike what is now common knowledge in Eskom or Transnet, state capture at local level has largely escaped public attention. Many of these stories are still to be told. The one lens we do have on the situation is the auditor-general reports. In 2018, the auditor-general reported that his office had audited 257 municipalities and 21 municipal entities. Only

33 municipalities, or 13%, managed to produce quality financial statements, as well as complied with all key legislation and, as a result, received clean audits. This was down from the 48 municipalities that obtained clean audits in the 2015/16 financial year. Out of all the municipalities that were audited, the audit outcomes of 45 regressed while those of 16 improved.[3]

Economic growth and inclusion

Attending to these governance concerns is a prerequisite for investment and growth. No one will invest in a local economy where integrity issues are consistently being questioned, and where the basics are not being done well. Crime, grime and non-enforcement of by-laws are major investment constraints.

We should have learnt from the last 25 years that simply being South Africa, having survived apartheid and experienced a remarkable political transition counts very little in the mind of the investor. After all, they have an obligation to their shareholders, not South Africa as a whole. While we have been concerned with a race to the bottom in terms of reducing the costs of labour, we are assured of reaching that bottom if we do not prioritise job creation. Competitiveness is not measured exclusively in labour costs; on the contrary, government has a whole range of levers to pull relating to the cost of doing business that have no bearing on labour inputs and may, indeed, if handled correctly, raise the return to labour.

A 2018 World Bank report showed that the ease of doing business in major South African cities varies significantly, with slow reforms since the last report three years before. The report 'Doing Business in South Africa 2018' surveyed nine major municipalities: Cape Town, Buffalo City, Ekurhuleni, eThekwini, Johannesburg, Mangaung, Msunduzi, Nelson Mandela Bay and Tshwane.[4] It measured the regulatory environment for small and medium-sized enterprises, such as time frames for obtaining construction permits, electricity connection, property registration and trade across borders for port cities. No city performed well across all areas measured, but Cape Town showed major improvement in the time it takes to obtain contractual permits for projects and getting electricity. Cape Town outperformed the average for Organisation for Economic Co-operation and Development

Location	Dealing with construction permits		Getting electricity		Registering property		Enforcing contracts	
	Distance to frontier score (0–100)	Ranking (1–9)	Distance to frontier score (0–100)	Ranking (1–9)	Distance to frontier score (0–100)	Ranking (1–9)	Distance to frontier score (0–100)	Ranking (1–9)
Buffalo City (East London)	71.66	6	59.4	5	57.81	6	51,.8	9
Cape Town	75.48	1	79.81	1	54.69	7	54.71	7
Ekurhuleni (Germiston)	71.81	4	52.09	6	58.48	4	55.58	5
eThekwini (Durban)	73.65	2	69.4	2	54.58	8	55.74	4
Johannesburg	68.16	8	68.77	3	59.68	2	54.1	8
Mangaung (Bloemfontein)	71.25	7	59.82	4	59.73	1	59.01	1
Msunduzi (Pietermaritzburg)	73.17	3	49.59	8	52.78	9	58.78	2
Nelson Mandela Bay (Port Elizabeth)	71.7	5	42.19	9	57.93	5	54.85	6
Tshwane (Pretoria)	66.25	9	51.24	7	59.39	3	56.14	3

Table 16.1: 'Doing Business in South Africa 2018': where is it easier?

high-income economies. By contrast, Tshwane's score placed it in the bottom half of global economies, behind Eswatini and just ahead of Namibia.[5] Buffalo City's ranking across the four indicators (Dealing with Construction Permits, Getting Electricity, Registering Property and Enforcing Contracts) was 6, 5, 6 and 9.

Reducing red tape is important. But red tape alone does not explain why cities are not powering South Africa's growth. Two case studies, of Buffalo City and Cape Town, are offered to illustrate local growth dynamics, both constraints and opportunities, and how these can be unlocked.

Buffalo City

Its seven million residents make the Eastern Cape Province the third largest by population in South Africa. But, it has the lowest per capita income,

241

ensuring it remains the source of constant migration to other, richer parts. One reason for this is that it includes the former homelands of Transkei and Ciskei and what was formerly the eastern region of the Cape Province. Another reason is due to the poor performance of the manufacturing sector in the region since 1994, whose contribution to the local economy fell from 17% to 11% between 2004 and 2014.

A drive through East London's run-down Wilsonia industrial area confirms the extent of the city's deindustrialisation. Unlike nearby Dimbaza, where factory buildings have all but vanished as the homeland subsidy scheme disappeared along with the apartheid imperative, in Wilsonia factories have been replaced by depots, conduits for goods made elsewhere and traded locally. There were little more than 1 000 workers signed up in the Metal Industry Bargaining Council in the 'border' area by 2018, from a peak close to 20 000 in 1994.

Today, the Buffalo City Municipality, which services East London, is the biggest proprietor, with 5 100 employees, more than Mercedes-Benz, the industrial doyen, with 3 300. Frame Park is another metaphor for the metamorphosis of the city. Once the site of a blanket manufacturer, the vast factory site has been converted into an office park, dominated by government bureaus. For jobs that once paid taxes, there are now jobs that spend tax income. As Buffalo City's executive mayor, Xola Pakati, admits, 'Things are moving too slowly. Investment rates are too low. Inequality and poverty remain, as a result, too high.'[6]

Mercedes-Benz has been manufacturing cars in South Africa since 1958. Since then, 24 different Mercedes models have been produced at the plant, including four generations of C-Class sedans. In 2015, it produced its millionth car. Today, it is one of four global production sites of the C-Class. Its R10-billion investment to build the latest C-Class was made because of incentives: a rebate for imports based on its exports, a capital-expenditure (capex) rebate on its investment and lower electricity costs. Without that, its executives admit, they would not have done so.

Mercedes is one of the few manufacturing investors not complaining about the difficulties of doing business, as the unemployment and closure statistics indicate. These difficulties include a lack of government integration between different levels (national, provincial and municipal), the high cost and quality of local services, from potholed roads to electricity and waste management, difficulty of access via the port and the premium on moving containers from Coega, the red tape and lack of responsiveness in government, and the disjuncture between macro-level economic policy (which has generally been sound, they state) and micro-level actions (which have generally been a failure).

Yet, many of the same people identify among Buffalo City's strong selling points its pristine unspoilt beaches; its lifestyle attributes, including medical facilities and schools; the untapped appeal of its tourism market; the ease of local access encapsulated in the term the 'Ten-Minute City'; the receptive political leadership; the strong emotional commitment of the business community to the city; and the co-location of its IDZ and Special Economic Zone (SEZ) with a large labour pool, agriculture and services sector, and unlimited sporting potential from motor-racing and boxing to triathlons.

Meeting some of these challenges is outside the control of government, including globalisation and the influx of cheap goods from Asia. But some are directly within its purview: labour inflexibility and low productivity, red tape, costly electricity inputs and high transport costs.

East London's resilient industrialists have a raft of positive suggestions for government, though they suspect no one is listening. Mostly, they look for greater subsidisation of their businesses not necessarily in the form of direct cash transfers but lower electricity and rates prices, and lower taxes such as those on offer at the IDZ/SEZ. Much of the dialogue between business and government seems to have failed, however, with the effect that some business people have simply given up.

There is light at the end of the tunnel if a few key opportunities are taken. Buffalo City could live up to the potential identified in the National Development Plan, being the country's fifth competitiveness node.

An immediate quick win will be to rename the East London grand prix track the Jody Scheckter Grand Prix Circuit, in honour of South Africa's only Formula 1 world champion and a local son done good, and promoting an international annual historic racing festival in the fastest-growing and wealthiest category of international motorsport.

More difficult to achieve, but more impactful, will be the widening and deepening of the port and the development of a fully fledged container terminal. This will do much to boost Buffalo City's export manufacturing potential. Two potential automotive original equipment manufacturer investors have been lost to Coega due to port constraints. The port, which processed just 65 000 TEU[7] containers in 2018 compared to 180 000 in Port Elizabeth and 774 000 in Coega, will either have to receive investment to allow larger vessels or concessioned to a private operator. Failure to seize this opportunity will consign the port to irrelevance and ultimately death, with negative consequences for the IDZ/SEZ.

The second big opportunity coming to the city is the undersea cable, connecting the East London IDZ to Mauritius and India. The cable will bring stable 54-terabytes/second data to the city. Already Buffalo City is being promoted as a business process service hub, with the first investor signed. Long-term plans include other ICT-enabled industries, such as a hyperscale data centre and a film studio. This could be the start of a new cycle of innovation-led growth, with planned Innovation Districts attracting and developing a 'creative class' as the agency for change. This will require the city's two host universities – Walter Sisulu and Fort Hare – to step up, or allow new universities into the space.

The third big opportunity speaks to the East London IDZ, which is one of eight SEZs in the country.[8] Like others, it is able to offer a discounted corporate tax rate of 15%, well under the usual 28%. The IDZ attracted 38 new investors in 2017, with investments totalling some R4.4 billion.[9]

It must be asked (a) why SEZ tax measures have taken so long to promulgate; and (b) whether they can be extended to other industrial parks in the metro. More than that, why should there not be an incentive scheme that rivals that available to the apartheid-era 'border industries', which encourage new, labour-intensive industries? The government was wrong in quickly dismantling everything Bantustan back in 1994. Subsidies and incentives must remain an essential tool in enabling labour market participation among the low and semi-skilled, as we transition towards a high-productivity workforce.

A twenty-first-century version of the Dimbaza subsidy scheme should look at the following:

- Tariff protection on textiles and related labour-intensive industries;
- A South African Revenue Service unit dedicated to cracking down on smuggling violators;
- A corporate tax rate aligned with the SEZs; and
- Electricity tariffs and capex support at the same level as Mercedes-Benz.

Such a package would retain and expand the industrial base of Buffalo City. The Da Gama fabric factory is a case in point. Once employing 9 000 employees, now down to a few hundred, Da Gama was taken over in 2014 by private investors led by Neil Cowie, whose Fort Jackson-based trading family had deep links with the region. Not only did they save the business and its iconic 'Three Cats' Shweshwe label from vanishing, but in so doing saved the only significant source of employment outside of government in an otherwise extremely deprived area. Expansion of the textile business, the owners contend, would be possible with the type of regime advocated above. Unlike politicians and bureaucrats, they speak from bitter experience.

We should heed their advice, and those of success stories elsewhere in our country.

For Buffalo City's economy to ignite, government must get a whole package of issues right to ensure inclusive economic growth, involving responsive bureaucracy and infrastructure and service delivery, along with a set of policies to attract investment.

Cape Town

The Cape Town experience is enlightening in a different way. We should not shy away from learning best practice from outside and especially from inside, no matter the political sensitivities in so doing.

Cape Town offers some of these best-practice lessons, not least concerning the way it has grown its economy faster than much of the rest of the country. Good governance underlies this growth. No fewer than 21 of those 33 municipalities which received a clean audit in 2018 are in the Western Cape.[10]

Other reasons include doing the basics well – keeping the city clean, investing in infrastructure maintenance, and investing in future infrastructure capacity such as water, electricity, waste, transport and ICT, which is now an important element of infrastructure. While Cape Town's lifestyle is a selling point, Tim Harris, CEO of Wesgro, the province's growth and investment promotion body, argued in a discussion that 'there are beautiful cities everywhere which don't work. If Cape Town was dysfunctional, its natural beauty would not help.' He observed that 'the biggest threat to major multinational investment (which would be a massive spur to growth) in recent years has been where the reliability of this infrastructure has been compromised (especially with regards to water and electricity)'.

Besides investing in economic infrastructure, the other area where Cape Town has done well is in investment promotion and aftercare. Province and the city work closely together, to reduce red tape and to address investor concerns. Vehicles have been established – a Red Tape Reduction unit and a One-Stop Shop – which complement rather than compete with each other. The city also has the lowest residential, commercial property and industrial property rates in the country.

Metro	Residential	Ranking	Commercial	Ranking	Industrial	Ranking
Buffalo City	R888.00	5	R2 221.00	6	R2 221.00	4
Nelson Mandela Bay	R974.00	8	R1 948.00	4	R2 434.00	5
Johannesburg	R612.00	2	R1 591.00	2	R1 591.00	2
Ekurhuleni	R815.00	4	R1 631.00	3	R2 040.00	3
Cape Town	R596.00	1	R1 192.00	1	R1 192.00	1
eThekwini	R933.00	6	R2 115.00	5	R2 729.00	7
Mangaung	R624.00	3	R2 564.00	7	R2 564.00	6
Tshwane	R967.00	7	R2 845.00	8	R2 845.00	8

Table 16.2: Comparative rates per city, 2018 financial year

The third big lesson we can learn from Cape Town is the value of partnerships. The Central City Improvement District, established as a public-private partnership in 2000, has been a real success in revitalising the central CBD, making it safer, cleaner and more vibrant.

Fixing the basics does not fix everything. Several challenges remain, including the need to ensure aviation links. The 'weight of history' is another constraint, whereby Johannesburg's commercial and consumer strength remains a significant business incentive. This is why Cape Town has focused on new sectors such as renewables, ICT and business process services. Moreover, that East London, Bloemfontein, Port Elizabeth, Cape Town and Durban are challenging Johannesburg 'should be a spur to national growth', Harris observed.

Finally, the 'absence of levers' remains a frustration and a disincentive to business. Top of the list is the challenge with the Department of Home Affairs and the issuing of permits and visas. Second, while the SEZs offer incentives, greater latitude by the provinces would again provide greater competition. Thirdly, Harris advocated the abolition of exchange controls, which disincentivise foreign investment.

Like most African cities, Cape Town has very limited scope to act independently of central government in dealing with its specific challenges – or, more positively, to play to its strengths. The reasons for this, as in other areas, come down to money and autonomy. Eighty per cent of the city's income comes from the premiums charged on utilities (especially electricity), property rates and other charges. The remainder comes from three sources: a tranche from the national government determined according to a country-wide formula; conditional grants from the Treasury (which remove the discretion for municipalities to spend as they may need to); and a portion of the fuel levy raised on sales within the municipal boundary. The vast proportion of these funds (like other municipal budgets) is spent on maintaining and expanding infrastructure, and delivering basic services, including water, electricity and refuse removal, on the back of that infrastructure. The shortage of funding is worsened by 'unfunded mandates', including library services and clinics.

This fiscal and political environment severely limits the room for manoeuvre of Cape Town and other South African cities to act independently in designing strong investment incentives. It can offer 'non-financial' incentives: accelerated planning approvals, biodiversity offsets, an investment facilitation touchpoint in the mayor's office, and the overall lifestyle advantages. On the financial side to support investments, the city has been able to offer discounted electricity tariffs and waive various application fees and development contributions that would normally be incurred by infrastructure projects. It can also offer discounted rates and land leases, though this is controversial within the administration, not least given the budgetary funding imperative.

Conclusion: Towards a new urban deal

In conclusion, it is evident that urbanisation and the growth of cities are inevitable facts. Countries must plan for urbanisation. At country level, we have the Integrated Urban Development Framework, which provides a relatively comprehensive framework for city planning and development. Worrying is the fact that over one-third of African countries have no urbanisation plans.

The National Treasury has developed a fairly comprehensive approach to shaping city development in line with the Integrated Urban Development Framework. This includes framing allocative decisions (conditional grants) around priorities of densification and inclusivity, and monitoring outcomes accordingly (through Circular 88). However, the next level of urban settlement – the secondary cities and large regional towns – currently has very weak control and support (through the Department of Cooperative Governance and Traditional Affairs). Many of these towns are bursting at the seams from in-migration, have weak governance, are bankrupt and have dilapidated infrastructure. This is a major area for attention going forward.

As good as the Integrated Urban Development Framework is, a country-level planning framework can only take you so far. Cities must develop their own plans as entry points for country-level urbanisation plans. A number of our cities have developed long-term growth and development strategies, but the extent to which these have been institutionalised and actually shape the Integrated Development Plan and budget planning is doubtful. Our cities need to up the game if they are to become globally competitive and able to navigate new risks associated with climate change.

Five sets of actions stand out at the centre of the new urban deal.

First, we must do more to encourage densification and making land available for human settlement close to economic opportunities. The private sector and banks must play their role. We must increase investment in strategic transport corridors and networks that connect marginalised residential areas with nodes of employment.

Second, cities must do more to attract and retain investment. This includes doing the basics well, cutting red tape, reducing the costs of doing business, and setting up politically backed investment promotion institutions.

Third, cities must ensure that the benefits of growth are shared. Part of the package must be inclusive innovation and technology transfer. This will require new kinds of partnerships with universities and the private sector, developing new platforms like technology hubs, incubators and innovation precincts.

Fourth, cities must get governance right. The starting point is to disentangle politics from local business interests. Good governance and new models of development cooperation must be politically championed. Local growth coalitions made up of state formations, established business and new entrant firms, universities and other stakeholders, must be assembled at city level to negotiate trade-offs and forge active partnerships. The new national consensus must find expression at local level.

Fifth, cities must prioritise financial sustainability and reduce dependence on the national fiscus. Revenue bases must be protected and expanded, and ratios of indigent to ratepayers carefully monitored. Innovative off-budget funding mechanisms must be utilised for large capital projects. Land parcels should be more effectively utilised for investment leveraging.

Conclusion

Getting the Politics Right

I believe that here in South Africa, with all our diversities of colour and race; we will show the world a new pattern for democracy. There is a challenge for us to set a new example for all. Let us not sidestep this task.
— Chief Albert Luthuli

The results of the 2019 election clearly show a decline in parties of the political centre and the growth in support for populist ideologues to the left and right. Perhaps more concerning, they show that, for the first time, less than half the adult population voted, with just a quarter supporting the winning party.

This rejection of political institutions and the accompanying rise in extra-parliamentary politics that is seen in service delivery protests are no accident. It is the result of more than two decades of growing unemployment and the exclusion of the youth from economic life. Unemployment has reached an astonishing 27.5%. Youth unemployment is believed to be as high as 50%.

The constituencies that benefited from the 1994 arrangement – established business, the new black elite and the trade unions – have begun to go their separate ways as their outlook hardens in the face of economic stagnation.

There are two attitudes to the 1994 deal that are pervasive. The first is nostalgic, viewing the arrangement as the foundation of the 'rainbow nation', emblematic of a time when South Africans broke out of their narrow ideological straitjackets and placed the national interest above all else. The second is outright cynicism, which views the 1994 consensus as a carve-up among elites with the interests of ordinary South Africans placed below those of the powerful.

Both are mistaken. It is far more useful to view the 1994 arrangement as a product of its time. It was, all those years ago, the only way that a peaceful, negotiated political settlement could be made to stick, and, whatever criticisms you might have of contemporary South Africa and its many faults, it has become a far better place to live in than it was back then.

Housing has been built on a vast scale and electricity, although flickering on and off due to recent failings, has been extended to far more people, as has access to potable water. South Africa has a social welfare network that effects a vast transfer of resources to the indigent, which places it at the forefront of the developing world.

But what was a necessary step forward in 1994 is now holding us back. It was primarily a political settlement with a Constitution protecting rights and exhorting the government to right the wrongs of the past. But it was silent about the economy, perhaps because the priority was to stop the bloodshed of apartheid's dying years and introduce democracy.

That economic policy lacuna has been filled by a succession of government plans to produce jobs and growth. With the exception of a few good years in the mid-2000s, which eventually collapsed under the weight of rising inflation, corruption in the form of state capture and a deteriorating global economy, these plans failed to keep pace with the growing numbers of people looking for work.

The evident policy confusion over the past two terms of government was a convenient cover for the accelerated looting of the state by corrupt and powerful people in business and in government.

Destructive disruption will be the logical outcome if there is a continuation of the 'muddling through' policy approach that has characterised the past decade, and if reformers in the ANC continue to lose the battle against those who consolidated their power under the old state-capture order.

If this situation persists, South Africa will see a continuation of the trends of the past decade: rent-seeking, corruption, declining state capacity and legitimacy, reduced investor confidence and fixed investment, economic stagnation, growing unemployment and inequality, and increased social tensions.

This scenario plays itself out like this: low growth and decreasing per capita income fuel frustration and discontent among the poor and lower-paid workers, with declining support for government and the ruling party. This creates a growing sense of crisis, with weakened revenue and legitimacy impacting on the state's ability to lead society out of the crisis. The ruling party turns to short-term populism to regain electoral support, at the direct expense of investment and employment. This further reinforces the vicious cycle of declining legitimacy, reduced investment, rising unemployment and increased social discord.

And as the political elite consolidates power around diminishing resources and rents, the room for buying acquiescence is reduced. The ability to increase the amount and reach of social grants is curtailed. This leads to growing authoritarianism, both to quell growing protest action and to weaken civil society demands for public accountability. This is a scenario we can ill afford. It would signal the end of the liberation project to entrench human rights and people's dignity.

The need for constructive disruption

What is needed is 'constructive disruption', which ushers in fundamental institutional and economic reform. And the two must go together. As our recent past demonstrates, strong institutions matter and shape the economic prospects of countries. Where economic governance is inclusive, countries are more likely to have shared and sustained prosperity. At the same time, institutions reflect the accumulation logic of different economies. Where wealth is created through rent-seeking, as opposed to innovation and productivity, institutions will always be under threat.

This presents something of a chicken and egg paradox – inclusive institutions are required to restructure an economy towards higher and more shared growth, but elite interests controlling rents actively prevent the necessary innovation and institutional change. The question is how to break this pattern.

South Africa finds itself in a middle-income trap, unable to compete in the low-skill, labour-intensive industries where low-income countries enjoy competitiveness, and without the spread of technological know-how and human capabilities to compete with high-income countries in more sophisticated industries and services. The result has been increasing deindustrialisation and a growth slowdown. Poor education, skills and a dearth of innovation outcomes have meant that the country has been unable to transition to higher-value activities. Less opportunity for wealth creation in the real economy has increased the stakes in the parallel, clientelist economy. This, in turn, has weakened the state and those very institutions central to inclusive growth.

This suggests that the break – the constructive disruption – must be sharp, deliberate and aimed simultaneously at impacting on the economy and state institutions. Minor and incremental policy changes at the margins will not be sufficient to change our development path. Instead, we require immediate and significant interventions at scale to create dynamism and confidence in the economy and institutions.

The need for new national obsessions

We need to build the momentum for a newly invigorated state and a growing and inclusive economy. Achieving this is not just about having 'the right person at the top', although obviously this is an important success factor. It is rather about embedding a change agenda in a diverse range of interest groups – political formations, the state, trade unions, civil society and business. We need to create new national obsessions around which stakeholders can cohere and push difficult policy decisions that will break our low-growth, high-inequality trap. This societal mobilisation is vital to combat the fightback by those hell-bent on destroying institutions that limit looting and rent-seeking.

The new consensus must be built on the logic that we need both growth and transformation. Economic growth without transformation will reproduce and exacerbate inequalities, which will make growth unsustainable; transformation without growth will lead to less investment, jobs and wealth to redistribute, which will trigger elite conflict, making any consensus impossible to manage.

There are three national obsessions around which we need to build consensus and mobilise.

An obsession with inclusive growth

The first is inclusive growth. In the immediate term this means putting jobs at the centre of economic policy while we restructure towards higher productivity and higher value-added activities. This will require new policy measures, including subsidies and incentives to encourage labour-intensive production.

Our obsession with inclusive growth should also tackle constraints on competitiveness and investment. These should be identified and resolved in collaboration with the private sector at industry level. In the immediate term, red tape can be cut to reduce bureaucratic burdens, taxation and onerous compliance processes, especially for small business. In the more medium term, we need to drastically cut costs of business, including port charges, costs of broadband and energy, and costs associated with cross-border trade. We must also nurture a new obsession with research and development and technology development and application, working with our tertiary education sector. The necessary fiscal instruments for this must be developed with urgency. The finance sector (including pension funds) needs to be intensely engaged to redirect new resources for productive capital expansion, including venture capital for technology development and start-ups.

Growth will generate much-needed revenue for the fiscus, which will allow us to expand transfers to the poor. This will begin to reverse levels of inequality, but will only be sustained if complemented by real shifts in wealth and asset ownership. This will require new sets of trade-offs, which need to be negotiated with the private sector and banking sector. These trade-offs must be at the heart of the industry-level compacts that will be negotiated as part of the consensus for inclusive growth.

An obsession with quality public education and training

Good-quality basic education is both a development goal itself and a crucial ingredient of economic development. It is crucial to the supply of skills necessary to run a modern, complex, competitive and expanding industrial economy. We have made huge strides in improving access to education, but the quality of this education leaves much to be desired. Despite the relatively high fiscal allocations to the sector, our basic education system has very poor learner outcomes by international comparison (in literacy, numeracy, problem solving and especially maths and science).

Our broken education and skills pipeline both exacerbates inequality and reduces economic competitiveness. In the short term, we need to radically improve school performance and accountability, the starting point of which would be to appoint competent school principals (and remove incompetent ones). We need to implement vigorous programmes for teacher retraining and development. All stakeholders must come on board.

In the immediate term we also need to relax visa requirements for the importation of scarce and critical skills, and even consider importing maths and science educators as required. Medium-term outcomes include strengthening early childhood development, which is critical to cognitive development. We must also fix and reconfigure the post-schooling vocation system to align the Technical and Vocational Education and Training Colleges and Sector Education and Training Authorities to the changing needs of the labour market. Similarly, the restructuring of the higher education sector must embrace a more dynamic understanding of the future economy.

An obsession with a stronger, more capable and less corrupt state

The third national obsession we need to cultivate as part of the new consensus relates to state capability and orientation. The extent to which the South African state was captured and repurposed for corrupt gain is a matter of public knowledge. Highly abusive patronage networks have become deeply embedded across state formations, and have eroded public service delivery, interfered with good governance and accountability, and destroyed the legitimacy of the state.

255

Important work has started to dismantle these patronage networks, especially in the state-owned enterprises (SOEs), and rebuild the security cluster to impartially uphold the rule of law as prescribed in the Constitution. This must be accelerated. Important going forward will be to dismantle these abusive networks in local and regional politics and governance institutions, where their impact on service delivery is possibly even more damaging.

Our work on state-building should start with stabilising our SOEs. Some SOEs, such as Eskom, bring contingent liability risks that, if not managed, actually threaten national sovereignty. In finding solutions, we must move away from rigid ideological positions, which have been used to serve and protect rent-seeking interests (masquerading as some kind of redistributive outcome). The state has a key role to play in correcting market failure, but we must be more alert to state failure and cognisant of the veiled interests that underpin some state decision-making. And where state-owned enterprises are using their monopoly positions in value chains to crowd out private investment and reinforce uncompetitive pricing, we need to take heavy-handed and decisive action.

In the short term we also must reduce consumption expenditure in favour of capital expenditure. Government's balance sheet has deteriorated with rising expenditure on wages and salaries, leaving less and less money for spending on service delivery and on infrastructure that enables economic growth. More money needs to be spent on creating an enabling environment for investment.

Part of reducing consumption spending must involve the reconsideration of the shape and structure of the state. President Cyril Ramaphosa has started consolidating the number of ministries, but far more is needed to address wastage and inefficiencies across the three spheres. We need urgently to implement practical solutions to address the service delivery challenges presented by the increasing number of unviable municipalities that are incapable of playing the developmental role they were established to perform.

Our record of executing policy and plans, especially over terms of government, suggests much room for improvement. This requires immediate attention. Without the necessary coherence, coordinating capacity and accountability, the new consensus that is being proposed will be stillborn.

The other deal-breaker for realising the new consensus is leadership, and the extent to which leadership across all formations has the appetite and maturity to put the national interest above narrow sectarian interests. To unite opposing and disparate interests in society behind a common agenda – and to manage those who cannot or will not be accommodated – will require a special kind of leadership: one that is able to make hard choices, placate the growing impatience among our people, and not succumb to populist solutions that may win the day but take us nowhere on the broader journey to restructuring the economy and society.

Acknowledgements

I considered writing a book for some time about the current political and economic moment in South Africa. But, as with any process that requires recording one's opinions and observations, I wanted to be absolutely sure that what I wrote would be relevant and useful to the national debate on how to progress our young democracy. I knew what I did not want, which was an autobiographical account of my experiences. I also knew what I wanted, which was to write a book that would fill that fairly awkward space between the nexus where economic growth meets the political economy but without losing the colloquialism of a read that would touch as wide an audience as possible. Answering the question of who my audience was raised some doubtful eyebrows when I explained that it was the array of constituencies that make our country whole.

I am not sure I have succeeded, but I do hope that this book helps to navigate committed South Africans, from all walks of life, who want to shepherd our country forward.

In this regard, I would like to thank the following people, who, at different stages of this book writing process, have been of great support:

About 20 people, all experts in their various fields, gave up invaluable family time to spend a weekend with us to critique an early draft of the book. Their feedback was instrumental in shaping the final product. They know who they are.

Professor Haroon Bhorat and his team provided critical support in checking that the data I use in the book is accurate, up to date and properly interpreted. Thank you to Solly Mapaila for his frank ideological engagement with the ideas, to Malusi Mpumlwana for his responses to the early drafts of the book and to Andrew Murray for his consistent support through the writing process. Thanks to Gillian Saunders, Ivor Chipkin, Ismail Momoniat and Ester Levinrad for their input. Several young people contributed to the process, especially Nomonde Ndwalaza, Lufefe Mkutu, Thabi Nkosi and Faith Pienaar. Their input was vital given my hope that this book will make a difference to the country's future. I also thank Mavuso Msimang for his wise counsel.

Greg Mills, an old friend, finally convinced me to take the plunge and write the book.

Ray Hartley, also an old friend, waded through reams of my previous writing to put form to an early draft of the book, and then gently nudged the process forward, as did Emily van der Merwe.

Thank you to Nomboniso Gasa, Raymond Suttner and Saul Musker for their contributions.

To Sis Daphne Mashile Nkosi and Enoch Godongwana for their advice along the way.

To the publisher Pan Macmillan, and in particular Andrea Nattrass, for their patience in driving this project to completion. Sally Hines, the editor, has worked tirelessly incorporating our multitude of changes without complaint.

Thank you to President Cyril Ramaphosa for his engagement with the manuscript and for writing the Foreword.

Finally, thank you to my family and friends who have steadfastly supported me.

Notes

All the website references in the notes below were working links when accessed during the researching and writing of this book.

Introduction: Can We Prosper?
1 See https://data.worldbank.org/indicator/SE.XPD.TOTL.GD.ZS.
2 South Africa today ranks in the bottom half of the 178 states measured by the Fragile States Index, published annually by the Fund for Peace. It is in the 'elevated warning' category, in which 15 of the 20 most vulnerable countries are African.
3 See https://data.worldbank.org/indicator/NY.GDP.MKTP.KD.ZG?end=2017&locations=ZA&start=1994.
4 Doi Moi is the term used to describe Vietnamese economic reforms implemented in the mid-1980s with the aim of creating a market economy within a socialist framework.
5 See https://data.worldbank.org/indicator/NY.GDP.PCAP.KD?locations=ZA.
6 Alec Hogg, 'Eskom: How It Turned from World's Best to Basket Case in 15 years', *BizNews*, 8 June 2015, https://www.biznews.com/undictated/2015/06/08/eskom-how-it-turned-from-worlds-best-to-basket-case-in-15-years.
7 Department of Finance, 'Budget Review 22 June 1994', http://www.treasury.gov.za/documents/national%20budget/Budget%20Review%201994.pdf.
8 Department of Finance, 'Growth, Employment and Redistribution: A Macroeconomic Strategy', http://www.treasury.gov.za/publications/other/gear/chapters.pdf.

Chapter 1: Eight Economic Realities
1 'Freedom Charter', 26 June 1955, https://www.sahistory.org.za/archive/74-freedom-charter-1955.
2 Antonio Gramsci, *Selections from the Prison Notebooks*, edited and translated by Quentin Hoare and Geffrey Nowell Smith. London: Lawrence & Wishart, 1971.
3 See http://www.treasury.gov.za/documents/national%20budget/2010/review/chapter3.pdf.
4 Stats SA, 'Quarterly Labour Force Survey Q2: 2018', http://www.statssa.gov.za/?p=11361.
5 'National Income Dynamics Study 2017, Wave 5', Southern Africa Labour and Development Research Unit, University of Cape Town. 2017.
6 GroundUp, 'Why is South Africa's Unemployment so High?' *Daily Maverick*, 14 February 2019, https://www.dailymaverick.co.za/article/2019-02-14-why-is-south-africas-unemployment-rate-so-high/.

7 Data released by Stats SA reveals that 40% of South Africans live below the lower-bound poverty line (R758 per month) and 55.5% of South Africans live below the upper-bound poverty line (R1 138 per month). See https://africacheck.org/factsheets/factsheet-south-africas-official-poverty-numbers/.

8 Nora Lustig, 'The Redistributive Impact of Government Spending on Education and Health: Evidence from Thirteen Developing Countries in the Commitment to the Equity Project', Working Paper No. 30, 2015, https://econpapers.repec.org/paper/tulceqwps/30.htm.

9 Haroon Bhorat, Safia Khan and Kezia Lilenstein, 'Labour Legislation, Active Labour Market Policy and Trade Unions in South Africa: Current Context and Future Trends', Development Policy Research Unit, University of Cape Town, 2018, p.11.

10 South African Reserve Bank, 'Quarterly Bulletin', No. 290, December 2018, https://www.resbank.co.za/Lists/News%20and%20Publications/Attachments/8985/01Full%20Quarterly%20Bulletin%20%E2%80%93%20December%202018.pdf.

11 World Trade Organization, 'Doha Ministerial Declaration', 2001, https://www.wto.org/english/thewto_e/minist_e/min01_e/mindecl_e.htm.

12 Gregory Ireland and Jesse Burton, 'An Assessment of New Coal Plants in South Africa's Electricity Future', Energy Research Centre, University of Cape Town, 2018.

13 World Bank, *South Africa – Systemic Country Diagnostic: An Incomplete Transition – Overcoming the Legacy of Exclusion in South Africa*. Washington, D.C.: World Bank Group, 2018.

14 'R10bn in Mining Investment Forfeited Yearly', *IOL*, 7 November 2006, https://www.iol.co.za/business-report/economy/r10bn-in-mining-investment-forfeited-yearly-826081.

15 Credit Suisse, *Credit Suisse Global Investment Returns Yearbook*, 2017, p.41.

16 See http://www.statssa.gov.za/?p=11129.

17 Enno de Boer, Diego Hernandez Diaz and Helena Leurent, 'The Fourth Industrial Revolution and the Factories of the Future', 17 August 2018, https://www.mckinsey.com/business-functions/operations/our-insights/operations-blog/the-fourth-industrial-revolution-and-the-factories-of-the-future.

18 'Full List – Here is Ramaphosa's New Cabinet', *Businesstech*, 29 May 2019, https://businesstech.co.za/news/government/319988/full-list-here-is-ramaphosas-new-cabinet/.

Chapter 2: The Developmental State Remains Elusive

1 CST is a South African Communist Party formulation of the apartheid era as 'colonialism of a special type'. The idea of CST was that the shape of apartheid society was conditioned by its colonial history, and that colonialism persisted in the division of South Africans into a rich elite (white) and an oppressed, impoverished underclass (black).

2 Russell Wildeman and Wellington Jogo, *Implementing the Public Finance Management Act in South Africa: How Far Are We?* Cape Town: Institute for Democracy in South Africa, 2012, p.18.

3 Ivor Chipkin and Mark Swilling, *Shadow State: The Politics of State Capture*. Johannesburg: Wits University Press, 2018.

4 Auditor-General South Africa, 'Auditor-General Laments Lack of Accountability as He Releases Declining Local Government Audit Results', Media Statement, 2017, http://www.agsa.co.za/Portals/O/ReportsMFMA/201617/Media%20Release/2016%20-17%MFMA%20Media%20Release.pdf?ver=2018-05-23-082131-353. For more detail see Auditor-General South Africa, *MFMA 2016–2017: Consolidated General Report on Local Government Audit Outcomes*. Pretoria: AGSA, 2017. In particular, the report notes 'accountability continues to fail in local government' (p.10).

Chapter 3: Successes and Failures of Policy

1 See https://afrobarometer.org/sites/default/files/publications/Summary%20of%20results/saf_r7_sor_13112018.pdf.

2 Alex Harrowell, 'The Populist Papers: 29 Years of Populism', 7 March 2017, http://fistfulofeuros. net/afoe/the-populist-papers-29-years-of-populism/.

3 Stats SA. 'Poverty Trends in South Africa: An Examination of Absolute Poverty between 2006 and 2015', 2017, p.19, http://www.statssa.gov.za/publications/Report-03-10-06/Report-03-10-062015.pdf.

4 Municipal IQ, '3 Key Trends from 2018's All-Time Service Delivery Protest Record', 16 January 2019, https://www.municipaliq.co.za/index.php?site_page=press.php.

5 Ibid.

6 Ibid.

7 See https://www.resbank.co.za/Lists/News%20and%20Publications/Attachments/9136/04%20 April%202019.pdf.

8 See https://wwwrs.resbank.co.za/webindicators/MonthlyIndicators.aspx?DataType=MRDMA.

9 See https://www.resbank.co.za/Lists/News%20and%20Publications/ Attachments/7870/20170630Long%20term%20trends%20in%20credit%20extension%20to%20 households%20and%20corporates.pdf.

10 Haroon Bhorat, Safia Khan and Kezia Lilenstein, 'Labour Legislation, Active Labour Market Policy and Trade Unions in South Africa: Current Context and Future Trends', Development Policy Research Unit, University of Cape Town, 2018, p.11.

11 National Treasury, 'Employment Tax Incentive Descriptive Report', August 2016, http://www. treasury.gov.za/comm_media/press/2016/20160810%20-%20ETI%20descriptive%20memo%20 With%20Exec%20summ%20For%20Nedlac.pdf.

12 Haroon Bhorat, Karmen Naidoo, Morné Oosthuizen and Kavisha Pillay, 'Demographic, Employment, and Wage Trends in South Africa', WIDER Working Paper 2015/141, https://www. wider.unu.edu/sites/default/files/wp2015-141.pdf.

13 Stats SA, 'General Household Survey 2016', https://www.statssa.gov.za/publications/P0318/ P03182016.pdf.

14 Anna Orthofer, 'Wealth Inequality in South Africa: Evidence from Survey and Tax Data', REDI3x3 Working Paper 15, June 2016, http://www.redi3x3.org/sites/default/files/Orthofer%202016%20 REDI3x3%20Working%20Paper%2015%20-%20Wealth%20inequality.pdf.

Chapter 4: State-Owned Enterprises and the Growing Burden of Debt

1 See https://pmg.org.za/briefing/26382/.

2 'State Capture and the Economics of Corruption: The Case of Transnet', Development Policy Research Unit, University of Cape Town, February 2019, forthcoming.

3 Total SOE capex for the same group has declined since 2010 when it reached R212 billion. See 'Betrayal of the Promise: How South Africa is Being Stolen', Public Affairs Research Institute, 25 May 2017, https://pari.org.za/betrayal-promise-report/.

4 Nancy L. Clark, Manufacturing Apartheid: State Corporations in South Africa. New Haven: Yale University Press, 1994, p.43.

5 Clarke, Manufacturing Apartheid, p.48.

6 For a full account of this policy shift, see OECD, State-Owned Enterprises in the Development Process. Paris: OECD Publishing, 2015.

7 See http://www.dpe.gov.za/newsroom/Pages/Address-by-Minister-Malusi-Gigaba-MP,-on-the-occasion-of-a-business-breakfast-hosted-by-the-Black-Management-Forum-(BMF)-in.aspx.

8 National Planning Commission, 'Our Future – Make It Work: National Development Plan 2030: Executive Summary', 2012, p.28, https://www.gov.za/sites/default/files/Executive%20Summary-NDP%202030%20-%20Our%20future%20-%20make%20it%20work.pdf.

9 Department of Trade and Industry, 'Industrial Policy Action Plan 2018/19–2020/21', 2018, https:// www.gov.za/st/node/779706.

10 Department of Economic Development, 'The New Growth Path', 2011, www.gov.za/about-government/government-programmes/new-growth-path.

11 Department of Planning, Monitoring and Evaluation, 'Medium-Term Strategic Framework 2014–2019', 2014, https://www.gov.za/documents/medium-term-strategic-framework-2014-2019.

12 Sunita Kikeri, *Corporate Governance in South African State-Owned Enterprises : Background Note for the South Africa Systematic Country Diagnostic (English)*. Washington, D.C. : World Bank Group, 2018, http://documents.worldbank.org/curated/en/798071529303940965/Corporate-governance-in-South-African-state-owned-enterprises-background-note-for-the-South-Africa-systematic-country-diagnostic.

13 State Capacity Research Project, 'Betrayal of the Promise: How South Africa is Being Stolen', 2017, https://pari.org.za/wp-content/uploads/2017/05/Betrayal-of-the-Promise-25052017.pdf.

14 Ibid.

15 Matthew Hart, 'How to Steal a Diamond', *The Atlantic*, March 1999, https://www.theatlantic.com/magazine/archive/1999/03/how-to-steal-a-diamond/305488/.

16 See 'Commanding Plights: South Africa's State-Owned Companies', *The Economist*, 27 August 2015, https://www.economist.com/middle-east-and-africa/2015/08/27/commanding-plights.

17 For a full account of these appointments and their effect on Alexkor, see Richard Poplak, 'Alexkor Meltdown: Northern Cape's State-Owned Enterprise Non-Gift that Keeps on Giving', *Daily Maverick*, 11 June 2018, https://www.dailymaverick.co.za/article/2018-06-11-trainspotter-alexkor-meltdown-northern-capes-state-owned-enterprise-non-gift-that-keeps-on-taking/.

18 See the report by amaBhungane and Scorpio, 'A Tale of Two Captures: Alexkor, Gupta Inc and "WMC"', *Daily Maverick*, 13 December 2017, https://www.dailymaverick.co.za/article/2017-12-13-amabhungane-and-scorpio-guptaleaks-a-tale-of-two-captures-alexkor-gupta-inc-and-wmc/#.Wx1PX1OFPOQ.

19 Cited in Poplak, 'Alexkor Meltdown'.

20 See https://www.gov.za/speeches/budget_vote.

21 NERSA agreed to a 9.41% hike for 2019/20, translating into an effective rate increase of 13.8%, more than double the inflation rate.

22 See their statement in J.P. Casey, 'South Africa Risks 150,000 Mining Jobs if Eskom Electricity Tariff Increase Goes Ahead', *Mining Technology*, 30 January 2019, https://www.mining-technology.com/news/south-africa-risks-150000-mining-jobs-if-eskom-electricity- tariff-increase-goes-ahead/.

23 'Eskom Looting Could be as Much as R500 Billion', *BusinessTech*, 24 February 2019, https://businesstech.co.za/news/energy/301496/eskom-looting-could-be-as-much-as-r500-billion report/.

24 Melanie Gosling, 'Eskom and the Multi-Billion Rand Mega Projects that Could Have Saved SA', *fin24*, 13 February 2019, https://www.fin24.com/Economy/eskom-and-the-multi-billion-rand-mega-projects-that-could-have-saved-sa-20190213.

25 Interview anonymous.

26 Interview, anonymous.

27 Telephonic interview, 19 March 2019.

28 See https://www.resbank.co.za/Lists/News%20and%20Publications/Attachments/8985/01Full%20Quarterly%20Bulletin%20–%20December%202018.pdf.

29 'South African Airways is on Verge of Bankruptcy', *BBC News*, 3 August 2017, https://www.bbc.co.uk/news/business-40813582.

30 For a full account of their agreement, see the amaBhungane exposé titled 'Gupta Link in R647m Train Deal', 20 May 2018, https://amabhungane.org/stories/gupta-link-in-r647m-train-deal/.

31 At the time of writing, the Werksmans report was publicly available at https://www.dropbox.com/sh/jfyps27c17evb83/AAAHALEIY7p_qlvK4aqUzT0xa?dl=0.

32 According to the Auditor-General of South Africa, *Annual Report 2017/2018*, www.agsa.co.za/.

33 Bekezela Phakathi, 'Finances at SABC are so Dire That It Cannot Pay Content Providers', *Business Day*, 2 August 2018, https://www.businesslive.co.za/bd/national/2018-08-02-finances-at-sabc-are-so-dire-that-it-cannot-pay-content-providers/.

34 Linda Ensor, 'SABC's Financial Year Loss of R622 million is Somewhat Less Terrible than 2017's Figure', *Business Day*, 3 September 2018, https://www.businesslive.co.za/bd/companies/2018-09-03-sabcs-financial-year-loss-of-r622m-is-somewhat-less-terrible-than-2017s-figure/.
35 'South African Airways is on "Verge of Bankruptcy"', *BBC News*, 3 August 2017, https://www.bbc.co.uk/news/business-40813582.
36 Genevieve Quintal, 'Denel Posts Dismal Financial Reports, Again', *Business Day*, 31 October 2018, https://www.businesslive.co.za/bd/national/2018-10-31-denel-posts-dismal-financial-results-again/.
37 Genevieve Quintal, 'Government Extends Denel Guarantee to 2023', *Business Day*, 29 October 2018, https://www.businesslive.co.za/bd/national/2018-10-29-government-extends-denel-guarantee-to-2023/.
38 See Caiphus Kgosana, 'State-Owned Entities are "Sewers of Corruption": Ramaphosa', *The Times*, 31 May 2018, https://www.timeslive.co.za/news/south-africa/2018-05-31-state-owned-enterprises-are-sewers-of-corruption-ramaphosa/.
39 OECD, *State-Owned Enterprises in the Development Process*. Paris: OECD Publishing, 2015, p.168.
40 Ibid.
41 Stephan Hofstatter, *Licence to Loot: How the Plunder of Eskom and Other Parastatals Almost Sank South Africa*. Johannesburg: Penguin, 2018.

Chapter 5: Schools but No Learning

1 Thokazani Mathebula, 'People's Education (for People's Power) – A Promise Fulfilled', *South African Journal of Education* 33(1), January 2013, http://www.scielo.org.za/scielo.php?script=sci_arttext&pid=S0256-01002013000100002.
2 *Back to Learning: The National Education Conference*. Johannesburg: Ravan Press, 1992, pp.8–9.
3 Nic Spaull, 'Strategies for Long-Term Prosperity', 22 November 2018, https://www.sun.ac.za/english/faculty/economy/Documents/N_Spaull_RamaphosaRoundtable.pdf.
4 Ibid.
5 Ibid.
6 Unicef, 'Education Budget South Africa, 2017/2018', 2017, https://www.unicef.org/esaro/UNICEF_South_Africa_--_2017_--_Education_Budget_Brief.pdf.
7 See work by Nic Spaull at https://nicspaull.com/presentations/.
8 See, for example, Raj Mestry, 'Empowering Principals to Lead and Manage Public Schools Effectively in the 21st Century', *South African Journal of Education* 37(1), February 2017; and Mgadla Isaac Xaba, 'The Possible Causes of School Governance Challenges in South Africa', *South African Journal of Education* 31(2), January 2011.
9 Ashley Westaway, 'Towards an Explanation of the Functionality of South Africa's "Dysfunctional" Schools', February 2015, https://www.ru.ac.za/media/rhodesuniversity/content/uhuru/documents/Functionality_of_SAs_dysfunctional_schools.pdf.
10 Gertrude Makhafola, 'MEC Exposes Corruption at Joburg School', *IOL*, 10 August 2015, https://www.iol.co.za/news/south-africa/gauteng/mec-exposes-corruption-at-joburg-school-1897684.
11 'Report of the Ministerial Task Team Appointed by Minister Angie Motshekga on the Selling of Posts of Educators by Members of Teachers Unions and Departmental Officials in Provincial Education Departments', 18 May 2016, p.199, https://nicspaull.files.wordpress.com/2016/05/dbe-2016-volmink-report.pdf.
12 Spaull, 'Strategies for Long-Term Prosperity'.
13 Tertiary students are handicapped by poor basic education. Moreover, Technical and Vocational Education and Training (TVET) colleges and Sector Education and Training Authorities (SETAs) are of dubious quality.

Chapter 6: Youth Exclusion

1 'NDP: Population Profile Poses Opportunity', 15 August 2012, https://www.iol.co.za/business-report/economy/ndp-population-profile-poses-opportunity-1363179.
2 Claire Bisseker, 'SA's Unemployment Moderates, but No Cause for Celebration', *Financial Mail*, 14 February 2019, https://www.businesslive.co.za/fm/fm-fox/2019-02-14-sas-unemployment-moderates-but-no-cause-for-celebration/.
3 Stats SA, 'Quarterly Labour Force Survey: Quarter 1: 2019', http://www.statssa.gov.za/publications/P0211/P02111stQuarter2019.pdf.
4 The Economist, *Pocket World in Figures 2019*. London: Profile Books.
5 See http://www.statssa.gov.za/?p=12121.
6 Department of Higher Education and Training, 'Statistics on Post-School Education and Training in South Africa', 2016, http://www.dhet.gov.za/Research%20Coordination%20Monitoring%20and%20Evaluation/6_DHET%20Stats%20Report_04%20April%202018.pdf.
7 See http://www.statssa.gov.za/wp-content/uploads/2019/05/Youthdatastorygraph.jpg.
8 See https://equaleducation.org.za/2017/01/09/matric-results-and-south-africas-youth-unemployment-crisis/.
9 Bongani Nkosi, 'Of the 18% of Matrics Registered at Universities, Half Drop Out', 21 May 2015, https://mg.co.za/article/2015-05-21-18-of-matrics-register-at-universities-half-drop-out.
10 Haroon Bhorat, Arabo Ewinyu, Kezia Lilenstein, Christopher Rooney, François Steenkamp and Amy Thornton, 'Economic Complexity and Employment Expansion: The Case of South Africa', Development Policy Research Unit, University of Cape Town, September 2017.
11 Stats SA, 'Quarterly Labour Force Survey: Quarter 1: 2019', http://www.statssa.gov.za/publications/P0211/P02111stQuarter2019.pdf.
12 See Gordon Hands, 'Roberto Michels and the Study of Political Parties', *British Journal of Political Science* 1(2), April 1971, https://www.jstor.org/stable/193505?seq=1#page_scan_tab_contents.

Chapter 7: Politics: The More Things Change, the More They Stay the Same

1 The adult population figure was derived from Stats SA population estimates with two-thirds of the 15–19 age cohort being counted as 'adult'.
2 Joel Netshitenzhe, 'Competing Identities of a National Liberation Movement Versus Electoral Party Politics: Challenges of Incumbency', 31 May 2012, https://cisp.cachefly.net/assets/articles/attachments/40100_competing_identities.pdf.
3 Ibid.
4 Ibid.
5 Ibid.
6 Gwede Mantashe, 'Organisational Report to 54th ANC Conference', 19 December 2017, https://www.politicsweb.co.za/documents/gwede-mantashes-organisational-report-to-54th-anc-.
7 Ibid.
8 eNCA, 'ANC Faces 5 Court Battles just Days before Conference', 11 December 2017, https://www.enca.com/south-africa/5-days-to-conference-anc-faces-court-battles-in-5-provinces.
9 Gwede Mantashe, 'Organisational Report to 54th ANC Conference', 19 December 2017, https://www.politicsweb.co.za/documents/gwede-mantashes-organisational-report-to-54th-anc-.
10 'Constitution of the Republic of South Africa, 1996 – Preamble', https://www.gov.za/documents/constitution-republic-south-africa-1996-preamble.
11 Public Protector South Africa, 'Secure in Comfort', March 2014, https://cdn.24.co.za/files/Cms/General/d/2718/00b91b2841d64510b9c99ef9b9faa597.pdf.
12 Ibid.
13 Constitutional Court of South Africa, Cases CCT 143/15 and CCT 171/15, https://cdn.24.co.za/files/Cms/General/d/3834/24efe59744c642a1a02360235f4d026b.pdf.
14 Ibid.

15 Ibid.
16 Pierre de Vos, 'Public Protector: Court Judgment Provides More Evidence of Incompetence and Misconduct', *Daily Maverick*, 21 May 2019, https://www.dailymaverick.co.za/article/2019-05-21-public-protector-court-judgment-provides-more-evidence-of-incompetence-and-misconduct/.
17 Ibid.

Chapter 8: Setting the Basis for a New Agenda

1 Stats SA, Community Survey 2016, http://www.statssa.gov.za/?page_id=6283.
2 Both these figures are generously more than at present.
3 See Stats SA, General Household Survey 2015, http://www.statssa.gov.za/?p=7765.
4 See Anna Orthofer, 'Wealth Inequality: Striking New Insights from Tax Data', *Econ 3x3*, 24 July 2016, http://www.econ3x3.org/article/wealth-inequality-%E2%80%93-striking-new-insights-tax-data.
5 Haroon Bhorat, Karmen Naidoo, Morné Oosthuizen and Kavisha Pillay. 'Demographic, Employment, and Wage Trends in South Africa', WIDER Working Paper 2015/141, December 2015, https://www.wider.unu.edu/sites/default/files/wp2015-141.pdf.
6 The national lower-bound poverty line is equivalent to US$3.50 (purchasing power parity) a day. The national poverty line was updated in 2011 to make it more relevant to the current average basket of consumption goods.
7 Nora Lustig, 'Inequality and Fiscal Redistribution in Middle Income Countries: Brazil, Chile, Colombia, Indonesia, Mexico, Peru and South Africa', Commitment to Equity Working Paper Series, No. 31, Department of Economics, Tulane University, 2015.
8 Arden Finn, Murray Leibbrandt and Vimal Ranchhod, 'Patterns of Persistence: Intergenerational Mobility and Education in South Africa', South African Labour and Development Research Unit, October 2017, http://opensaldru.uct.ac.za/handle/11090/830.
9 Including financial intermediation, insurance, real estate and business services (including the legal profession, built-environment professionals and labour brokers).
10 See http://microdata.worldbank.org/index.php/catalog/1790/study-description.
11 See, for example, Arthur M. Okun, *Equality and Efficiency: The Big Tradeoff*. Washington, D.C.: Brookings Institution Press, 2015.
12 Raquel Ramos, Rafael Ranieri and Jan-Willem Lammes, 'Mapping Inclusive Growth', Working Paper No. 105, International Policy Centre for Inclusive Growth, https://econpapers.repec.org/paper/ipcwpaper/105.htm.
13 African Development Bank, 'Briefing Notes for AfDB's Long-Term Strategy', Briefing Note 6, 10 April 2012, https://www.afdb.org/fileadmin/uploads/afdb/Documents/Policy-Documents/FINAL%20Briefing%20Note%206%20Inclusive%20Growth.pdf.

Chapter 9: A Conducive Environment for Investment and Business

1 See http://www.statssa.gov.za/?p=11983.

Chapter 10: A Twenty-First-Century Economy

1 See https://data.worldbank.org/indicator/NY.ADJ.NNTY.PC.KD.ZG?locations=ZA.
2 Haroon Bhorat, Arabo Ewinyu, Kezia Lilenstein, Christopher Rooney, François Steenkamp and Amy Thornton, 'Economic Complexity and Employment Expansion: The Case of South Africa', September 2017, Development Political Research Institute, University of Cape Town, p.3.
3 See Haroon Bhorat and Morné Oosthuizen, 'Foresight Africa 2015: The Pursuit of Inclusive Growth in South Africa – Constraints and Opportunities', *Brookings*, 29 January 2015, https://

www.brookings.edu/blog/africa-in-focus/2015/01/29/foresight-africa-2015-the-pursuit-of-inclusive-growth-in-south-africa-constraints-and-opportunities.

4 Margaret S. McMillan and Dani Rodrik, 'Globalization, Structural Change and Productivity Growth', Working Paper 17143, National Bureau of Economic Research, https://www.nber.org/papers/w17143.pdf.

5 See http://atlas.cid.harvard.edu/learn/glossary.

6 Bhorat et al., 'Economic Complexity and Employment Expansion'.

7 Bhorat et al., 'Economic Complexity and Employment Expansion'.

8 Bhorat et al., 'Economic Complexity and Employment Expansion'.

9 Bhorat et al., 'Economic Complexity and Employment Expansion'.

10 Bhorat et al., 'Economic Complexity and Employment Expansion'.

11 Enno de Boer, Diego Hernandez Diaz and Helena Leurent, 'The Fourth Industrial Revolution and the Factories of the Future', 17 August 2018, https://www.mckinsey.com/business-functions/operations/our-insights/operations-blog/the-fourth-industrial-revolution-and-the-factories-of-the-future.

12 Parliamentary Monitoring Group, 'National Minimum Wage: Input by COSATU, NUMSA, SATAWU, Free Market Foundation & National Employers' Association of South Africa', 5 September 2014, https://pmg.org.za/committee-meeting/17489/.

13 Deloitte, 'An Overview of Electricity Consumption and Pricing in South Africa', 24 February 2017, http://www.eskom.co.za/Documents/EcoOverviewElectricitySA-2017.pdf.

14 According to the National Planning Commission, 'Our Future – Make it Work: National Development Plan 2030: Executive Summary', 2012, https://www.gov.za/sites/default/files/Executive%20Summary-NDP%202030%20-%20Our%20future%20-%20make%20it%20work.pdf.

15 Johann Kirsten and Wandile Sihlobo, 'Is South African Agriculture Really Dominated by Big Commercial Farms? Evidence Suggests Not', News24, 27 February 2019, https://www.news24.com/Analysis/is-south-african-agriculture-really-dominated-by-big-commercial-farms-evidence-suggests-not-20190227.

16 Wandile Sihlobo, 'How Does the Youth See Agriculture in South Africa?' Agricultural Economics Today, 18 May 2018, https://wandilesihlobo.com/2018/05/18/how-does-the-youth-see-agriculture-in-south-africa/.

Chapter 11: We Need a Legitimate and Capable State

1 'How Much Does Government Spend on Civil Servant Salaries', IOL, 24 October 2018, https://www.iol.co.za/business-report/economy/how-much-does-government-spend-on-civil-servant-salaries-17615778.

2 Genevieve Quintal, 'New NPA Chief Batohi Stresses Good Governance and Independence', Business Day, 4 December 2018, https://www.businesslive.co.za/bd/national/2018-12-04-new-npa-chief-batohi-stresses-good-governance-and-independence/.

3 Ibid.

Chapter 12: State-Owned Enterprises Must Become Smart Growth Enablers

1 See the extensive analysis in Chris Yelland, 'Understanding the Cost of Electricity from Medupi, Kusile and IPPs', Engineering News, 21 July 2016, http://www.ee.co.za/article/understanding-cost-electricity-medupi-kusile-ipps.html/.

2 Dirk de Vos, 'Eskom, Tariffs, Bailouts and IPPs: Let's Cut through the Chaos', Daily Maverick, 20 February 2019, https://www.dailymaverick.co.za/article/2019-02-20-eskom-tariffs-bailouts-and-ipps-lets-cut-through-the-chaos/.

3 Isabel Sim, 'Does State Capitalism Work in Singapore? A Study on Ownership, Performance and Corporate Governance of Singapore's Government-Linked Companies', University of Western

Australia Business School, 2011, https://research-repository.uwa.edu.au/en/publications/does-state-capitalism-work-in-singapore-a-study-on-ownership-perf.

4 'Presidential Review Committee on State-Owned Entities', 30 April 2013, https://www.gov.za/documents/report-presidential-review-committee-prc-state-owned-entities-soes.

5 Ibid.

6 World Bank Group, *An Incomplete Transition: Overcoming the Legacy of Exclusion in South Africa*. Washington, D.C.: World Bank, 2018, p.4.

7 'Presidential Review Committee on State-Owned Entities', Volume 1, https://www.gov.za/sites/default/files/gcis_document/201409/presreview.pdf.

8 World Bank Group, *An Incomplete Transition*, p.8.

9 National Planning Commission, 'Our Future – Make it Work: National Development Plan 2030: Executive Summary', 2012, https://www.gov.za/sites/default/files/Executive%20Summary-NDP%202030%20-%20Our%20future%20-%20make%20it%20work.pdf.

Chapter 13: Transform Our Labour Market and Reap Our Youth Dividend

1 Thomas Piketty, *Capital in the Twenty-First Century*. Cambridge, MA: Belknap Press.

2 Meeting with Tharman Shanmugaratnam, May 2018.

3 See https://educatingforthefuture.economist.com/.

4 Joey Lee, 'Singapore's Education System is No.1 in Asia – But There's More to be Done beyond the Classroom', *Business Insider Singapore*, 21 September 2017, https://www.businessinsider.sg/singapores-education-system-is-no-1-in-asia-but-theres-more-to-be-done-beyond-the-classroom/.

5 See http://ventureburn.com/2018/01/funding-startup-ventureburn-investors/.

6 Finmark Trust, 'Report of the South African Financial Inclusion Workshop', 2017, http://www.finmark.org.za/wp-content/uploads/2017/12/South-Africa-Workshop-Report.pdf.

7 Isabelle Coetzee, '32% of South Africans Do Not Have a Bank Account – Here's Why', *Just Money*, 21 June 2018, https://www.justmoney.co.za/news/2018/06/21/32-of-south-africans-do-not-have-a-bank-account-here-s-why/.

8 See https://www.banking.org.za/what-we-do/overview/towards-a-financial-inclusion-strategy.

9 Ibid.

10 World Economic Forum, '6 Challenges to Financial Inclusion in South Africa', 27 April 2019, https://www.weforum.org/agenda/2017/04/financial-inclusion-south-africa/.

11 Ibid.

12 Bombi Mavundza, 'South Africans Will Save So Much Money through Stokvels this Year that They Could Buy Pick n Pay in Cash and Still Have R10 Billion Left Over', *Business Insider*, 22 February 2018, https://www.businessinsider.co.za/stockvels-could-buy-pick-n-pay-and-still-get-change-2018-2.

13 World Economic Forum, '6 Challenges to Financial Inclusion in South Africa', 27 April 2019, https://www.weforum.org/agenda/2017/04/financial-inclusion-south-africa/.

Chapter 14: It Is Time to Release Our Tech Potential

1 Martin Ford, *The Rise of the Robots: Technology and the Threat of Mass Unemployment*. London: Oneworld, 2015.

2 Quoted in David Pilling, 'African Economy: The Limits of "Leapfrogging"', *Financial Times*, 13 August 2018, https://www.ft.com/content/052b0a34-9b1b-11e8-9702-5946bae86e6d.

3 GSMA Intelligence, 'The Mobile Economy Sub-Saharan Africa', 2018, https://www.gsma.com/r/mobileeconomy/sub-saharan-africa/.

4 Duncan McLeod, 'First-Ever Southern Transatlantic Cable in Service Soon', *Tech Central*, 28 June 2018, https://techcentral.co.za/first-southern-transatlantic-cable-in-service-soon/82101/.

5 Chris Baynes, 'Entire Country Taken Offline for Two Days after Undersea Internet Cable Cut', *Independent*, 10 April 2018, https://www.independent.co.uk/news/world/africa/mauritiana-internet-cut-underwater-cable-offline-days-west-africa-a8298551.html.

6 See Worldwide Broadband Speed League 2018, https://www.cable.co.uk/broadband/speed/worldwide-speed-league/#highlights.

7 Competition Commission SA, 'Data Services Market Inquiry: Summary of Provisional Findings and Recommendations', 24 April 2019, http://www.compcom.co.za/wp-content/uploads/2019/04/Data-Services-Inquiry-Summary.pdf.

8 Interview, 14 April 2019.

9 See the two-part series of articles by Alan Knott-Craig, 'How 4IR will Benefit South Africa', *Bizcommunity.com*, 22 and 24 October 2018, https://www.bizcommunity.com/Article/196/706/183302.html.

10 See '10 Things the ANC Got Right in South Africa', *BusinessTech*, 6 May 2016, https://businesstech.co.za/news/general/122723/10-things-the-anc-got-right-in-south-africa/.

11 See https://soundcloud.com/biznews-com/getsmarter-cape-company-disrupting-worlds-higher-education-one-mit-cambridge-at-a-time.

12 Interview, Cape Town, 4 March 2019.

13 On the details of African internet and cell usage, see David Smith, 'Internet Use on Mobile Phones in Africa Predicted to Increase 20-Fold', *The Guardian*, 5 June 2014, http://www.theguardian.com/world/2014/jun/05/internet-use-mobile-phones-africa-predicted-increase-20-fold.

14 Patrick Kihara and Juliet Njeri, 'Africa Cracks Down on Social Media', *BBC News*, 10 September 2016, http://www.bbc.com/news/world-africa-37300272.

15 'The African Tech Hubs Fostering Innovation', *CNN World*, 22 February 2018, http://edition.cnn.com/2015/06/19/africa/gallery/african-tech-hubs/.

16 Bill Gates, 'The Secret Decoder Ring: How Cell Phones Let Farmers, Governments, and Markets Talk to Each Other', in *African Farmers in the Digital Age*, 2016, pp. 89–90, http://www.kofiannanfoundation.org/app/uploads/2016/01/African-Farmers-in-the-Digital-Age-1.pdf.

17 Victor Kiprop, 'Africa: Mobile Industry to Add U.S.$150 Billion to Africa's Economy by 2022, as Subscribers Rise', *AllAfrica*, 31 January 2018, https://allafrica.com/stories/201807310736.html.

18 'Editorial: The Smart Road to Lasting Recovery', *Financial Mail*, 1 November 2018, https://www.businesslive.co.za/fm/opinion/editorial/2018-11-01-editorial-the-smart-road-to-lasting-recovery/.

19 'Tech and Telecom Sector in Africa to Thrive in 2018 and 2019', *IT News Africa*, 16 March 2018, http://www.itnewsafrica.com/2018/03/tech-and-telecom-sector-in-africa-to-thrive-in-2018-and-2019/.

20 Toby Shapshak, 'Sub-Saharan African will have 500m Mobile Users by 2020, Already Has over Half Mobile Money Services', *Forbes*, 11 July 2017, https://www.forbes.com/sites/tobyshapshak/2017/07/11/sub-saharan-african-will-have-500m-mobile-users-by-2020-already-has-over-half-mobile-money-services/#3245c5a62456.

21 Milicent Atieno, 'How Technology can Improve Healthcare in Sub-Saharan Africa', *innov8tiv*, 3 November 2017, http://innov8tiv.com/technology-can-improve-healthcare-sub-saharan-africa/.

22 'Could Nigeria's Music Industry do as much for the Economy as Nollywood?', *ACCA*, 1 April 2018, https://www.accaglobal.com/pk/en/member/member/accounting-business/2018/04/insights/music-industry.html.

23 Anna Nicolaou, 'Universal Targets Africa for Growth in Music Streaming', *Financial Times*, 4 November 2018, https://www.ft.com/content/463e2b04-dfbe-11e8-a6e5-792428919cee.

24 Isshak Abdullai, 'Africa's Fastest Growing Music Streaming and Download Platform Boomplay Reaches 10 Million Installations', *Yfm*, 13 July 2018, https://www.yfmghana.com/2018/07/13/africas-fastest-growing-music-streaming-and-download-platform-boomplay-reaches-10-million-installations/.

25 'How E-Commerce with Drone Delivery is Taking Flight in China', *The Economist*, 9 June 2018, https://www.economist.com/business/2018/06/09/how-e-commerce-with-drone-delivery-is-taking-flight-in-china.

26 Cynthia Luo, 'Africa's Largest Ecommerce Player, Jumia, Finally Flexes Its Muscles Overseas', *ecommerceIQ*, 19 April 2018, https://ecommerceiq.asia/africa-ecommerce-jumia/.
27 'Transferring Intellectual Property Offshore', *Michalsons*, 2019, https://www.michalsons.com/ focus-areas/intellectual-property-copyright-protection/transferring-intellectual-property-offshore.
28 Interview, 6 March 2019.
29 Bradley Wattrus, CFO, Yoco, Interview, Cape Town, March 2019.
30 Ibid.

Chapter 15: Rural Development Must Look to the Future, Not the Past

1 Christian Lund, 'Negotiating Property Institutions: On the Symbiosis of Property and Authority in Africa' in Kristine Juul and Christian Lund (eds), *Negotiating Property in Africa*. Portsmouth: Heinemann, 2002, p.11.
2 For detailed statistics on the South African deciduous fruit industry, see Hortgro, 'Key Deciduous Fruit Statistics 2015', https://www.hortgro.co.za/wp-content/uploads/2017/08/key-deciduous-fruit-statistics-2016.pdf.
3 See http://www.wapa-association.org/asp/page_1.asp?doc_id=446.
4 Hortgro, 'Key Deciduous Fruit Statistics 2017', https://www.hortgro.co.za/wp-content/uploads/ docs/2018/07/key-deciduous-fruit-statistics-2017.pdf.
5 Frans Cronje, 'How Much of SA's Land is Really in Black Hands?', *Politicsweb*, 27 February 2012, https://www.politicsweb.co.za/opinion/how-much-of-sas-land-is-really-in-black-hands.
6 'Massive Land Reform Scam Uncovered: Report', *Businesstech*, 24 January 2019, https:// businesstech.co.za/news/government/295032/massive-land-reform-scam-uncovered-report/.
7 According to leading agricultural economist Mohammad Karaan, personal communication, 13 April 2019.

Chapter 16: Thinking Globally and Acting Locally: A 'New Urban Deal' for South Africa's Towns and Cities

1 World Bank, 'Urban Population', https://data.worldbank.org/indicator/SP.URB.TOTL.IN.ZS.
2 'Managing Urbanisation to Achieve Inclusive Growth: A Review of Trends in South African Urbanisation and Suggestions for Improved Management of Urbanisation', 2018, https://csp. treasury.gov.za/Resource%20_Centre/Conferences/Documents/Urbanization%20Review%20 Papers/Managing%20Urbanisation.pdf.
3 'Regression in Municipal Audit Outcomes', *SANews*, 23 May 2018, https://www.sanews.gov.za/ south-africa/regression-municipal-audit-outcomes.
4 World Bank, 'Doing Business in South Africa 2018', http://www.doingbusiness.org/content/dam/ doingBusiness/media/Subnational-Reports/DB18_South-Africa.pdf.
5 'Slow Progress in Business Environment Reforms for SA Cities – World Bank', *Fin24*, 19 September 2018, https://www.fin24.com/Economy/South-Africa/ slow-progress-in-business-environment-reforms-for-sa-cities-world-bank-20180919.
6 Discussion, Buffalo City Hall, 18 February 2019.
7 Twenty-foot equivalent units.
8 These are Coega, Richards Bay, Saldanha Bay, East London, Dube Tradeport, Maluti-a-Phofung in the Free State, OR Tambo IDZ and Atlantis in the Western Cape. See Zeenat Vallie, 'Gallery: View the List of Special Economic Zones in SA', *IOL*, 13 September 2017, https://www.iol.co.za/ business-report/economy/gallery-view-the-list-of-special-economic-zones-in-sa-11183315.
9 See http://www.elidz.co.za/.
10 Janine Myburgh, 'WCape Shows Where SA Could Be Were It Not for Corruption – Cape Chamber', *Politicsweb*, 15 February 2019, https://www.politicsweb.co.za/ politics/a-clear-picture-of-where-sa-could-be-without-corru.

Index